CARLO AYMONINO

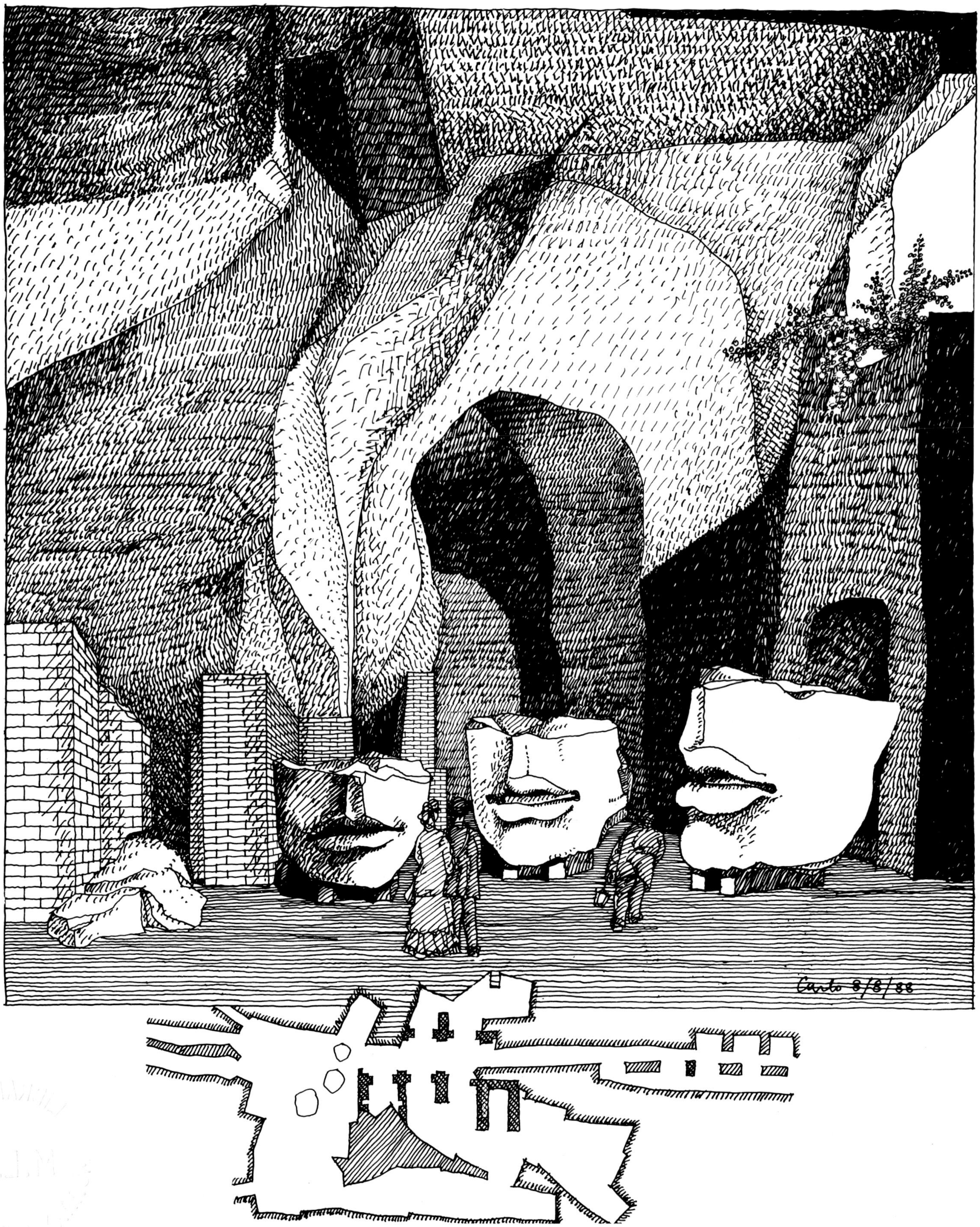
Carlo 8/8/88

Architectural Monographs No 45
CARLO AYMONINO

A.D. ACADEMY EDITIONS

ACKNOWLEDGEMENTS

I would like to thank Andrea Bettella for his patience and dedication in designing this book. My thanks also to Maggie Toy, Stephen Watt, Alex Young and Iona Baird for their hard work.

Front Cover: College Campus, Pesaro, 1970-84
Frontispiece: Sotto Napoli, Naples, 1988
Back Cover: The Colossus, Rome, 1982-84

All illustrative material is courtesy of the architect unless otherwise stated. Photographic credits: *Front Cover*: Mauro Tamburino (Pesaro); *Gallaratese, Milan*: Studio Foto Molfa p24; Alessandro Carlotto (Rome) p26; Luigi Filetici p21 – the model of Gallaratese, © Solomon R Guggenheim Museum (New York); Stefano Topuntoli (Milan) pp23, 27; *College Campus, Pesaro*: Alessandro Carlotto (Rome) pp32, 33; Studio 33 of Mauro Tamburino (Pesaro) pp34, 35, 38-43; *Court House, Ferrara*: Bruno Segato (Ferrara) p54; *Three Squares, Terni*: Sergio Coppi p63; Coca Color (Rome) p65 (photomontage); *Theatre Complex, Avellino*: Daniel Mularoni (Rome) p68; *The Roman Garden, Rome*: Luigi Filetici (Rome) pp122, 123 (of drawing); Zeno Colantoni (Rome) pp121, 123 (of models)

Architectural Monographs No 45

First published in Great Britain in 1996 by
ACADEMY EDITIONS
An imprint of

ACADEMY GROUP LTD
42 Leinster Gardens, London W2 3AN
Member of the VCH Publishing Group

ISBN 1 85490 283 0

Copyright © 1996 Academy Group Ltd. *All rights reserved.* The entire contents of this publication are copyright and cannot be reproduced in any manner whatsoever without written permission from the publishers.

Distributed to the trade in the United States of America by
NATIONAL BOOK NETWORK, INC
4720 Boston Way, Lanham, Maryland 20706

Printed and bound in Singapore

CONTENTS

Un Gentil Uomo Peter Eisenman	6
The Search for Carlo's Marks Giorgio Ciucci	8
Carlo Aymonino: From the Tiburtino Quarter to the Gallaratese Francesco Dal Co	12
The Trans-Architecture of Carlo Aymonino Achille Bonito Oliva	16

PROJECTS

Monte Amiata Housing Complex, Gallaratese Quarter, Milan	18
College Campus, Pesaro	30
Court House, Ferrara	48
Piazza del Popolo, Piazza Solferino and Piazza Europa, Terni	56
Theatre Complex, Avellino	66
Piazza del Mulino, Matera	76
St Mark's Basin, Venice	84
The Colossus, Rome	90
Sotto Napoli, Naples	96
Campo di Marte, Giudecca Island, Venice	102
Palazzo del Cinema, The Lido, Venice	108
The Roman Garden, Palazzo dei Conservatori, Rome	118
Biography	126
Complete Works	126
Selected Writings by Carlo Aymonino	127
Selected Writings on Carlo Aymonino: Foreign Publications	127
Selected Writings on Carlo Aymonino: Italian Publications	127

UN GENTIL UOMO
PETER EISENMAN

Looking back on the Italian architectural scene in the seventies, it was unique not only within its own cultural milieu but also to that period of architecture in general. This was mainly as a result of the relationships that were forged between the schools of architecture, the practice of architecture and the practice of power. It was a time when a famous art historian could become the mayor of Rome; a time when a practising architect could be the head of one of the most successful schools of architecture in the world and simultaneously become an *assessore* – an elected councillor of sorts – in Rome. (One should not neglect to mention that the present mayor of Venice is also an academic and practising philosopher, though architecture is clearly different from philosophy.)

This post-war renaissance was catalysed by the publication of Manfredo Tafuri's *Progetto e Utopia* and Aldo Rossi's *L'Architettura della Città* in the late sixties. Both these texts proposed a new attitude towards the relationship of architectural thinking to the city, and immediately preceded Rossi's *triennale* on a new rationalism growing out of an historical, as opposed to an abstract, awareness. From this, the only didactic and in a sense ideological movement of the seventies, the Tendenza, developed and soon became a hotly debated issue in the magazines and the schools. All of this seemed to coalesce around the University Institute of Architecture Venice (IUAV) that was headed by an architect named Carlo Aymonino.

Aymonino was simultaneously a patrician and card-carrying Communist, an unlikely combination that would be almost impossible to understand from the western side of the Atlantic; a man raised in the court of King Vittorio Emanuele, who fought with the *Bersaglieri* and in an instant, following Badoglio's surrender, joined the *partigiani*, a move which would eventually lead him to the Communist Party. He was to teach me that there were many sides to the idea of a party member. I was also to learn that his capacity to move easily in academic and political circles was both natural to him personally and facilitated by the particular conditions of Italian politics. Because of these connections he was able to bring about both real buildings and theoretical urban projects, whilst remaining a most subtle entrepreneur, hardly seeming to fit the part in his quiet, seemingly unassuming demeanour.

I remember clearly one evening, when, since Aymonino was the *capo* of the party, we had a reservation for the corner table upstairs at Harry's Bar which was reserved for important dignitaries, usually members of the party. As an American I always found this rather strange, since Harry's always seemed to be the height of capitalist, if not tourist, chic. In any case, our reservation was for late, around ten o'clock. When we arrived, Arrigo, the Harry of the said bar and air controller of that tiny corner of Venice, told us that our table was not yet ready. After some moments at the bar with Carlo, drinking I suppose Bellini's and choking on cigarette smoke, we noticed, with some excitement, the departure of Simone de Beauvoir and Jean-Paul Sartre, who brushed by us at the bar. We were to find out moments later that they had just vacated our table. I knew then that I was not only in the right place but also with the right person.

Venice seemed to be the centre of 'where it was happening' in Europe at that time, and the Venice-New York axis – with particular reference to the IUAV and the Institute for Architecture and Urban Studies (IAUS) – was already legendary in certain academic circles. Of personal significance to me are two events which happened in the summers of 1976 and 1978 respectively. During the first, I was in charge of the American half of the first international architectural *biennale* 'Europa-Amerika' held in Venice, which featured twenty-two architects equally divided between Europe and the United States. The highlight of this extended week installing the exhibition was the symposium at the Cinema Lido, which sparked a confrontation between Manfredo Tafuri and Aldo Van Eyck. It was on this visit that I first met, the laconic, always smiling, Carlo Aymonino. Since my Italian was, as it is today, a series of well studied sounds that tend to repeat what someone has just said with the addition of a modest *si* or *non*, and Aymonino's English was also as it is today, hardly recognisable as such, we communicated empathically.

As a result of our meetings during the time of the *biennale* I saw Carlo several times in New York and Rome. We had a mutual fondness and admiration that transcended our respective positions and inability to communicate conversationally. It was then that Carlo organised the theoretical urban project '10 Projects for Canarregio', which was, in retrospect, a turning point in my own career. This programme involved inviting five foreign and five Italian architects to spend the summer working on proposals for the Canarregio site. John Hejduk, Raimund Abraham, Rafael Moneo, Bernard Hoesli and myself were the international contingent, and we worked in the school's studios along with our Italian counterparts. It was an incredible experience, not only because of who we were with but also because of the opportunity to live and work in a foreign country. I remember the daily discussions at the end of each day, concerning the work of the previous hours, and the great feeling of pride and accomplishment, when I returned that winter to see the giant banners waving from the Museo Correr, Piazza San Marco, announcing our exhibition.

One cannot forget other moments which concern Aymonino's enormous personal generosity; specifically giving the design of a large building at Gallaratese to his friend Aldo Rossi. This was all the more magnanimous considering that the latter's work would come to overshadow his own, not only here but in other projects. While Gallaratese and the Modena Cemetery projected Rossi onto the international scene, Aymonino, although part of it, always remained behind the scenes. I have often thought how much better architecture would be if others had followed his lead, and with large building complexes extended similar benevolent gestures.

In the end, relationships between institutions, plans and structures are made not by circumstance or abstraction, but by people. While others will perhaps be remembered as the celebrities of that period – Rossi, Tafuri, Valle, Gregotti and Portoghesi – no one did more to create the conditions enabling that history to be written than Aymonino. It is often said of influential architects that they can choose between power in the present or a critical presence in the future. In a curious way Aymonino will have had neither, while perhaps making it possible for others to have had both. This is the irony of the patrician Communist who, because he had 'both' of sorts, never desired either power or recognition. He lived his life as a just and warm human being, and for this we should be thankful to him.

THE SEARCH FOR CARLO'S MARKS
GIORGIO CIUCCI

I would not be revealing anything strictly personal by observing that Carlo Aymonino has always collected, in very neat and tidy albums, photographs relating to his life. These are images that portray moments in which he was, directly or indirectly, a participant, and, considering his character, probably a protagonist. The private and the public life, the marriages and the travels, the offspring with their families and friends, all bear witness – to those leafing through these albums – to a lifetime that is the sum of many experiences; yet one cannot detect either nostalgia or regret for what has been lost. Every fragment represents an instance that Aymonino lived through, with the playful disposition of someone who lets themselves be transported by events whilst involving other people in the process. To neatly gather these fragments, to always have them in front of our eyes, is to render our past as a constant present.

However, these collections do not represent the search for a sense of security, by way of a coherent assembly; rather, they record events, that pin-point critical moments in a process that has often been discontinuous.

Similar feelings are engendered when one considers the albums Aymonino has gathered of his designs. Even here, he has not attempted, through the artificial placement of formal images and solutions, to show any continuity. Instead he selected the evidence he wanted to leave, marking his passage. There has been no attempt to construct a theory illustrating a coherent line of research or communication. Both photographic and architectural albums gather together traces which reduce the complexity of a lifetime to its essence. Within their pages we find all the protagonists – relatives, friends, architects, buildings, paintings, books – that he encountered. Admittedly they are primarily architectural but aspects of other disciplines, art, sculpture and literature, are also evident. If we concentrate on the architectural, avoiding his private life, we discover images that describe the multifarious and contradictory nature of Italian architecture for the last fifty years. Aymonino has always remained open towards contributions and suggestions from his contemporaries, although this should not be confused with passive acceptance, for throughout his many collaborations he has maintained his own identity, stamping every project with his individual mark.

I cannot expect to tackle, in a brief essay, such complex themes which have developed over such a prolonged period of time. Instead, I would like to emphasise, starting from my initial observations, one particular aspect of his body of work. This runs from his participation, as a young man having just attained his degree, with the group project for the Tiburtino quarter, Rome (1950-51), to his involvement, as an affirmed designer, with the Gallaratese residential complex, Milan (1967-70). I believe that these architectural marks left by Aymonino can reveal something of those twenty years, which represent for the Italian culture a lively and exciting period. In these projects there is an identifiable line of research centred on the relation between the mark and the urban space, a hypothesis – constantly verified through Aymonino's work; his designs, university teaching, research and essays. The testimonies that Aymonino left to his architecture not only reveal a valuable insight into his design philosophy, but also elucidate the discourse that occurred between architecture and its urban context that characterised Italian architecture in the fifties and sixties.

For instance, at Gallaratese there is a public mural – depicting the figures of Lenin, a young baker and a comrade lifting a clenched fist – symbolising the communal values that this complex articulates within the surrounding urban periphery. These references, within the linguistic and formal composition of the complex, express a new phase in Aymonino's work, with a political and cultural emphasis. Similar themes – the protest against political power, and its demand for a radical renovation of society after the struggle for liberation – were expressed in the Tiburtino quarter's language and forms, utilising realistic and popular images. However, at Gallaratese twenty years later, this conscious affirmation was limited to describing the spatial relationships between the various elements of the complex.

It could be said that the difference between the neo-realism of Tiburtino and the realism of Gallaratese – with its invitation to operate outside the myth of progressive architecture – and the distance between the moral and empirical, indicates the divergence between the generation of Quaroni and Ridolfi and successive movements. Aymonino, and Rossi, represent this generation's minority, through their attempts to explore new meanings in design without confusing architecture and politics.

However, even if the ideological differences between the proposals of Tiburtino and answers of the Gallaratese are

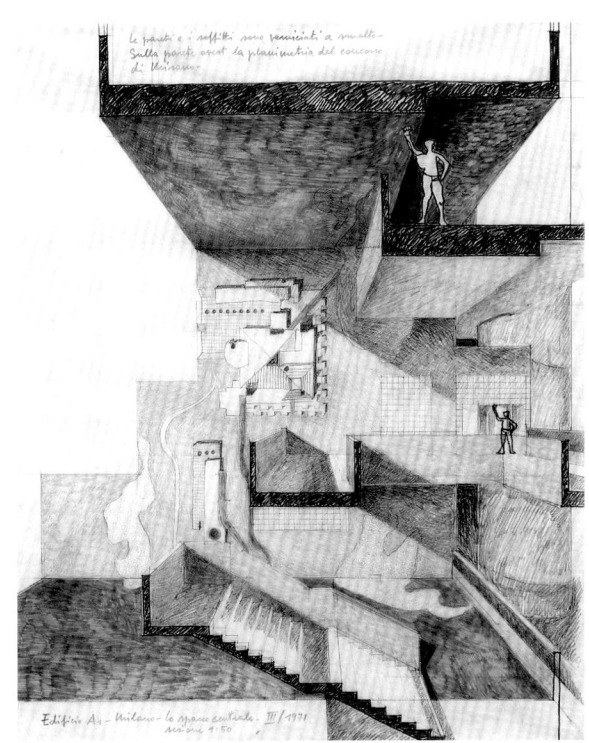

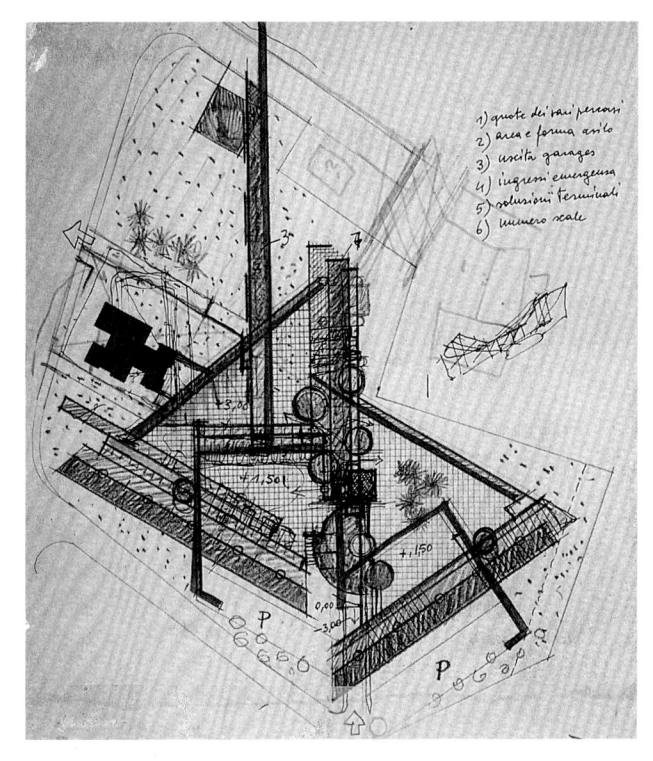

MONTE AMIATA HOUSING COMPLEX, GALLARATESE QUARTER, MILAN
ABOVE: Elevations; BELOW, L TO R: Sectional perspective; plan sketch

Giorgio Ciucci

profound, there are notable links between the two interventions. The estrangement of Tiburtino from the faceless suburb and its call for a recognisable urban fabric – based on the fact that it must be self-sufficient whilst presenting an image linked to the urban reality – does not appear to be entirely removed from the idea expressed in the Gallaratese through its refusal of a complex urban image, and in both settlements, the social services are the organising principles for inhabitants. At Tiburtino the social centre, school, church and other educational institutions are the focal points that enable democratic relationships, whilst the split-level square and the spaces between the houses provoke encounters that the suburb denies. Alternatively, at Gallaratese the internal streets, connections and public spaces recreate *in vitro* the complexities of urban reality, whilst the theatre, situated at the junction of the blocks, is intended for both formal and social exchange.

Similarly at Tiburtino and Gallaratese there is an attempt to illustrate an urban reality. In the first instance an ideal community, or village, is constructed that allows social interaction, and in the second a formalisation of the variety of form and the richness of interactions that already exist in the city is represented. In each case we find a form of spontaneity in the composition of the spaces which gives life to the architecture of a city. At Tiburtino this is evident from the composition of the master plan, whilst at Gallaratese it has no logical points of reference and is justified by the geometric construction which regulates the fundamental relationships. Paraphrasing what Quaroni has written, that in the drive towards the city we stopped at the village, it could be said that Aymonino, in his drive towards an area of the city arrived at the city. It is true to say that by closing itself off from the city Tiburtino becomes a village, and that by being a partial intervention Gallaratese manages to contain all of a city's urban complexity within a single structure.

Tiburtino and Gallaratese are consistent interventions within their respective cities, separated from, yet visually significant to, their urban context, but there are differences between the two. However, Aymonino cannot be held entirely responsible for this as Tiburtino was the result of bitter and involved cultural intervention, while Gallaratese was an expression of the architect's cognitive process. He was conscious of the fact that contradictions were present, within him and around him, even before Gallaratese, and was acutely aware of the problems created by contemporary society. When the police stormed the barely finished complex, to remove the homeless people who were occupying it, he felt no guilt but was aware of the dramatic reality his intervention had created. In Aymonino's view, architecture does not solve the housing problem and therefore architectural debate should be extended to consider it.

As he wrote in 1957, 'Tiburtino was the research, with extreme consequences, of an empirical experimentation . . . total freedom from any compositional constraint, the casualty of mobile elements'; after which it became apparent that he could not reduce the problem of popular housing to the preparation of prototypical modules, to be repeated time and time again until the demand for post-war housing was met. This highlights the strength and the limitation of Aymonino's argument. Architecture is a representation of reality, an expression of its implicit contradictions, and the architect is not simply the co-ordinator and synthesiser of a shattered, but nonetheless re-unifiable whole: on the contrary, he uses this fragmentation as a starting point to acquire knowledge of the real world. Despite this Aymonino has not taken refuge in the esoteric, isolating himself from the real world and building his own frame of reference, but has undertaken an impassioned investigation of architectural form based on reality.

Compared to other architectural ideologies in the fifties this represented an enormous methodological and cultural jump, illustrated by his entry for the National Library competition, which displayed a confidence of linguistic reference and novelty of form that belittled all the other designs submitted. This ideological break was epitomised by Aymonino's attempts with AYDE – the company formed by the two Aymonino brothers and the two de Rossi brothers – to realise an integral project from concept to completion, through the organisation of the professional studio and the contractors. Such a commitment to the rationalisation of the building industry should have enabled AYDE to practice without having to compromise with contractors, who were renowned for their paralysing technological and cultural backwardness. In fact their experiences with the integral project revealed the two faces of Italian architecture; the contractor's indifference to architecture and the inadequacy of strictly private answers to the problems of intervention in the building industry.

What then was the intention at Via Anagni, Rome, the firm's

most interesting project, which was built chronologically halfway between Tiburtino and Gallaratese? A prototype? An experimental project? An alternative? We can answer yes or no to all of these questions, but every affirmation or negation must be followed by an observation. In the first instance, the *naïveté* of the attempt to demonstrate, through examples, that it is possible to organise society to operate differently is comparable only to the illusion of being able to find space for such propositions. In the case of a negative answer, any attempt to alter the process of building construction through the restructuring of the architectural studio reveals an ignorance of the industry's actual problems. However, AYDE's proposal for Via Anagni deserves more complex answers that reveals their awareness of these fundamental problems. Admittedly the building is a formal model, an experimental project, but one which was realised; it is a professional alternative, but one which is far removed from the monopolies of the large studios tied to the industry. Was AYDE then, dissolved even before the formation of those practices, an impossible dream or even worse a failure? Again, yes and no. Yes, it was a failure within the context of Italy's evolving building industry, but considering the experience gained by the individual members, Aymonino in particular, it was a success. On the whole there were both positive and negative elements to this journey that allowed the contradictions from which Aymonino acquired knowledge.

This duality reflects Aymonino's personality and work. Not so much because there are negative and positive aspects within him, that would be too banal – nor because he is two-faced or too unkind – but because he had a disposition to explore every aspect of a problem with an open mind. The numerous collaborations that Aymonino made during his career are a sign of a willingness to verify his process of design; a fact that is once again illustrated by Tiburtino and Gallaratese. The former represents collaboration as a unity of intents, where like a village, the parochial spirit silences the discordancy; whereas the latter represents the plurality of positions as a conflicting space exposing the problems of the relations between architectural signs and urban possibilities. It is also true to say that in the first instance the rationalism does not allow contradictions, whereas the realism of Gallaratese, as defined by Aldo Rossi's contribution, is willing to confront issues beyond the physical. Aymonino's willingness to collaborate does not indicate a passive acceptance or a lack of choices, instead it implies a willingness for confrontation.

Once a mark has been left – whether it is a project, essay, intervention, lecture or personal experience – a certain amount of time must pass before a valid judgement on its value can be passed, yet during this period the confrontation still goes on. Quaroni's theory that architecture makes the present the past, is modified by Aymonino into a constant present: the empirical experimentation of the Tiburtino, or the formal dissolution of the Gallaratese; the formal synthesis of individual functions, as in the integral project for Via Anagni; the city that becomes architecture, as in the project for the centre of Bologna; the geometry that becomes the organising trait, as in the psychiatric hospital in Milan, or the network of routes which defines the architectural composition, as in Pesaro, are all monuments to this constant present, without implying continuity. In fact we can exchange the terms and the result is unaffected; the integral project is also a typological renovation, the architectural composition a formal dissolving, and the city by parts an empirical experimentation. The figures drawn on the sections of the Gallaratese spring back to mind, reflecting the spirit with which Aymonino neatly gathers his photographs in albums; private marks of an existence made up of events.

Giorgio Ciucci

CARLO AYMONINO: FROM THE TIBURTINO QUARTER TO THE GALLARATESE

FRANCESCO DAL CO

Carlo Aymonino's most important work, the residential complex in the Gallaratese quarter in Milan (1967-73), is in an expressionistic vein. The architecture is dominated by a formal anxiety which translates into a troubled search for correlations, in an attempt to absorb every value in a programmed chaos. Where language finds itself lacerated, Aymonino re-threads it; where the rule is in contrast to the exception, he nullifies the conflict. The architecture becomes a petition for continuity; even if, in order to express itself, it has to make use of uncovered stratagems. It is not by chance that Aymonino has felt the need to place an ascetic building by Aldo Rossi in the Gallaratese complex, almost as if to declare a compelling desire to comprehend the 'opposite'. It is an architecture that does not draw inspiration from remote suggestions or abandon itself to the most obvious citations; it is an autobiographical essay. To clarify its ideological significance it is necessary to pinpoint its cultural origins in the neo-realistic lesson – learnt by Aymonino in the fifties – the Italian cultural experience which more than all else, through social transfiguration, has highlighted the role of the autobiography. In this sense, the Gallaratese buildings acquire a significance that transcends their own formal coherence. As Federico Fellini's $8\frac{1}{2}$ ends a cycle of cinematographic culture by bringing to the extreme consequences its oneiric components, Aymonino's work similarly closes an era of Italian architecture, of which the hopes and the motivations had their origin in the Populism of the Tiburtino quarter in Rome, in the pluralistic dreams of culture, in the narration of the self elevated to 'genre'.[1]

These views should be partially reformulated in the light of Aymonino's latest works, although the critical premise that inspired them is still valid. Similar considerations, however, read almost ten years on, are a testimony to the impact that the construction of the Gallaratese complex made on contemporary Italian culture.

As with all important works – the significance of which dilates beyond the intrinsic implication of form and becomes part of the web of events that influences the intellectual climate of an historical period – the Gallaratese has come to represent a turning point. Such a creation has marked the limit for the architectural vicissitudes of the sixties and the seventies, separating the outcomes from subsequent developments. However, it must be said – and is confirmed by other episodes – that Aymonino's intelligence has always been practically applied by picking up the implications of similar moments of tension in culture, giving original design interpretations of them and resisting the temptation of fashions.

Ever since taking part in the competition for the construction of the new Paganini theatre in Parma (1964), the Roman architect has shown signs of such inclinations. On this occasion he designed a complex but paradigmatical building which was destined to become part of an unnerving urban environment, such as the one represented by the monumental centre of Farnese's city. In so doing, Aymonino submitted to the stringent critique of architectural organicism, thus questioning the neo-organic theories which at that time were still deeply embedded in the Italian culture. The network of routes from which the building would have developed, like a montage of figures confronting the surrounding urban environment, seems to put forward an ensemble of connections aimed to mimic the complexity of the functional structure of the historic city. The design of the building, on the other hand, refuses introversion, instead opening itself up to the morphological continuation of accumulation, modelling the form of the existing city. In the same vein, nine years later, the Gallaratese condensed and regenerated the experiences of the closing decade.

Given such considerations, it is easy to understand why Aymonino's best works occupy a privileged position in the panorama offered by Italy's contemporary architecture. No less peculiar is the cultural role the Roman architect has played during the course of his career, a fact critics have not always taken into account. Nevertheless, Aymonino is not an imposing protagonist. For reasons of an intellectual order and for professional reasons, beginning in the second half of the sixties, he represents a focal point for the Italian design culture.

Aymonino has lived with equilibrium, tangentially at first and later as a main protagonist, through some of the most significant experiences since the end of the War. Reconsidering his extensive career, it must be recognised that Aymonino has moved on the professional scene with measure and generosity. For these reasons he has carved for himself a very particular niche in the thorny world of Italian architects.

If Aymonino has proven to be generous in his professional assignments (one has only to think of the design opportunity offered to Aldo Rossi on the creation of the Gallaratese), he has involved himself in university and political life with as much grace. Before joining Rome's city administration in the eighties, as Councillor for Interventions in the Historic Centre, Aymonino was Dean at Venice's University Institute of Architecture. During his directorship of Italy's most prestigious architectural school he defended its traditions while renovating its organisation, opening the Institute's doors to the best exponents of design culture. At the same time, however, he has never given up maintaining a clear cultural line, frequently involving himself in lively debates, often with a subtle irony.

Hence, within Aymonino's complex personality solid formation merges with the legacies of experiences accomplished with open curiosity. For these and other reasons of a biographical nature – too great to explore here – Aymonino is the last relevant exponent of the 'Roman School', an expression not intended as academic formation but as a characteristic way of interpreting the undertaking of the project common to various architects formed or active in Rome since the early decades of the twentieth century.

Naturally, when speaking of the 'Roman School', one makes an historical distortion, because there is a risk of homologising very diverse experiences. When one thinks of architectural protagonists such as Marcello Piacentini, Adalberto Libera, Ludovico Quaroni or Enrico del Bebbio, Mario Ridolfi or Mario De Renzi of the Roman professional vicissitudes starting from the thirties, the multiplicity of the cultural perspectives motivating their works is undeniable. Nonetheless, such diverse designers are all influenced by the cultural climate characteristic of Rome, where the profession is subjected to pressures which do not exist in most other Italian cities.

Rome's modern architecture, in fact, is open to stimuli derived from a promiscuous relationship with the most diverse forms of power; whether they are contingents in which the dominant political regimes are determined, or are those in which the legacy of the past, or the weight of history, is perhaps more compellingly expressed. Consequently, particular attention is paid to the question of tradition and a professional practice is developed which is implicitly sceptical of the temptations of the avant-garde. In fact, a kind of circumspect adhesion to the canons of modern styles distinguishes the activities of even the more gifted exponents of the generation immediately antecedent to that of Aymonino. Even the 'Roman Rationalism' of the thirties is characterised by less schematic experiences compared to those occurring at the same time in other environments, mainly Lombardy (Milan) and Turin. The works of the two designers destined to become the protagonists of architecture after the War – Mario Ridolfi and Ludovico Quaroni – demonstrate the sceptical and measured reception reserved by Roman architects for the 'modern'. Though very different characters, they still managed to collaborate, with generous tolerance, on the work which was to become the most significant *program manifesto* to be conceived by the Italian architecture of the difficult, but hopeful post-war years.

By designing and building the Tiburtino quarter in Rome (1949-54), Quaroni and Ridolfi not only compiled the most important document left to us in the neo-realistic lyricism field of architecture but also demonstrated how the profound motives of this lyricism could be traced back to what had matured, especially within the Roman environment, during the years of Fascism. Construction expertise, a sense of tradition, enhancement of community values and a disinterest for every stylistic codification are the characteristics of the quarter created by Quaroni and Ridolfi; on this occasion leading a group of designers comprised of some of the most gifted exponents of a younger generation of architects, from Mario Fiorentino to Federico Gorio and Carlo Melograni. Carlo Aymonino was part of that working group, having just obtained his degree at the Faculty of Architecture in Rome, to which he had enlisted after being encouraged to do so by Mario Piacentini. The experience of working with Quaroni and Ridolfi is of primary importance. From it, Aymonino drew further stimulus for his intellectual curiosity, and from that stemmed the anti-dogmatic attitude which characterised, in the years to come, his approach to the problems of architectural design.

Realism without avant-garde marked the activities of the 'Roman School' after the War (the atmosphere which can be felt in the neo-realistic films of Rossellini and De Sica is also present in many of the works created by Roman architects in the decade after 1945). Aymonino's exploration of this, over the years, resulted in *narrative realism*. Even in this, he remained faithful to the tradition of which he was a participant in his youth, despite extending the range of his interests, over the years, to either the neo-organic experiences of Aalto, or to

Francesco Dal Co

the research conducted by the British profession during the sixties. The narrative vein, however, has never been neglected in Aymonino's work. Instead of expressing itself in a kind of 'lyricism of the fragment' – as indeed a scholar of Aymonino's, Claudia Conforti, has suggested – his figurative world is constructed of montages, destined in time to simplify themselves, of figures and images. On the other hand, a characteristic trait of the 'Roman School' consists of the privilege accorded to the image rather than the fragment, which is the result, amongst other things, of a particular attitude regarding the design procedure intended essentially as a 'craft'.

Aymonino, in fact, perceives his activity as a 'craft', attributing implicitly to the term all the traditional significance that can be associated with it. Intending design as a craft, Aymonino treasures the lessons both of Ridolfi – inspired by the concreteness of the practice – and of Quaroni – motivated by constant theoretical doubts and by unresolvable poetic tension. The project as the expression of a craft, of a complex knowledge, of a practice that communicates the poetic freedom of the forms but that cannot ignore the constraints of needs and necessities, is the foundation of the knowledge of the architect and the purpose of all his experiences. In this sense, the craft of the project is meant as a necessary antidote to the intransigence of thought, to the *univocity* of ideology, the dogmatism of poetry – the traits, in fact – of Aymonino's practices.

Intending the project as the factual mediation between ideas and things (one could add between desires and needs), Aymonino is naturally induced to emphasise the figures (the images) of which his buildings are composed. Thanks to this coherence, the *regest* of Aymonino's work allows us to appreciate the linearity of a research that maintains itself in time on a path marked by episodes in which the accumulation of experiences creates more elan.

In the fifties Aymonino designed a series of residential complexes for low-income users, financed by public funds, which capitalised on the experience attained when collaborating on the Tiburtino quarter. Between 1954 and 1957 Aymonino designed the popular 'White Thorns' housing project of Matera (which established a precedent for building complexes in the Puglia region) – the 'Tratturo dei Preti' borough in Foggia (1957-59), and 'Commenda Ovest' in Brindisi (1960-61), and the residential building in Via Arbia in Rome (1960-61). These mark the departure from the neo-realistic lesson, and a maturing of new cultural interests concurrent with those taking place on the international scene. Through the play of blocks intersecting one another and the curved surfaces, the building in Via Arbia was the development of what had already been presented for the National Library in Rome competition (1959), a marked homage to Alvar Aalto and a confirmation of the debt owed to the more or less coeval experimentation by Quaroni.

The early sixties represented a period of intense activity for Aymonino, but not only from a professional point of view. Operating within the university, he dedicated himself to research, which was to result in rich theoretical work, and a few notable historical contributions. At the centre of these activities Aymonino continued to nurture the interrelations between the building phenomena and urban configurations.

The study of the relationship between topology and morphology, between the phenomena of architectural scale and those constituting the structure of urban fabric, was developed by Aymonino from 1963 through the IUAV and through close collaboration, with, amongst others, Aldo Rossi. The result of this period of research was a series of publications dedicated to the problems of urban analysis, including a notable volume edited by Aymonino himself in 1970, *The City of Padua*. The series marks one of the moments of high originality and striking theoretical development for the Italian design culture following the War. At the same time Aymonino elaborated a few projects based on the themes examined in the theories: for example, he expanded on the hypotheses formulated while participating in the competition for the Paganini theatre in Parma. In 1967 he proposed a design for the Parliament offices in Rome, followed by a project for a psychiatric hospital in Mirano, Venice (1967), in collaboration with Costantino Dardi. In this last instance, the figurative narration Aymonino favoured was realised through a rich and dense montage of geometrical images, which through juxtaposition *disintegrate* the residual integrity of the organism. This practice, also experimented with in the multi-functional complex designed in Savona (1963-67), found its final expression in the Gallaratese.

It is not by chance that Aymonino attributes great importance to the definition of the system of circulation between different parts of building complexes. Far from being defined as having simple functional values, the varied connecting networks which criss-cross Aymonino's works are entirely related to the narrative vein that inspired them. As demonstrated in the Savona building and the Gallaratese, the ramps, galleries, walkways and internal squares emphasise the adjacent related spaces. The system is also evident in the project for the Paganini theatre which offers true 'promenades through the figures', since such promenades disclose the successions of ever-changing images of the architectural landscape. These routes reveal and tie together the complexity and the multiplicity of the figures. They are the dialectical connection of organisms that disintegrate under the relentless prodding of plastic emergences, that will not pull away from suggestions nor renounce the use of complex citations. The dramatic 'breaches' of the Gallaratese amply demonstrate this, in cuts reminiscent of Constructivism and Expressionistic details.

Collecting figures – a practice that found its most characteristic expression in the theoretical project Aymonino prepared for the XV Triennale in 1973 (with Costantino Dardi and Raffaele Panella) – and mounting a series of architectural models of works by Le Corbusier, rather than of Libera or Quaroni, in a sort of catalogue of his own 'elected affinities' allows Aymonino, within the context of more limited professional occasions, to make use of an expanded formal repertoire from which he draws the material corpulency of his figures. These constitute the platforms upon which rest the semantics that animate the multi-faceted universes Aymonino designs. The anxiety accumulated in the projects of the sixties and seventies was destined to resolve itself with the building of the vast residential complex in Milan. The following work, in fact, appears concerned with regaining a restrained poise, as in the example, albeit not yet mature, of the Court House in Ferrara (1977-79); the design and realisation of the college campus in Pesaro with a complex of built edifices (science college, 1970-73, technical and business studies institutes, 1978-79), all of which marked a turning point in the work of the Roman architect. Whilst the general setup of the intervention seemed still to be influenced by the experiences of the preceding decade, favouring a complex game of geometric *slippings*, the buildings presented simplified volumes, inspired by the restrained reductionism which was manifest in the simplicity of the overriding design, in the repetition of the roof and the emergence of the images.

It is precisely with the college campus project, which marked an apparent 'return to order', that the knowledge acquired with the theoretical research and the practical experimentation conducted since the beginning of the sixties comes to fruition. Due to its particular location on the city limits, the Pesaro college complex became, with its geometrically articulated set up and its simplified volume, a sign of ordered complexity within the shapeless anonymity of the urban periphery. By simplifying his own procedures, Aymonino managed to establish a close relationship between the morphology of the entire complex and the typology of the single buildings. Thus, the essential components that generate his research into the problems of urban analysis found a practical verification in the project. Reclaimed from a purely historical and theoretical framework, the urban analysis ceased to be purely a starting point and became a design tool, allowing Aymonino to prove his maturity. This is only logical, since the work carried out in Pesaro coincided with the beginning of the umpteenth youth of this energetic septuagenarian.

Notes
1 M Tafuri and F Dal Co, 'Architettura contemporanea', Electa (Milan), 1976, pp400-403, Eng trans, Abrams (New York), 1979, pp394-97.

Francesco Dal Co

THE TRANS-ARCHITECTURE OF CARLO AYMONINO
ACHILLE BONITO OLIVA

Post-modernism and the trans-avant-garde seem to have arisen in response to a crisis in art and design – particularly in the fields of architecture and painting – that occurred in the second half of the seventies. Up to that point the modern and historic avant-gardes had presided unquestioned as the revered ancestors of a rigid line of descent, guaranteeing legitimate offspring and development in the assured forward movement of history.

The moment this continuity was challenged, however, a crisis occurred: how were art and architecture now to evolve? What was in question was the successful re-transmission of meaning if there was to be experiment in the realms of the figurative and the environment. In terms of art the answer found was the trans-avant-garde, strategies of retrieval that involved self-conscious memory and past reference; the prefix 'trans' – rather than 'post' – reflecting the cultural nomadism and stylistic eclecticism endemic to the age of transition at the end of the twentieth century. Architecture, on the other hand, generated its own post-modernism out of its clash with the historical Modernist Movement.

Art, in terms of painting and sculpture, thus chose to evade confrontation and embrace the earlier object-based and conceptual movements in a form of cultural and stylistic co-existence. In architecture Carlo Aymonino adopted a similar stance and endorsed interrelation as a strategy that enabled him to work in terms of 'soft' design. This means a tempering of the firmly political internationalism of the term 'design', relocating it again in the sphere of the individual ethos of the architect, the urge to construct and achieve. This entailed a dramatic return to the traditional terms of design as they had shaped the architecture of the previous period, in particular the industrious quest for Utopia.

Aymonino's constructions embody a personal stance free of totalitarian ideologies, one capable at the same time of nourishing a richly differentiated range of options within the order of relationships. It was this that enabled him to escape involvement in the principles of conflict which dominated the post-modernism of the eighties. Aymonino finds room for a diversity of styles in the design and execution phases of his work, accommodating them within a poetic genre that permits the formal co-existence of numerous architectural elements that encourage contemplation and public availability. A subtle vein of expressionism binds the whole together, voicing the expressive urge of an architect who will not allow his work to be taken hostage by either the discipline of pure form or that of function, thus preserving it from the schematic conflict engaged in by post-rational and post-modern architects.

The strength of Aymonino's work lies in his ability to combine diverse architectural elements without diluting their meaning: the lightness of Mies van der Rohe's design with a firm sense of the volume's *gravitas*. As a consequence his designs are capable of distilling the values of the past and synthesising them in a monument to the present. This process enabled Aymonino to celebrate the Utopian aspirations of the Modern Movement without demeaning its vocabulary by employing it in an arbitrary and ornamental fashion. The resemblance to the aims of the trans-avant-garde is evident once again.

Aymonino's explicit borrowings are never engaged in for their own sake, but as a way of taking a strong personal grip on his own drawing, as a stylistic and conceptual input that allows him to reshape his work with fresh passion and lucidity. This grasp, which mirrors Aymonino's potent insight into the contemporary cultural milieu, requires him to set forth the rational element through a metaphysical perplexity – as if the connection with reason were a transitory occurrence rather than a permanent anchoring.

There was nothing casual in Aymonino's design of the three squares in Terni, the urban strategy in Matera, the restructuring of the Campo di Marte on the Giudecca Island in Venice and the Colossus in Rome. They were all part of his attempt to provide a link between past and present, architecture and sculpture, and the possibility of the design with the necessity of the reference, and in all these cases the calm metaphysics of an entirely Italian attitude, aimed at the formal conciliation of the whole, rests on the cosmopolitan spirit of the various styles. The aim of this approach is to avoid the superimposition of architecture over place; the realisation of a principle of continuity. As Heidegger said:

> What this word *raum*, space, indicates, is given by its ancient significance. *Raum* means a space made free for a settlement of colonisers, or for an encampment. A *raum* is something vacated, made free, between defined limits, what in Greek is called *peras*. The limit is the place where something finishes but, as the ancient Greeks knew, the concept for the point where something begins its essence is *horismos*, in other words, limit.
>
> Space is essentially what is vacated, what is put within limits. What is thus vacated is accordingly arranged, in other words picked from a place, by something akin to a bridge. As a result, the spaces are given their essence not by 'space' but by 'place'.[1]

To build, to inhabit, to think appear to be the dictates governing Aymonino's way of laying out projects according to his complex continuity. Even in the intervention in St Mark's Basin in Venice, the 'Sotto Napoli' project for the area of Monte Nechia and the new theatre in Avellino, where there was no urban continuity, he used the archaeological remains as a *genius loci* and inspiration; an anthropological blueprint for the architecture. Hence, throughout Aymonino's work there are references to Canova, Guido Reni and Graeco-Roman sculpture. However, these are not the product of cultural reverence but belong within an iconography that works as a theoretical prop by providing conceptual support. The allusions are hints rather than real presence, a display of erudite reference rather than an ornamental harking-back, a skilful avoidance of that taming of the present on behalf of the past practised by post-modernism.

Again the metaphysical hovers over these projects, highlighting Aymonino's ironic awareness of the unresolved conflict between the contingencies of the present and a fetishistic adhesion to the past. The rigidly evolutionistic progress of architecture is diffused through the constant affirmation of the principles of continuity, and replaced with a sense of 'present history' that cannot be divided or sublimated. Aymonino is the bearer of a secular and stoical architecture in the late twentieth century, accepting the fact that 'the terrible has already occurred' to quote Heidegger again.

This facing up to the unavoidable truth does not, however, blunt Aymonino's creativity as he cannot deny his need for expressive intervention – albeit tempered by the awareness that there will be innate contradictions within any design. In this sense Aymonino's architecture represents a push towards his acceptance as an architect who knows he must oppose history, while remaining free of any sense of absolution or guilt. Aymonino's trans-architecture, from the Gallaratese to today, closes the circle of art.

Notes
1 Martin Heidegger, *To Build, to Inhabit, to Think*, 1954.

MONTE AMIATA HOUSING COMPLEX, GALLARATESE QUARTER, MILAN, 1967-72

With Maurizio Aymonino, Alessandro de Rossi and Sachim Massaré

Examples of the richest architectural developments during the last fifty years have almost always emerged through the development of prototypes. '*Il s'agit donc . . . d'un prototype, à vrai dire d'une proposition formelle de conditions de vie pour la civilisation machiniste presente*', declared Le Corbusier, with reference to the Unité d'Habitation, realised for 1,600 inhabitants. This model does not relate to its specific location but instead to self-contained units, responding to functional requirements. The Unité contained primary schools, shops and other services indispensable for living. However, the relationship between the defined purposes was very simple and established, enabling the architect to concentrate on the maximum repetition of the model. Today, specific formal solutions are notably diversified. Yet, although the methodology of the model is retained, in relating it to a specific city – with an existing morphological and typological relation – the design abstraction is nullified.

The statistic of '2,400 inhabitants' for the Gallaratese project is itself an indication of the 'imposed' conditions the architects had to work with. This anonymous statistic is the result of a conventional standard established between the local authority of Milan, the *comune di Milano*, and the owner of the land. Under the premise of law decree no 167, on the 52,700 square metres of possible building area permission would be given to build up to 169,000 cubic metres of living accommodation plus the extra percentage allowed for reception, technical services and garages. Dividing the total by an average of 70 cubic metres per inhabitant (according to low-budget restrictions), indicates the number of people to be housed. The manner was not specified, though percentages referred to large, medium and small apartments established by the standards of low-budget building according to the GESCAL regulations of 1967. Using this calculation, housing is only an anonymous quantity of economical investment, without any relation to its purpose – in this case, the occupant.

The advantage of having a single owner of the property, and the planned uniformity of the buildings (not for sale but rental), determined the solution, right from the start. This was that of an 'ensemble' volumetrically defined by diversified elements, but not identifiable by the purely quantitative sum of several isolated buildings, as was envisaged by the volumetric plan of the *comune*. With regard to the location of the complex, the area is totally deprived of either natural or artificial context. The site is flat, with no relevant characteristics, such as trees or a river; the roads are flat and the adjacent buildings are comprised of eight-storey rectangular blocks or twelve-storey towers, arranged in a repetitive and mundane pattern. The centre of the quarter, bordering the north of the project area, was represented by an area of no architectural significance. The location is thus defined by a 'general' reference (with the risk of becoming generic, if it is unrepresented by a manufactured form) to a different urban structure. This method, of course, is not specifically unique to that area, but would surely have been perceived had it involved the entire Gallaratese complex, as 'part' of the city of Milan.

Thus, the attempt was made to accentuate the isolation from its surroundings, resorting to the most compact general setup, almost a single building, or better still, a single construction. The initial idea of a single construction, compact but articulated, gradually had to resolve itself in five building blocks, of varied height and depth, related to each other by connecting elements (ramps, galleries, staircases and aerial passages between buildings); commercial units; and recreational spaces (open-air theatre, squares on the garage roofs destined for play areas and internal promenades).

The creation of several building blocks was not

done for technical reasons, nor for functional considerations. It was primarily to fulfil the requirements of the different regulations to which the first ideas were subjected: construction, relating to the height of the floors, size of the rooms, illumination of the hallways; sanitary, with regards to lighting and direct ventilation of kitchens, bathrooms, staircases; fire, for the basements, lifts, garages; the 167 law, with regard to the maximum height allowed for buildings, the percentage of parking spaces, green areas, playgrounds, distance from boundaries.

This confirmed, at the height of the design stage, the thesis of the urban analysis studies on the process of 'reduction' of the architectural intervention, in the case of buildings for habitation (and all typologically classified buildings), as a guarantee for quantitative technical controls and as a consequence of economic investments, also aimed towards strictly quantitative solutions. Within these parameters, the continuity of the pedestrian routes, either vertically or horizontally, breaks with the traditional concept of the 'private' building – in which the relation to the 'public' areas of the city is through the main door facing the street – by defining itself, instead, as an alternative method for structuring residences and services. From the parking lot on the ground floor one can reach the atrium halls, from there, the galleries, and on to the internal hallways serving the duplex apartments, interconnected from block to block, and return to the porticos on the ground floor, to the theatre on the higher level, or pause on any of the three different plazas.

As with the number of routes, the variety of flats, from studios to maisonettes, stems from an architectural desire to change the inhabitant's use of the space – which does not necessarily relate to the real use. This also does not correspond to the traditional coincidence between the type of apartment and the volumetric type of the building, but relates to compositional rules.

Hence, the project involved building a number of flats, with the relevant services and, above all, with additional spaces – envisaged as public in the project, in reality communal – as partial confirmation of urban character. One example is the great covered walkway that runs under block B which, crossing over the road, should have joined the hypothetical centre of the suburb. Another example is the three squares which assume different roles: the first two, at a level of 3.5 metres (at the level of the garage roofs), are mainly meeting places and playgrounds, different in character yet similar; the third, however, is created by the orientation and convergence of the various walkways, on which are distributed the commercial and cultural activities necessary to the complex.

The project, however, leaves open the question concerning the urban development of the formally completed parts: that is, which architectural instruments can define both the methods and schedules of the project and its execution. The model attempts to address this by revealing the possibilities for repetition and standardisation of the building and its components. In developing the technological possibilities, the 'specific' solution can invert the process. Occasionally, it is possible to devote an industry to a single building enterprise; but this inversion assumes quantities (of cubic metres, of infrastructures, of financing) far removed from the those of the complex examined here or other similar ones.

Without this kind of inversion, involving political instruments, economic means, inventive and organisational skills, projects like the Gallaratese quarter can offer the potential for a different urban structure. However, after taking five years to complete, only 2,400 inhabitants have found a home, compared to the tens of thousands that have settled in Milan during the same period.

Site plan

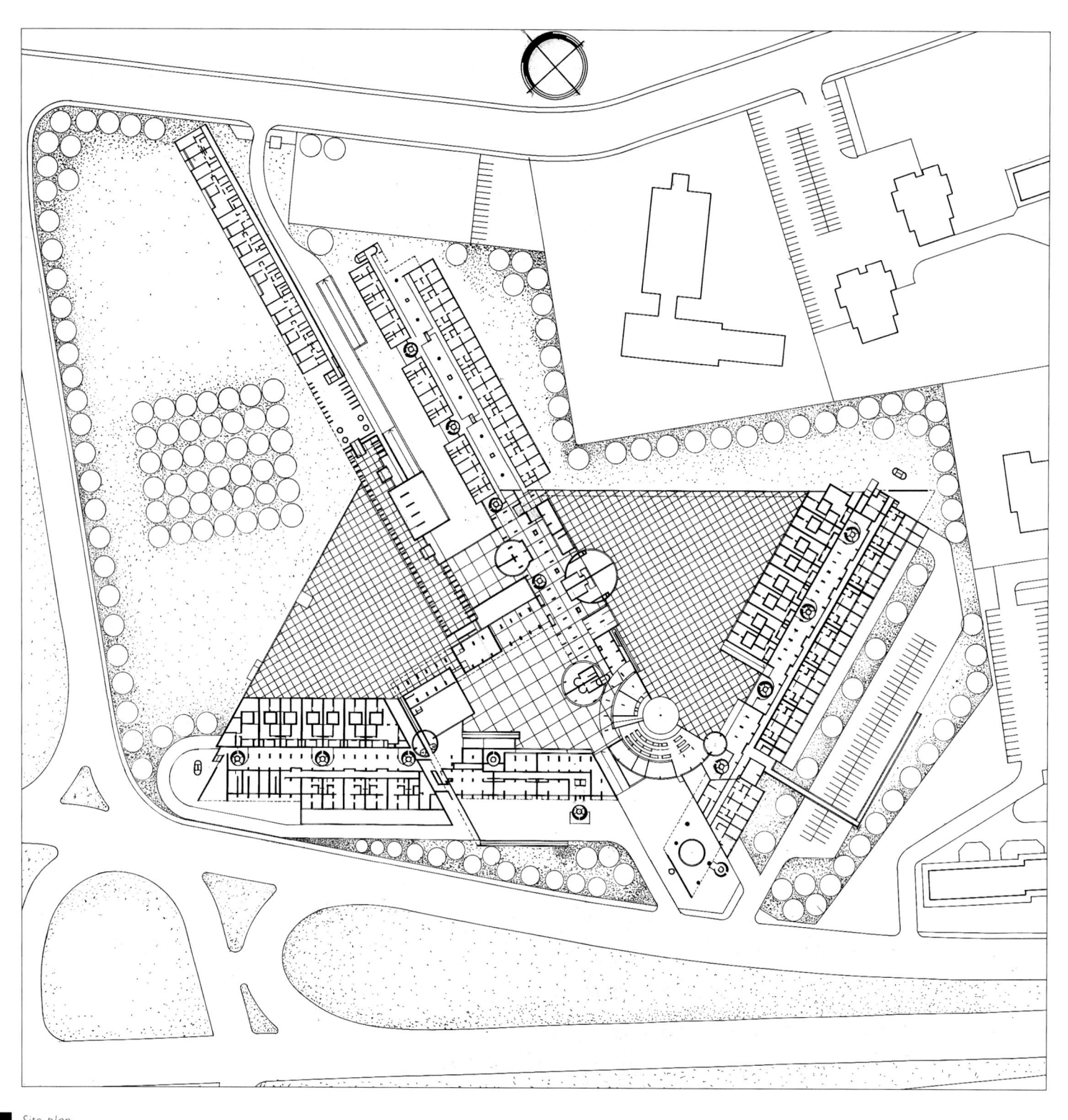

Monte Amiata

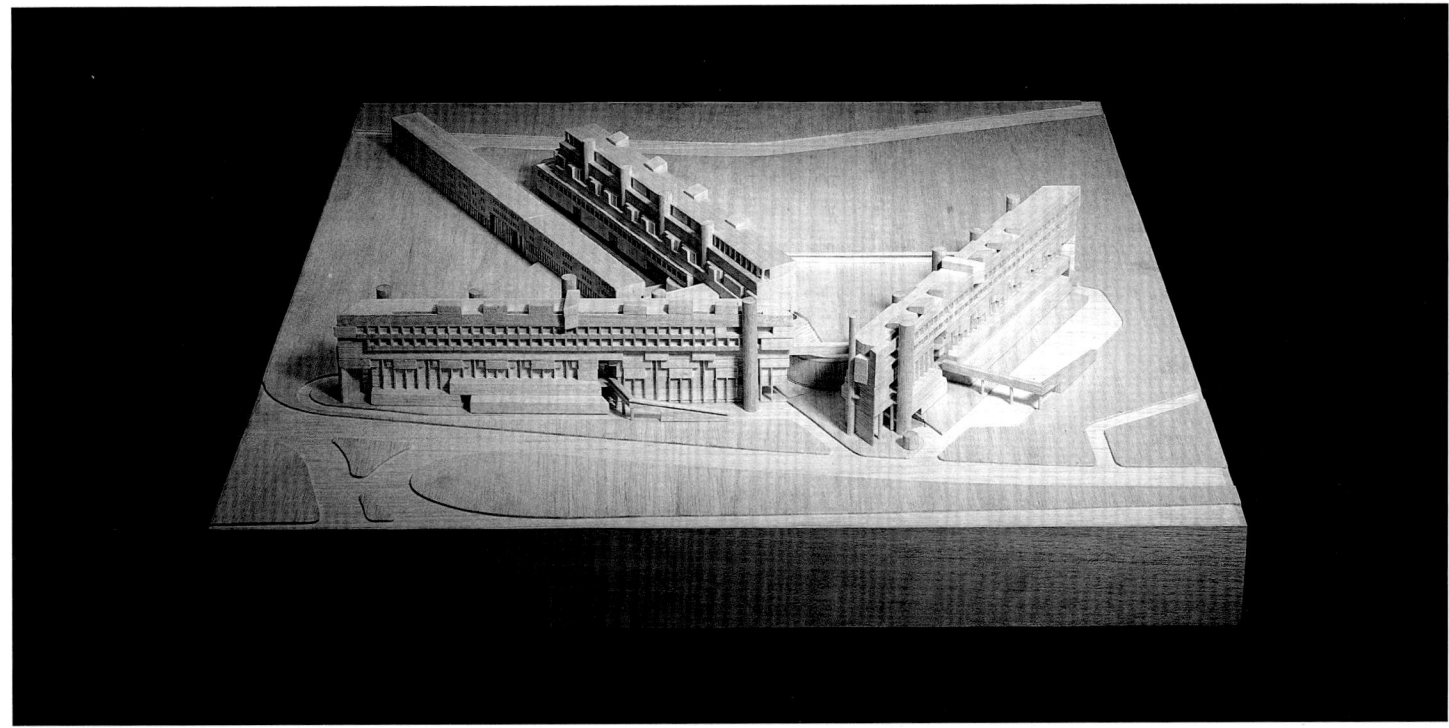

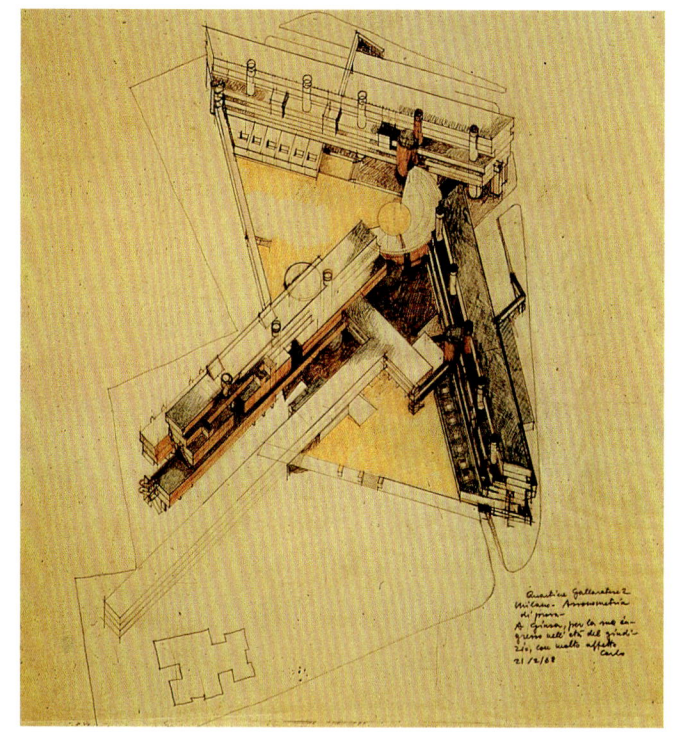

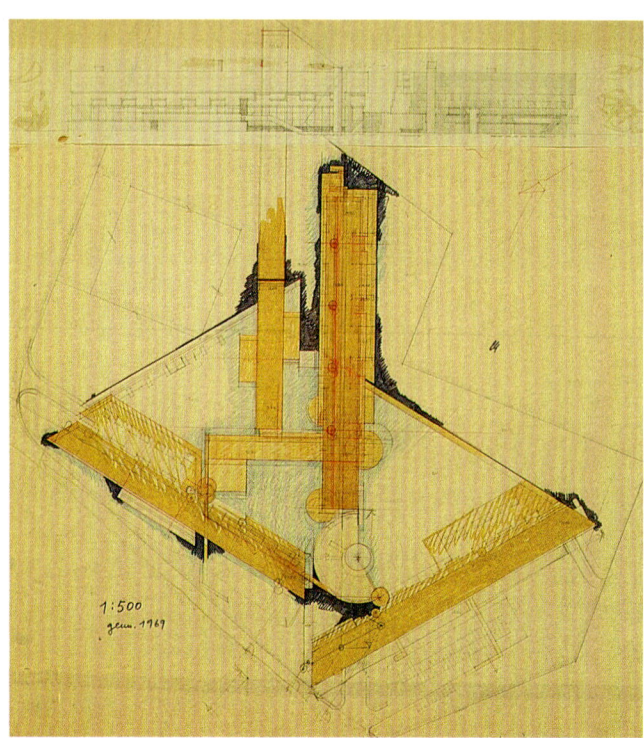

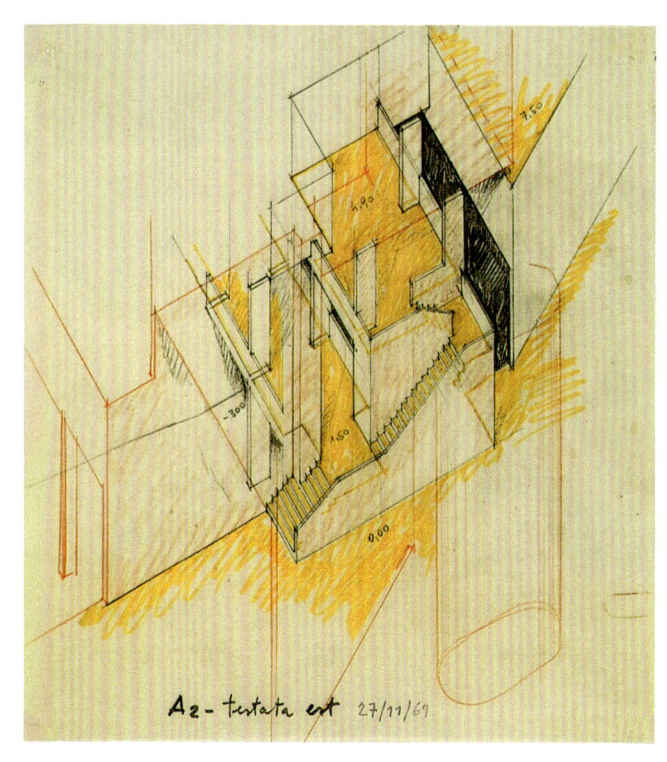

22 ■ *ABOVE: Isometrics; BELOW, L TO R: Plan; isometric*

Carlo Aymonino

Monte Amiata

Carlo Aymonino

Monte Amiata

Carlo Aymonino

Monte Amiata

Carlo Aymonino

Monte Amiata

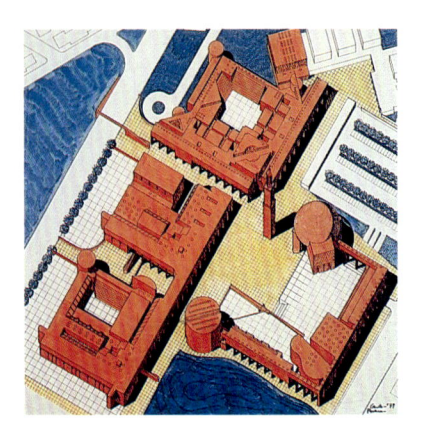

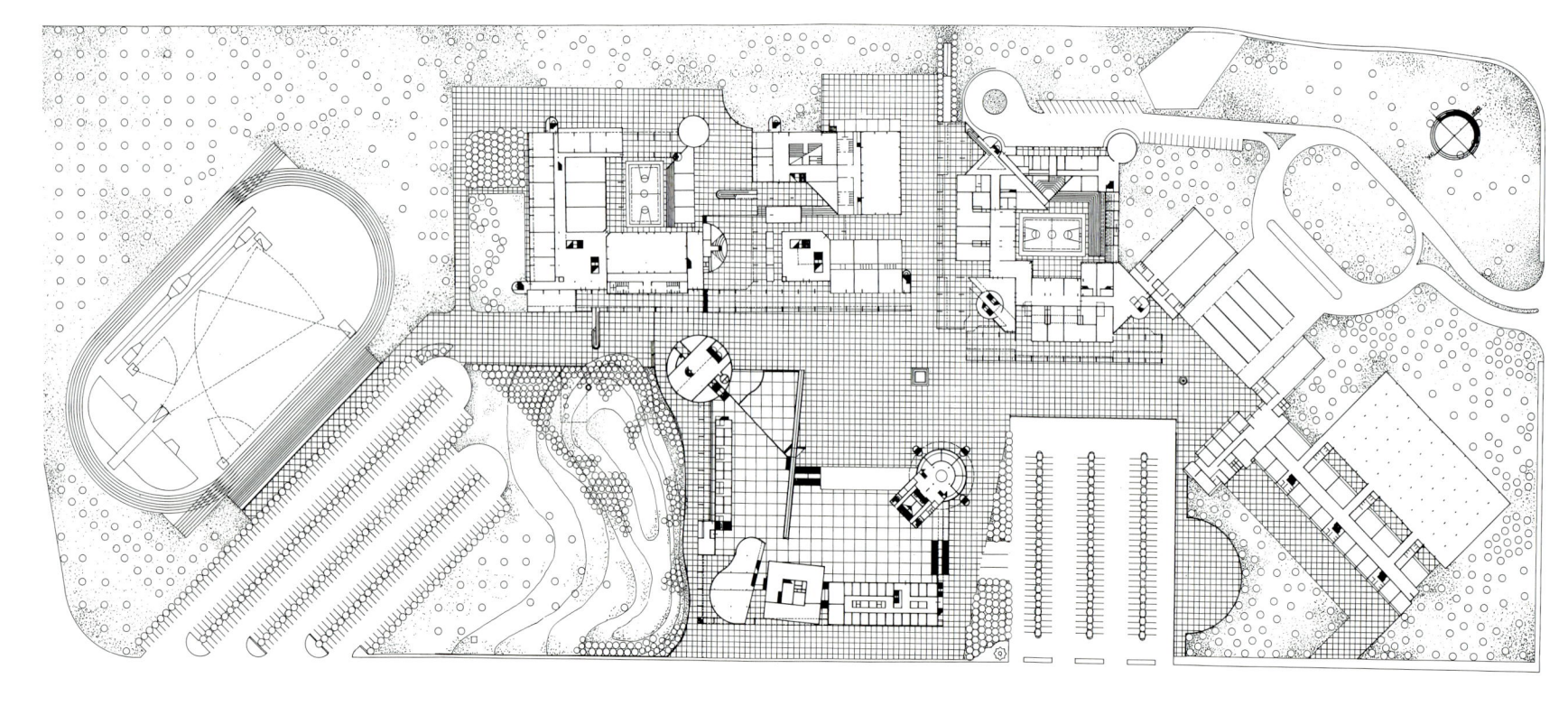

COLLEGE CAMPUS
FROM ABOVE: Isometric; site plan; PAGES 32-33: Perspective

Carlo Aymonino

COLLEGE CAMPUS, PESARO, 1970-84

With Cesare Montanari and Maria Luisa Tugnoli

The general regulatory plan allowed for a college complex within the expansion zone south of the city of Pesaro. In concentrating a professional institute, a business studies school, a technical school for accountancy and surveying, and a science college, for a total of about four thousand students within an area of twenty hectares, the plan quantified necessities and requirements, without proposing any ideas of 'architectural representation'. On the urban scale, a suitable area was selected and outlined which relates to the urban structure and to the various public routes. The architectural concepts were then directed and generated by the required density and the building programme.

These suppositions are necessary to support a project responding not only to functional requirements but also to the social conditions of its urban location. The influence of urban analysis studies is such that a project is expected to resolve not only a particular problem (in this case, the requirements of teaching) but a number of problems (here, those of teaching and those given by the context). The move to architectural scale has to take into account the existing urban surroundings, built or planned: in this particular case, an expanding residential area – mostly realised according to the economic principles of building – which will become an important part of the new city due to its relationship to the old city and the number of inhabitants.

On the other hand, the new city does not have any particular distinction: a commercial and a religious centre are planned; some residential services are assured (garages, primary schools, recreation and sports areas). The external spaces are different from those created by speculative building, even from those of spontaneous individual housing developments. What is missing, however, is a civic centre, and the architecture to represent it.

The architect has tried to identify an architectural methodology with which to focus the different needs of each building, in order to intervene on a more complex scale in single buildings, but as part of a larger co-ordinated programme. This unifying attempt conflicts with the differentiated, and above all, different sources of financing, the different agencies (the *comune* administration is responsible for the professional institute; the provincial administration is responsible for the other schools) and a non-unified management (for the time schedules, manpower, current expenditures). Suggested introduction of a civic, political, cultural and commercial centre in the campus, a meeting place for the student population and the social reality of the suburb, would also allow the concentration on one site of some of the services planned for each institute (library, canteen, clinic, assembly hall). This would provide higher quality, less expensive services, and above all, their utilisation for the benefit of the community. The opportunity is also there for an 'additional' architecture to add diversity to the composition of the campus (which is based around four school buildings); a point of reference visible and recognisable from areas of the city.

An early functional relation, not without formal implications, is determined by integrated vehicular and pedestrian routes: places have to be easily and comfortably accessible (streets and parking spaces), and once there, people have to be able to entertain themselves pleasurably (porticos, squares and pedestrian areas). The pedestrian walkway is the 'mark', the supporting structure of the composition. Indicating a collective and continuous use, it relates different functions, allows access to buildings, shops, gymnasia and common rooms.

The project for the science college attempts to satisfy two conditions: a single building, compact, without appendices, apart from the gym, and a corner building with urban qualities almost identical on both sides, facing similar parts of the pedestrian route, so both sides are porticoed and destined to public, cultural, or commercial activities. Similarly, the architectural composition of the two schools (technical and business) stems from the role they assume in the general context: the long porticoed facade that joins them in a single perspective towards the civic centre's square; the internal square separating the two buildings housing the volumes of the semicircular hall and the ramp; and the continuity between the internal covered spaces and the external open spaces.

The public space is structured as two squares, on two levels: the first, at ground level, gathers the diverse pedestrian circulation, architecturally ordered by the porticos (from here, the tower also provides an urban reference point); the other, at 3.5 metres above ground level, over the garages, gives access to the auditorium, the museum, the canteen and the library: a meeting place between academic and local life.

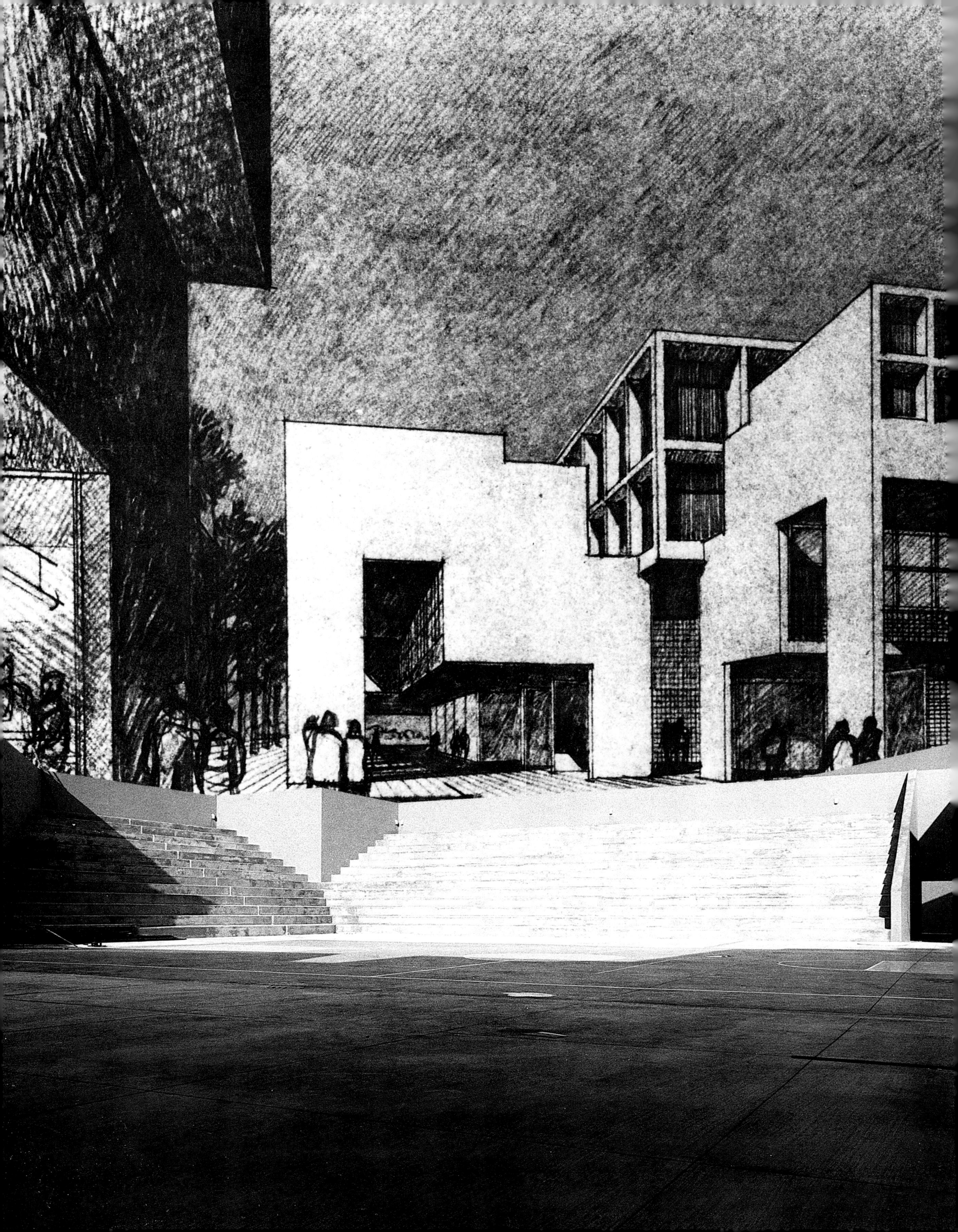

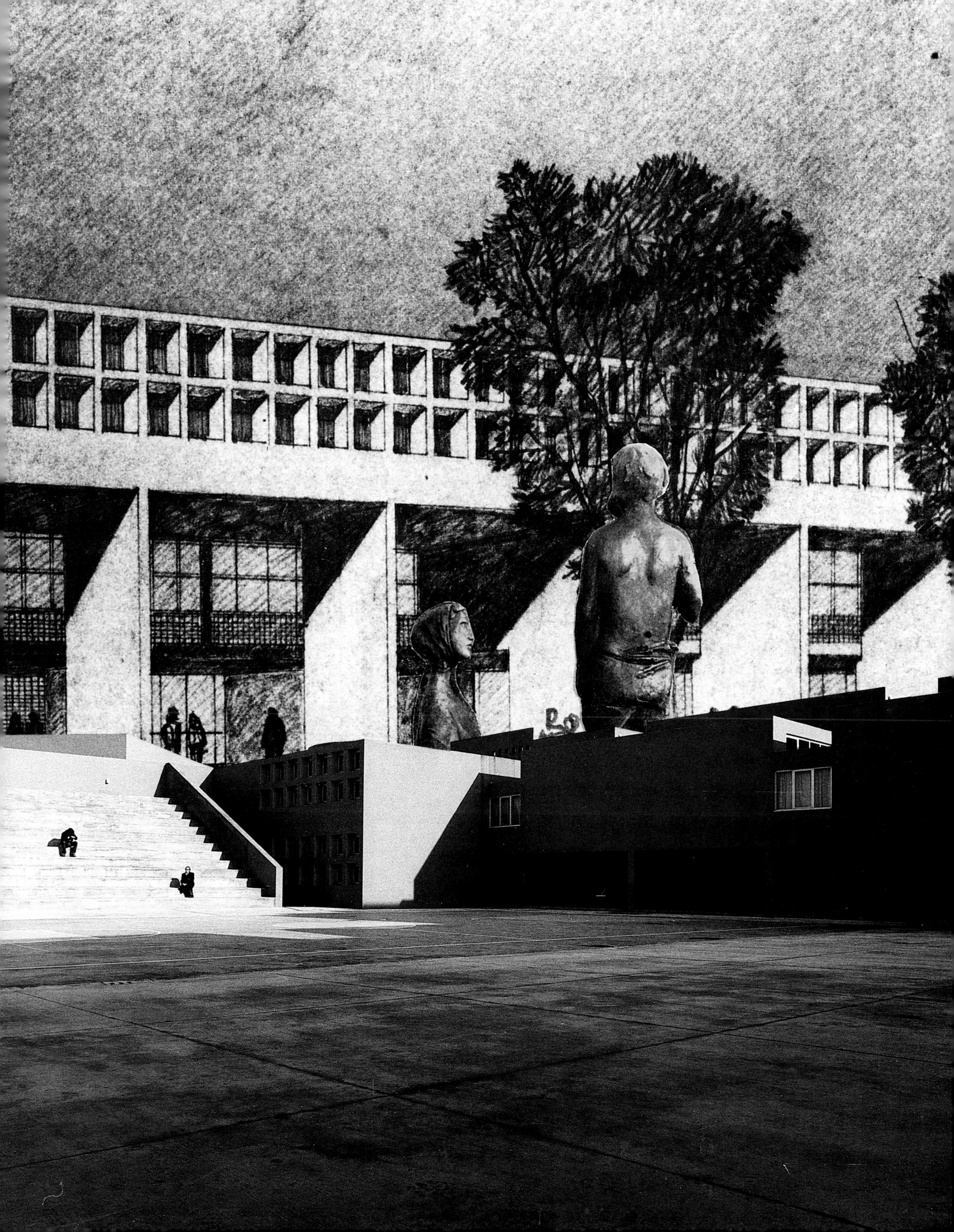

34 ■ SCIENCE COLLEGE
BELOW: South elevation

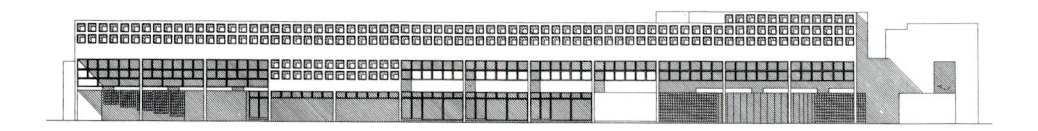

Carlo Aymonino

SCIENCE COLLEGE
BELOW: East elevation

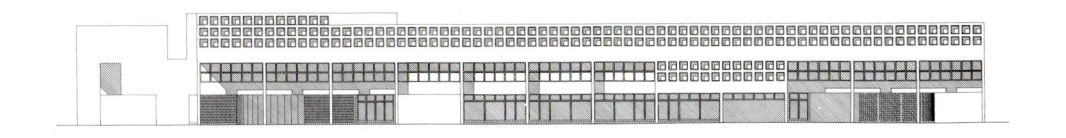

35
College Campus

Carlo Aymonino

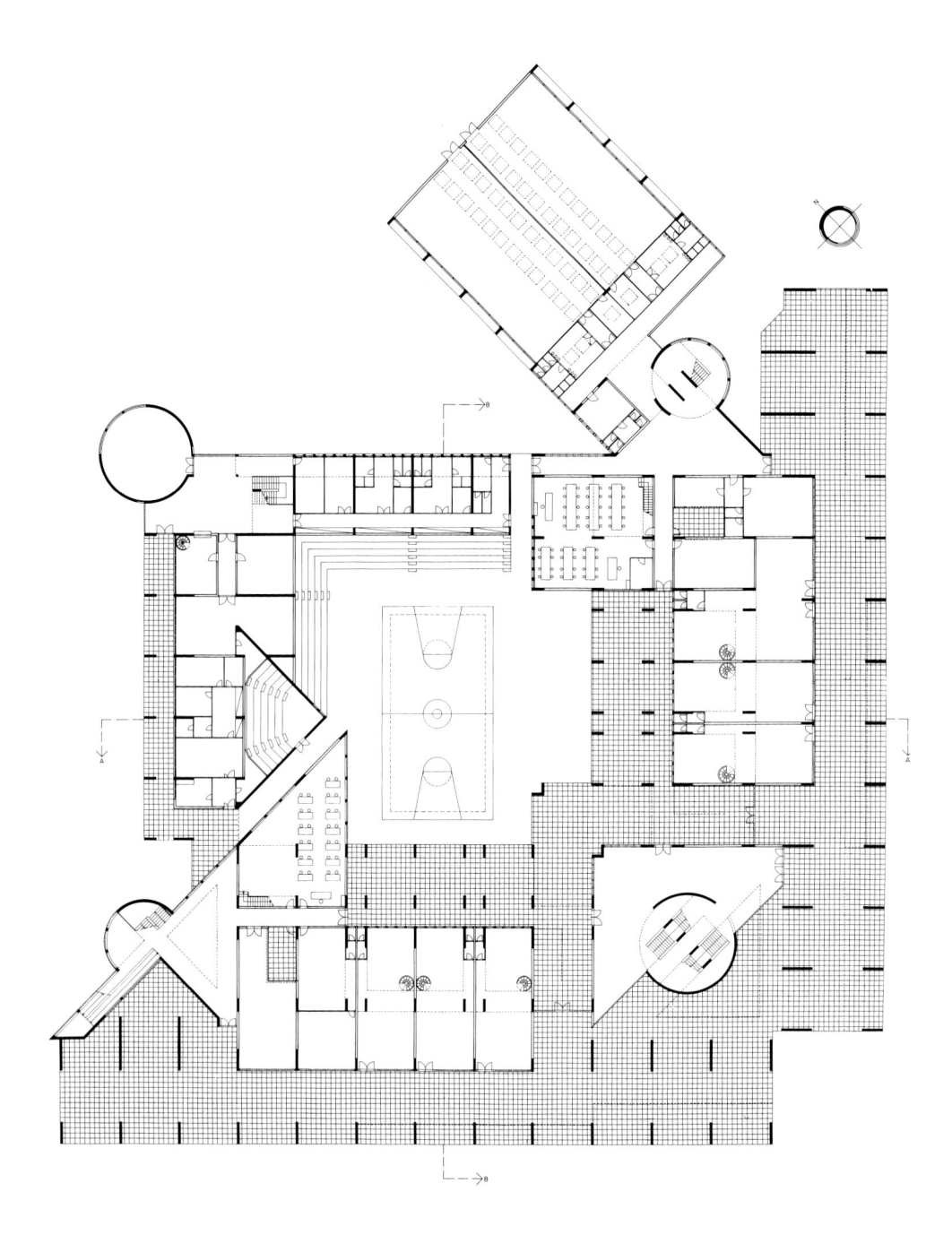

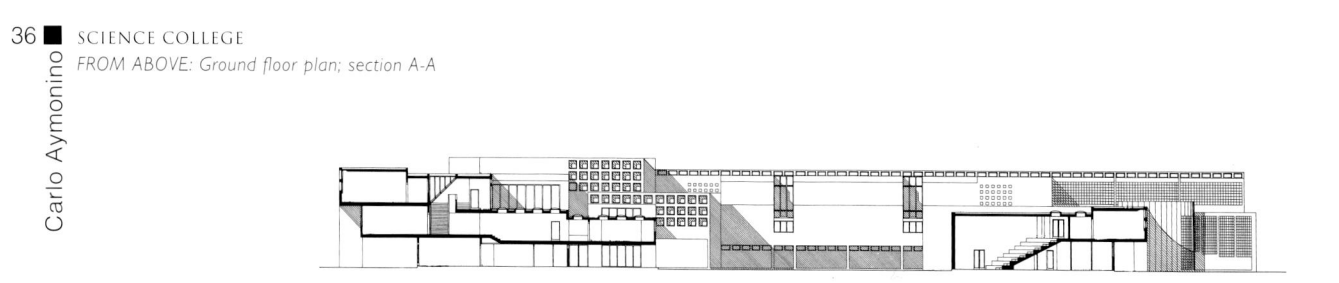

SCIENCE COLLEGE
FROM ABOVE: Ground floor plan; section A-A

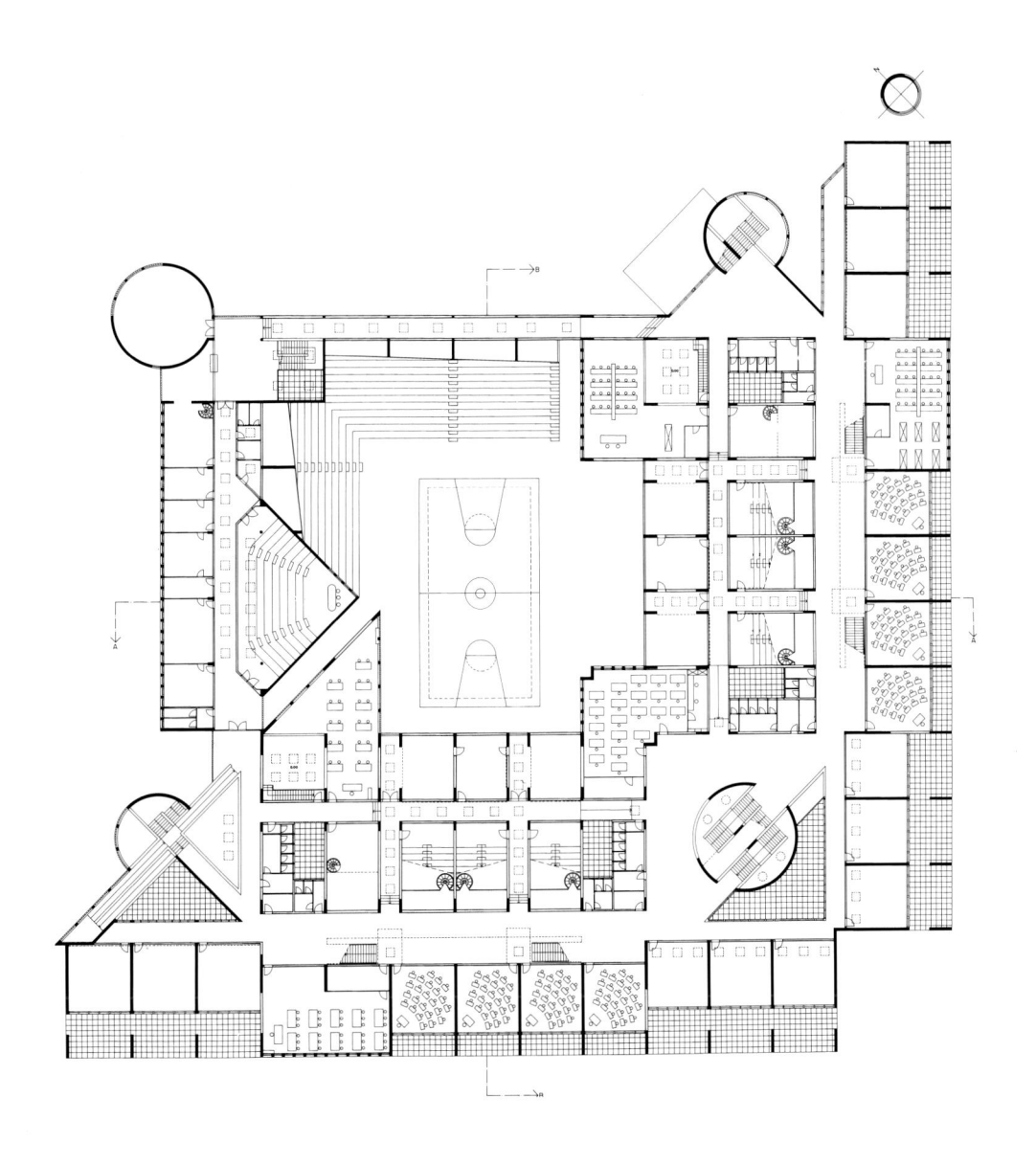

SCIENCE COLLEGE
FROM ABOVE: First floor plan; section B-B

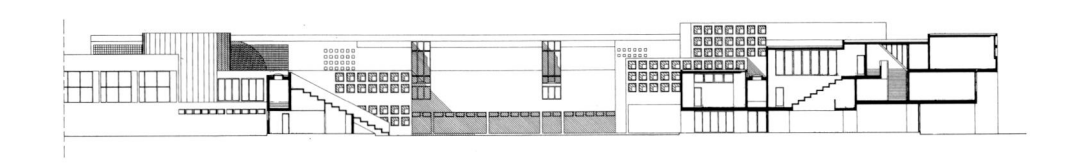

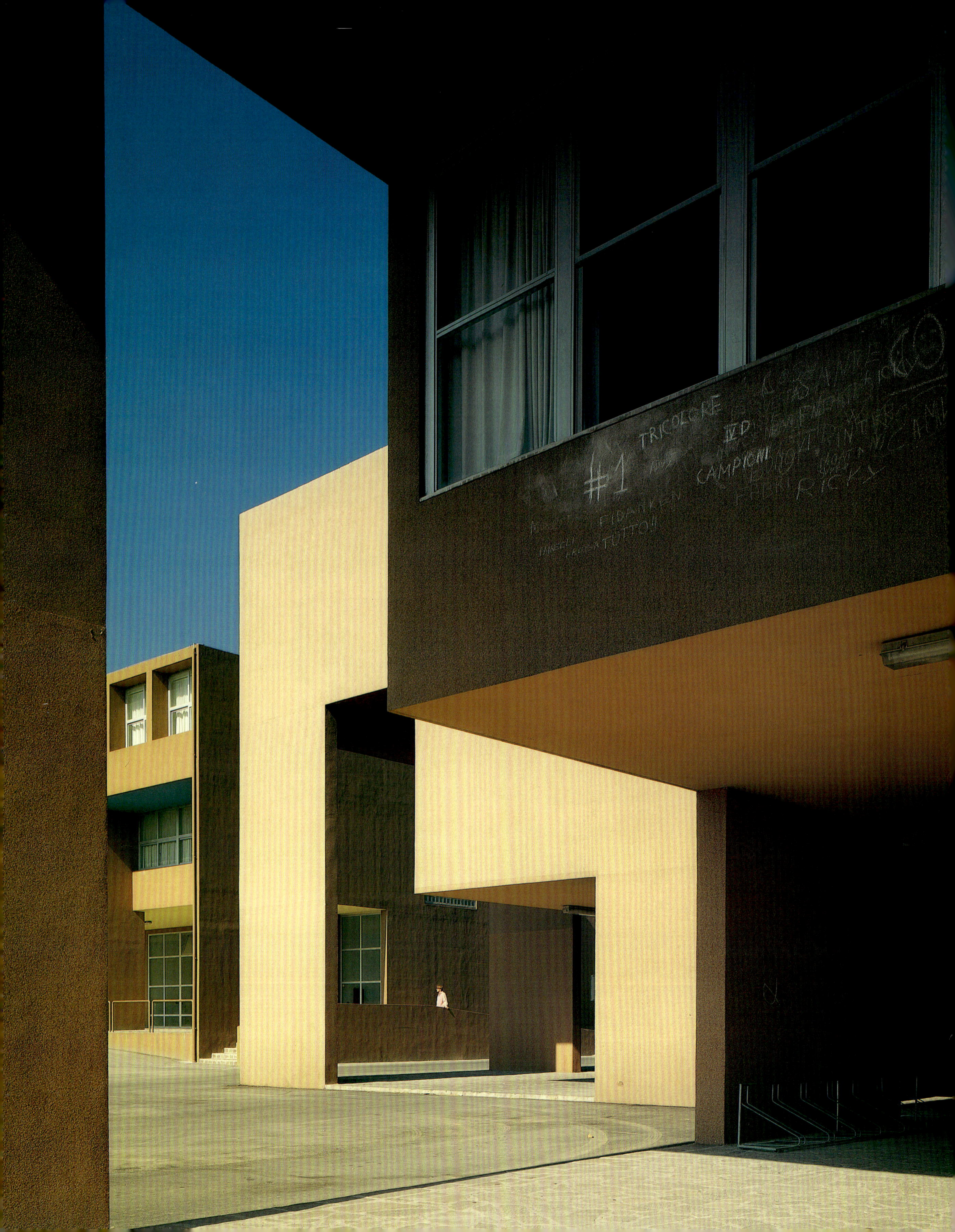
TRICOLORE
#1
CAMPIONI
RICKY

COMMERCIAL AND TECHNICAL INSTITUTE
RIGHT: Perspective sketch

39

College Campus

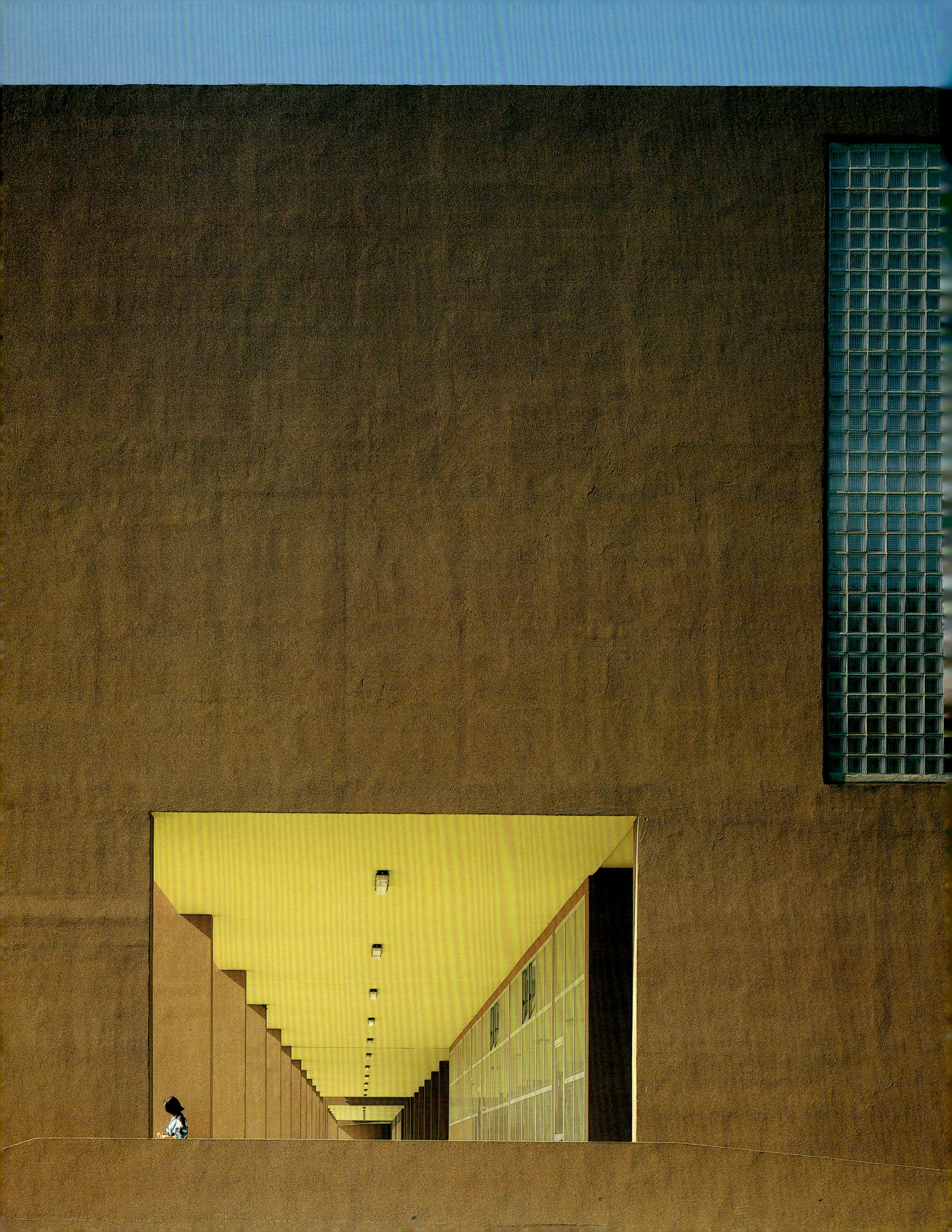

COMMERCIAL AND TECHNICAL INSTITUTE

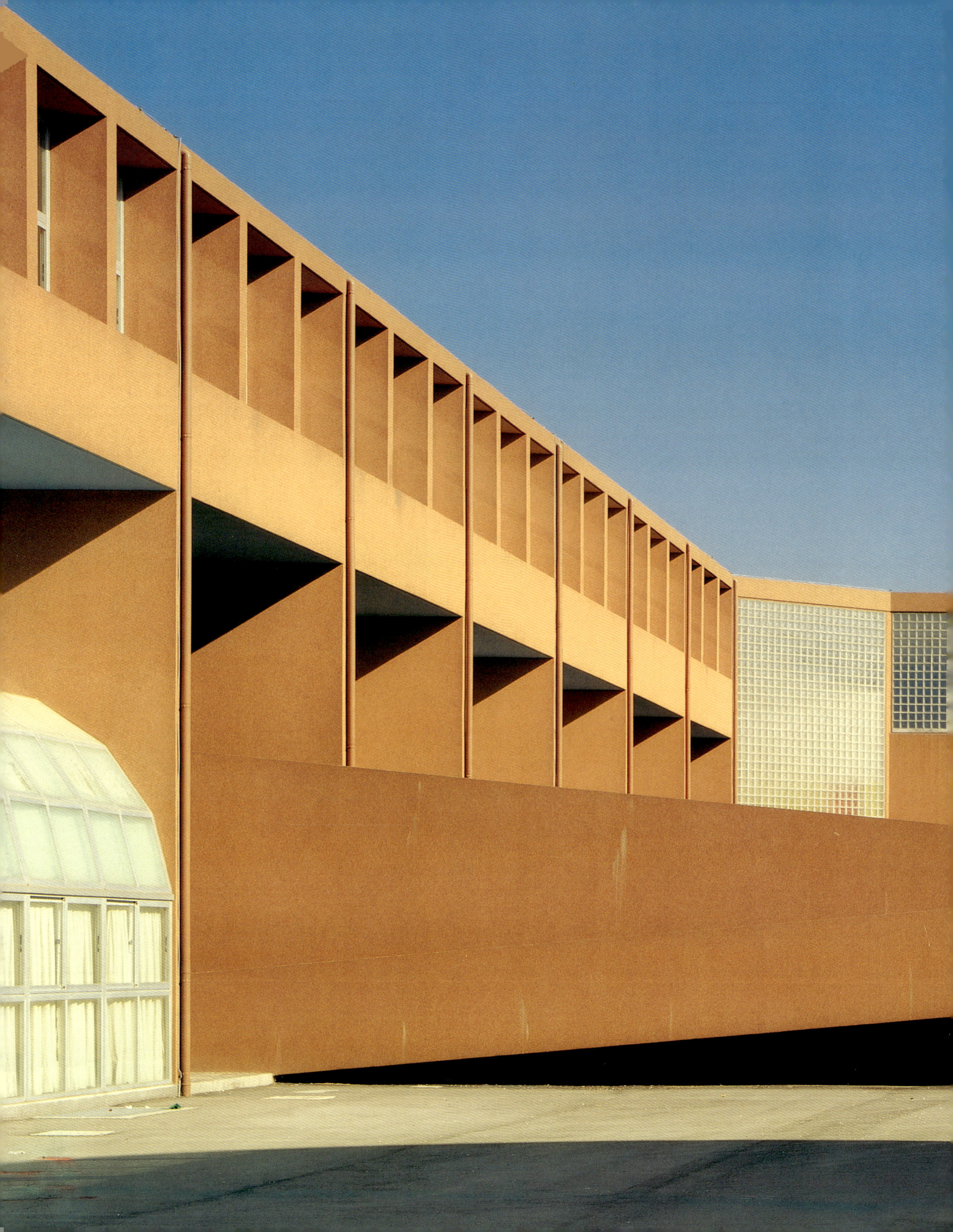

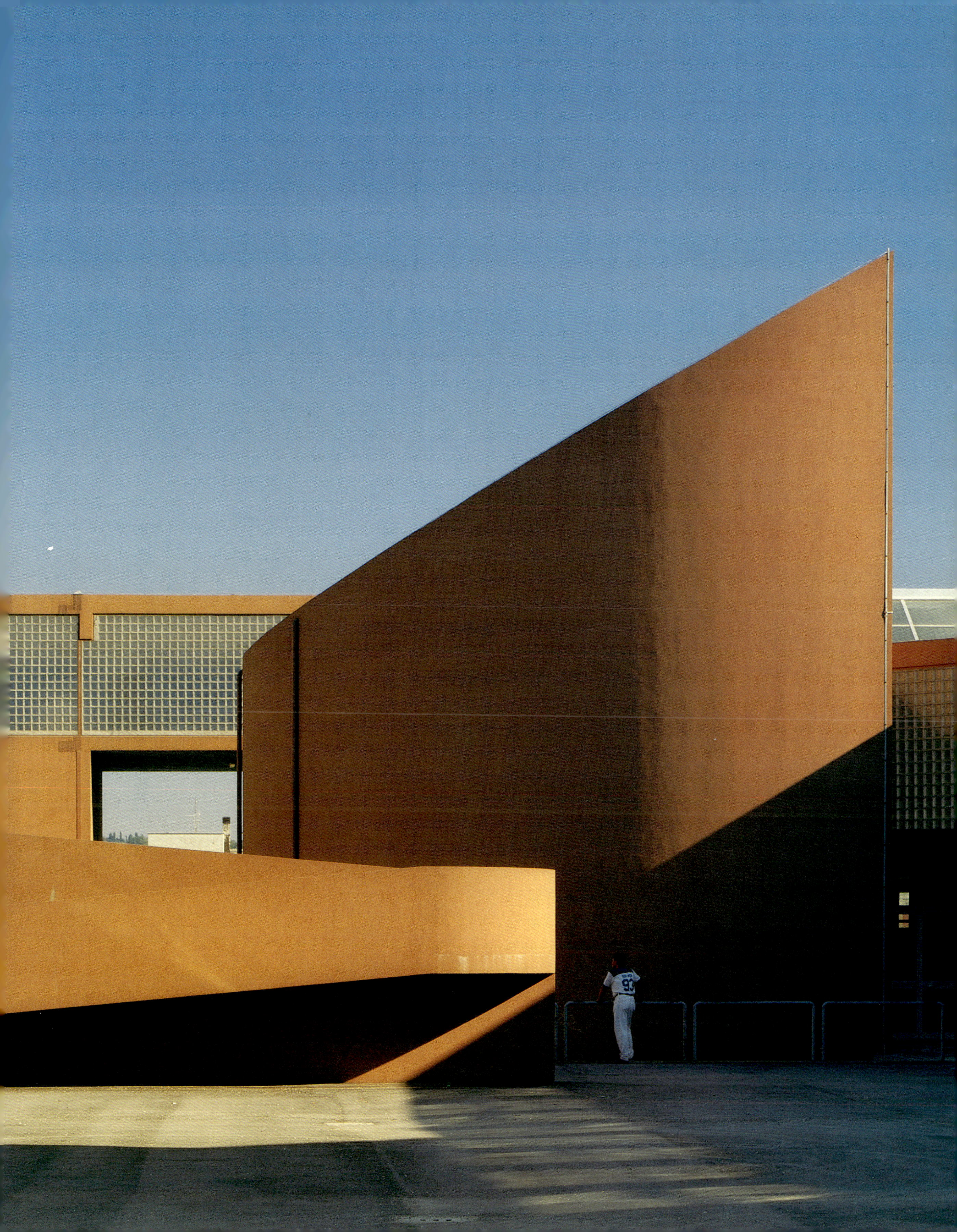

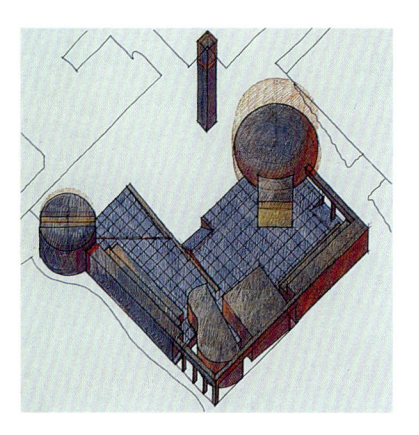

CIVIC CENTRE
FROM ABOVE: Axonometric; perspective view

Carlo Aymonino

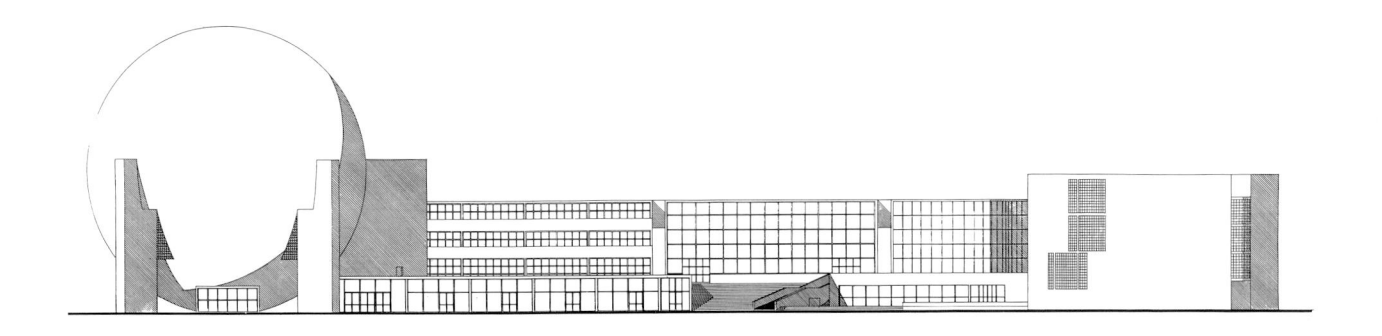

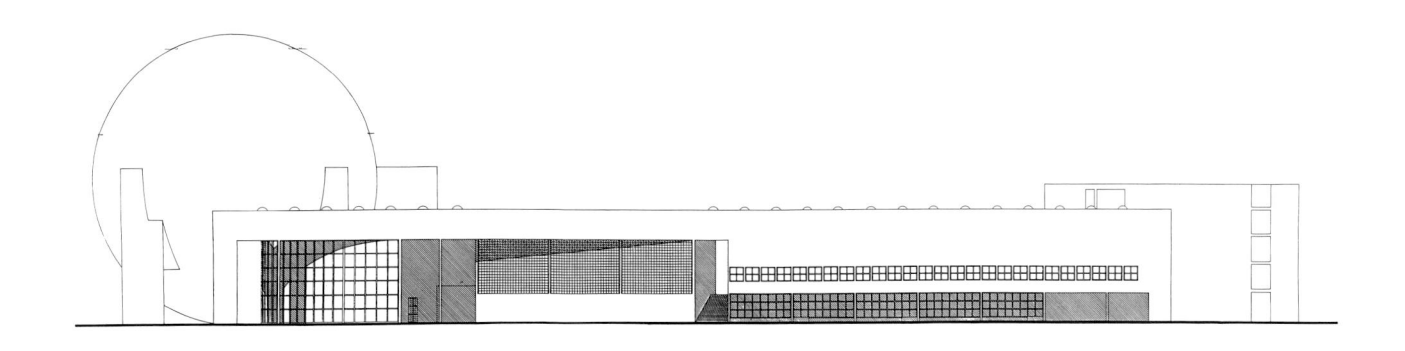

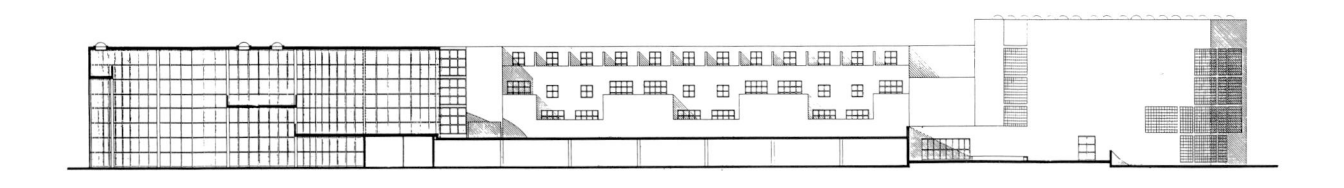

CIVIC CENTRE
*FROM ABOVE: North-west elevation; south-east elevation;
section B-B; south-west elevation*

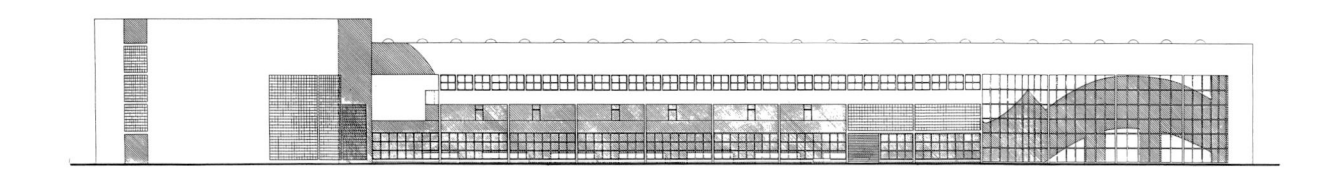

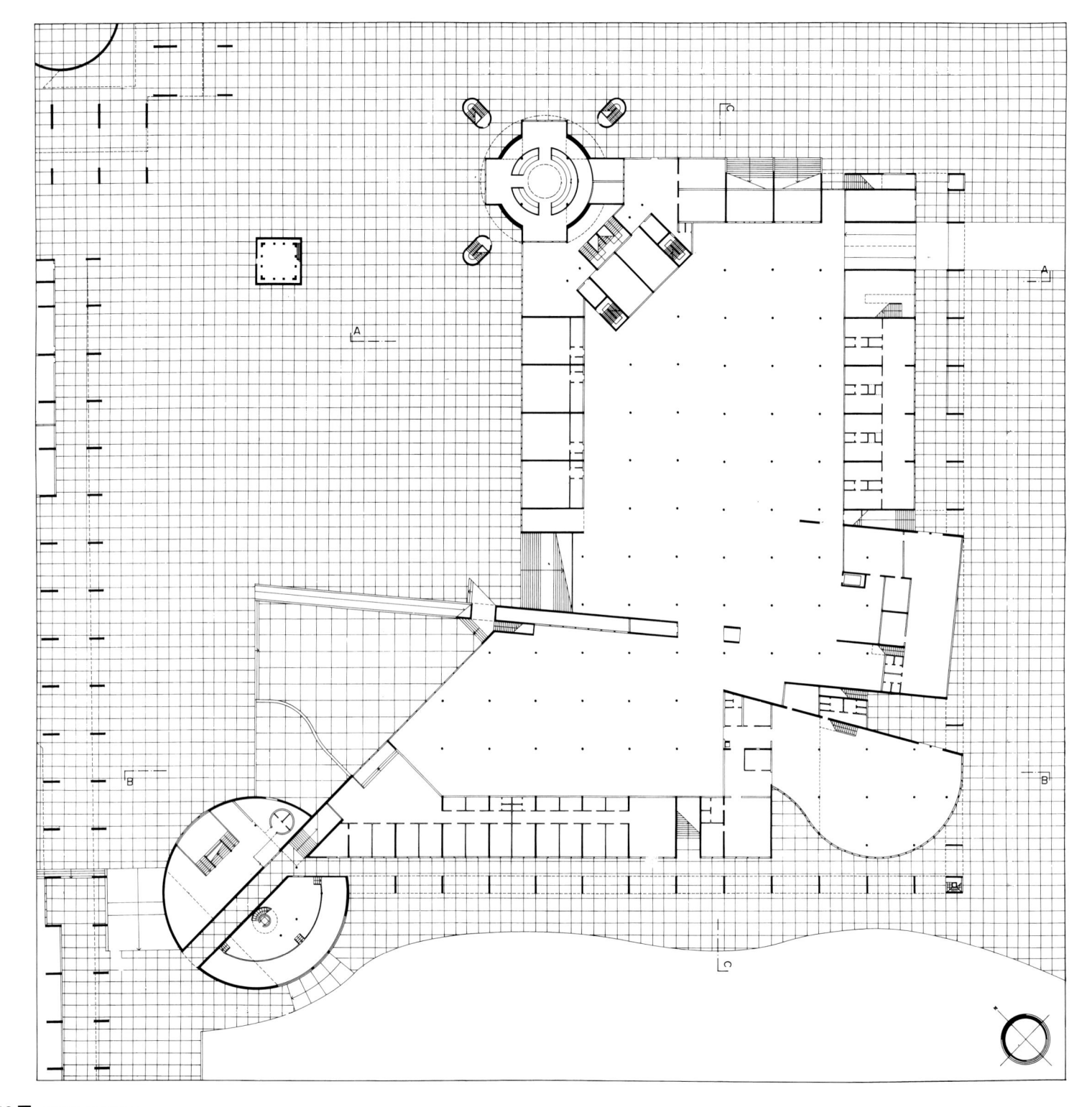

46 ■ CIVIC CENTRE
FROM ABOVE: Square level plan; north-east elevation

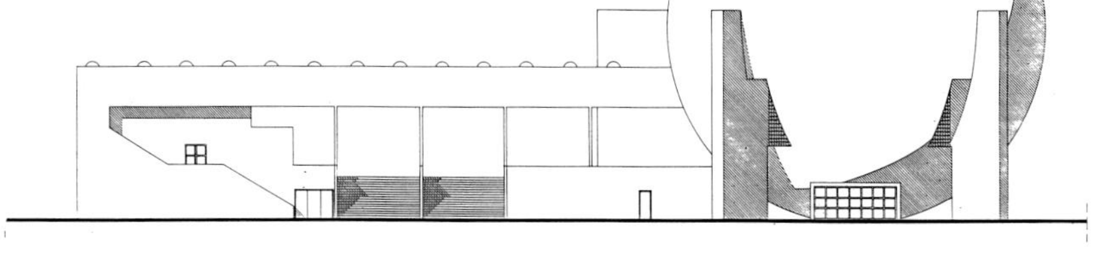

Carlo Aymonino

CIVIC CENTRE
FROM ABOVE: First floor plan; section A-A

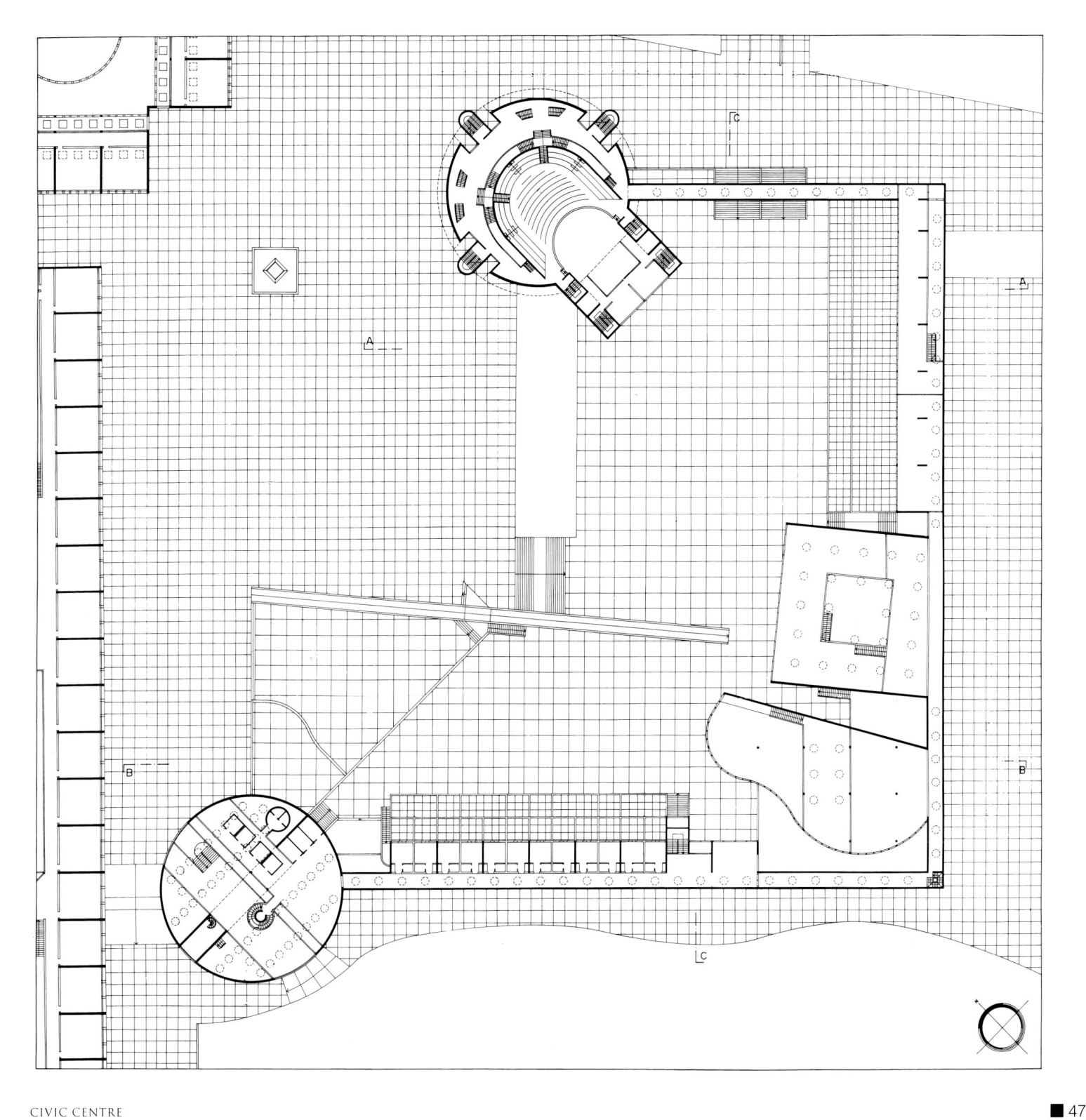

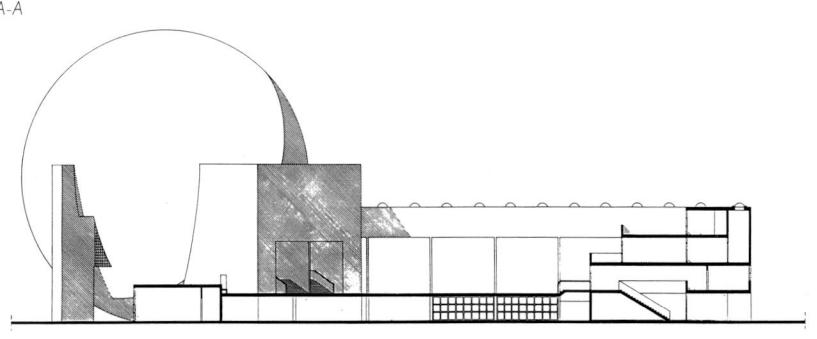

47

College Campus

Carlo Aymonino

Perspective

COURT HOUSE, FERRARA, 1977

With Alberto Torti

Founded as a convent annexed to the Chiesa del Gesù in the mid-sixteenth century, and rebuilt in 1676 for the new collegium, as two parallel wings joined by a transverse portico, this vast building complex was restructured again in the nineteenth century as a quadrilateral building by adding the building along Via Borgoleoni, next to the church. Its consecutive functions range from its religious beginnings as a convent to a prison for the court house, then a barracks for the civil guard and finally, higher education and technical institutes.

Equally diverse is the quality of the individual architectural styles that constitute the complex. While the imposing wing beside the church expresses its own monumental value in an extremely long and tall, cross-vaulted space, on to which open the apertures of the corridor that gives access to the upper floors (the simplicity of the building defies the peculiarities in height), the opposite wing finds itself, also as a consequence of its own historical vocation, as a massive, elementary (and often manipulated) container, deprived of any particular architectonic value, beyond its own *vetustas*. Even less worthy of consideration, a decidedly mediocre and superfluous recent addition, the building enclosing the courtyard on Via Borgoleoni is the only one not protected by the national heritage organisation, while the porticoed wing at the rear, housing the classrooms of a school on the adjacent lot, has unfortunately been modified by illegal and poor quality alterations, and has been, until now, beyond the control of the restructuring project for the area.

The former Jesuit convent, destined for use as a court of justice, has a vast amount of pre-existing structural fabric, albeit indifferent and of no significant quality. The project, which is based on a morphological and functional classification of an empirical nature, applies itself to providing diverse, partial answers, building by building. It puts forward an ensemble of specific approaches ranging from the 'scientific', and simple restoration for the two main wings, to the demolition and consequent rebuilding of the transverse structure with its main entrance from the street. In practice, the two four-storey buildings will maintain their own consolidated function of 'containers', the more valuable ones being entirely preserved, while the new construction of the two-storey transverse structure has been designed to house the court rooms. The idea of the project is to insert a modern architectural fragment, a new building that will instantly declare its foreignness to the context, but which, at the same time, in substituting new for old, can integrate and consolidate the physiognomy and spatial characteristics of the existing and remaining buildings.

Although further complicated by the necessity of fulfilling the contrasting demands of commissions imposed by the *comune*, the Ministry of Justice and the magistrates in turn, and also burdened by rigid technical and security restrictions, the project for the new building can adapt the compositional characteristics of the existing complex in the volumetric development of the two perpendicular axes.

A semi-arched suspended gallery, linking the four distinct court rooms, and emphasising the transverse axis, intersects the great glass gallery. This gallery, which begins at the main entrance, faces across the internal courtyard to the clock tower on the centre of the porticoed wing. On the semi-basement level are the security vaults and the most secluded judicial chambers and archives. On the ground floor are the four court rooms and related service spaces, and on the first floor more chambers on the entrance and street side.

50 ■ *Ground floor plan*

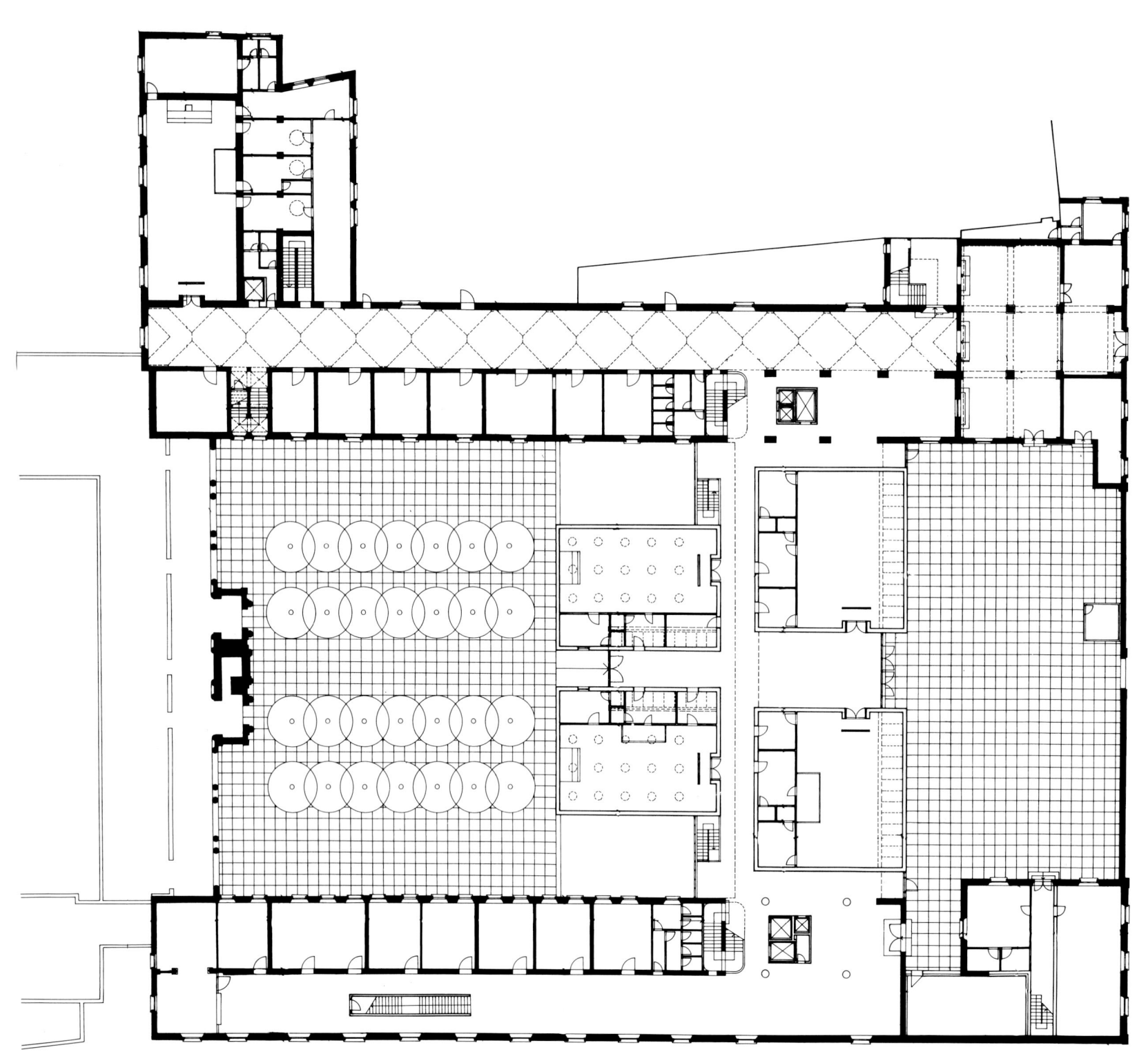

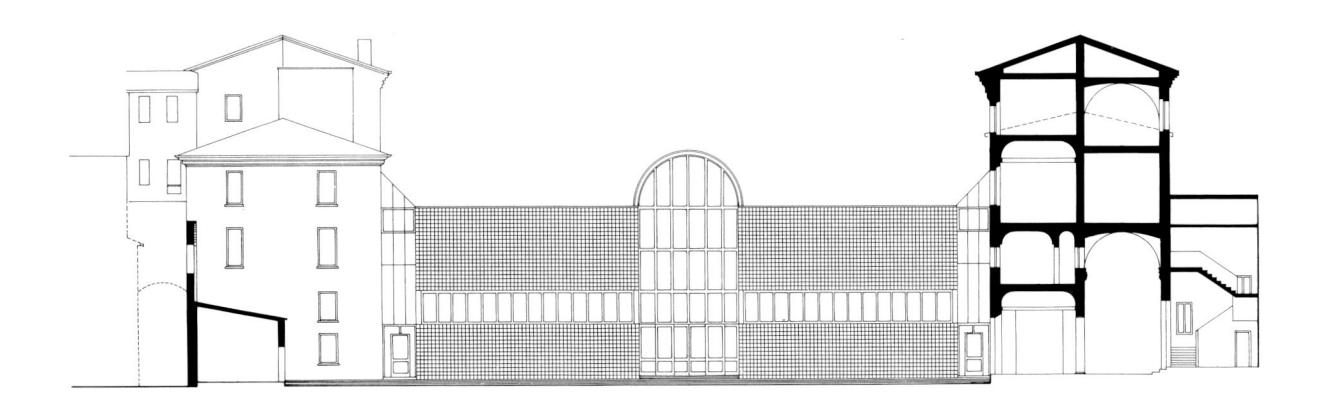

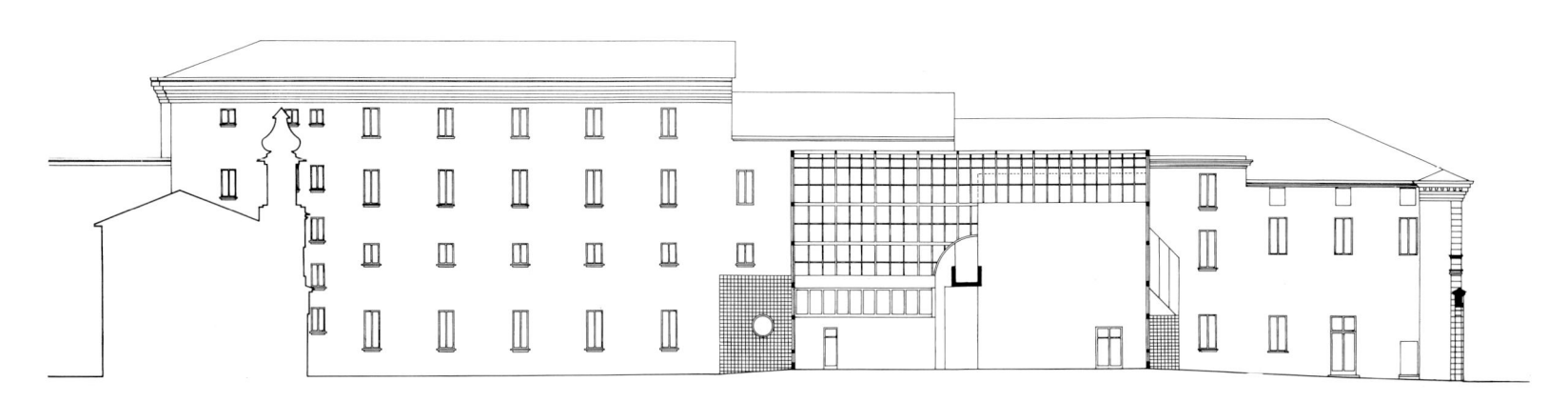

FROM ABOVE: Entrance elevation; longitudinal section showing the gallery and courtyard

52 ■ *First floor plan*

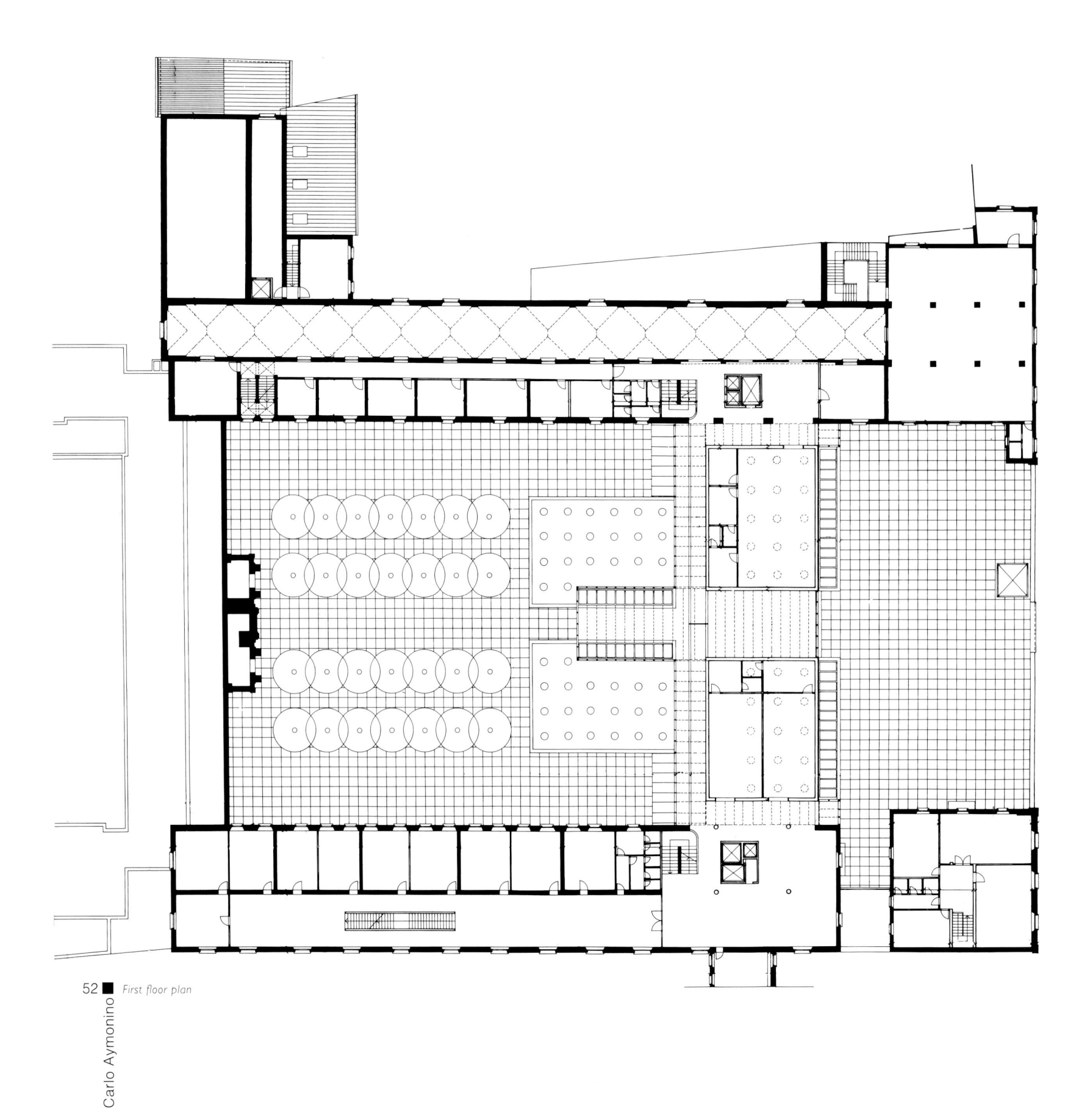

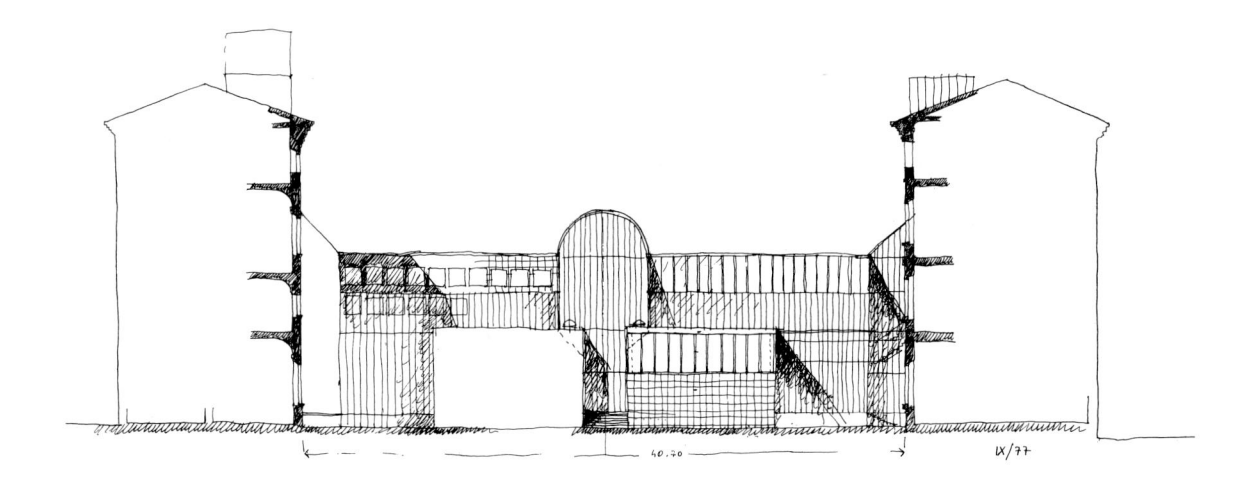

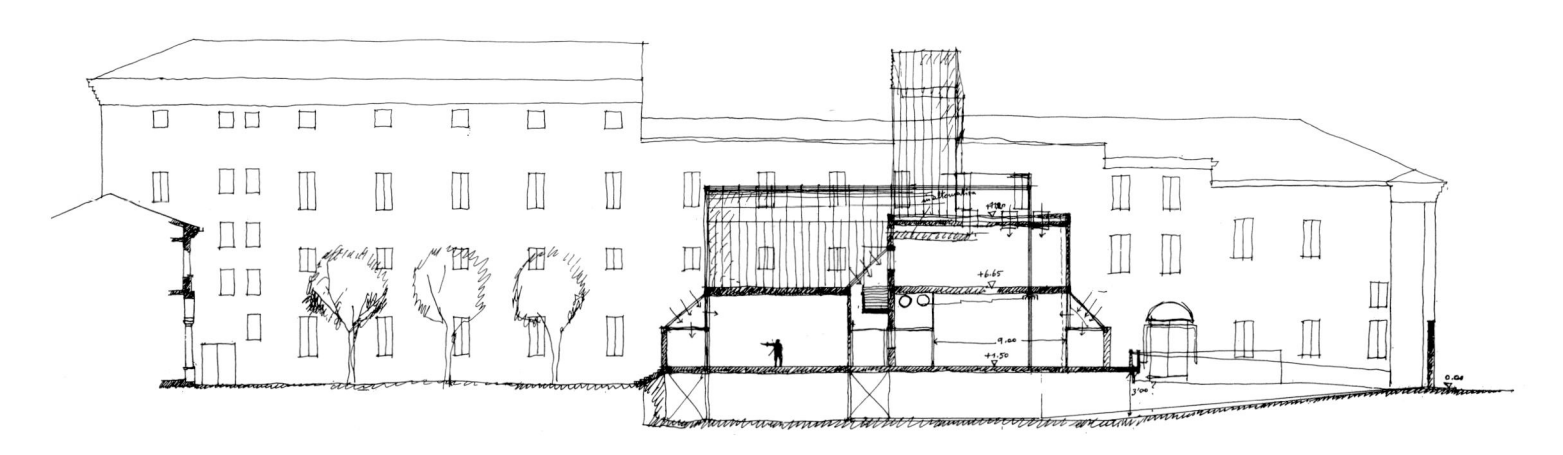

FROM ABOVE: Sketch of entrance elevation; sketch of longitudinal section

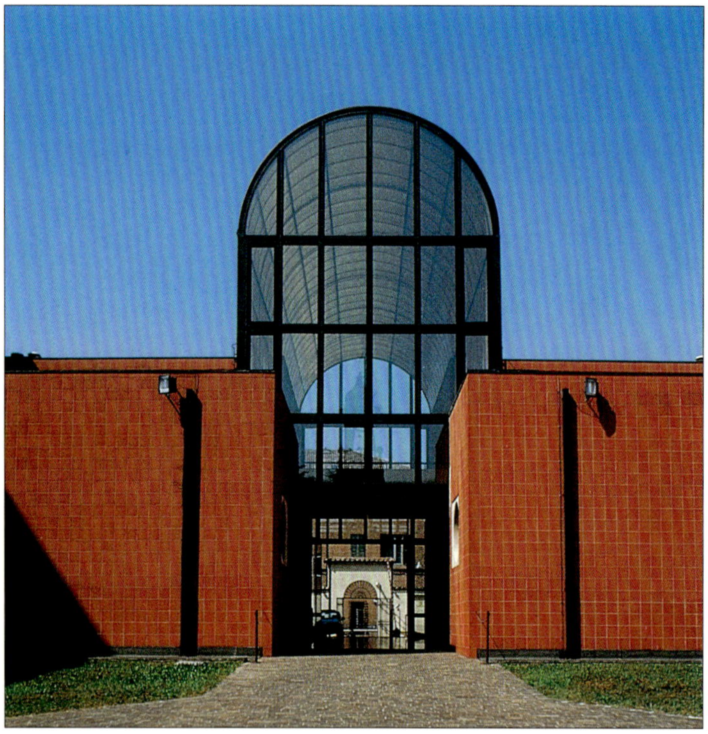

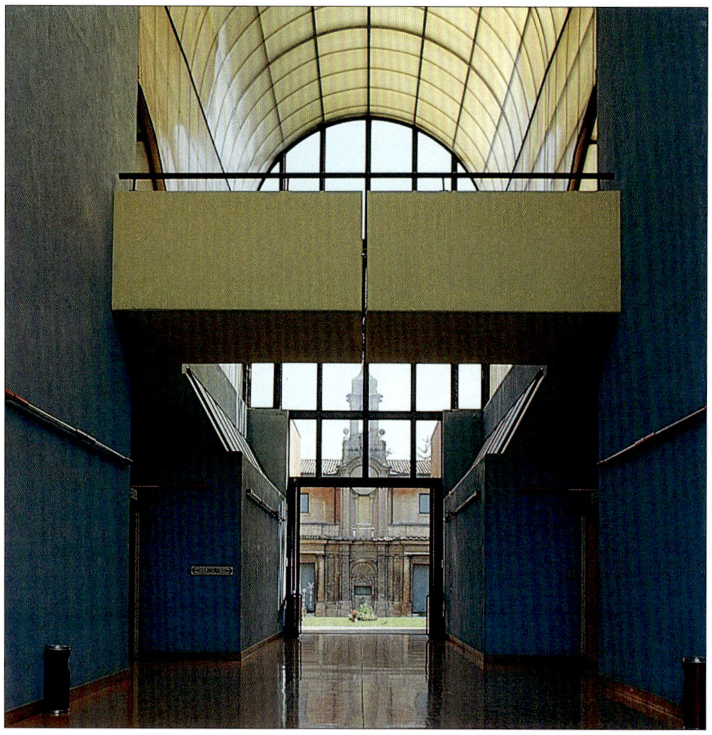

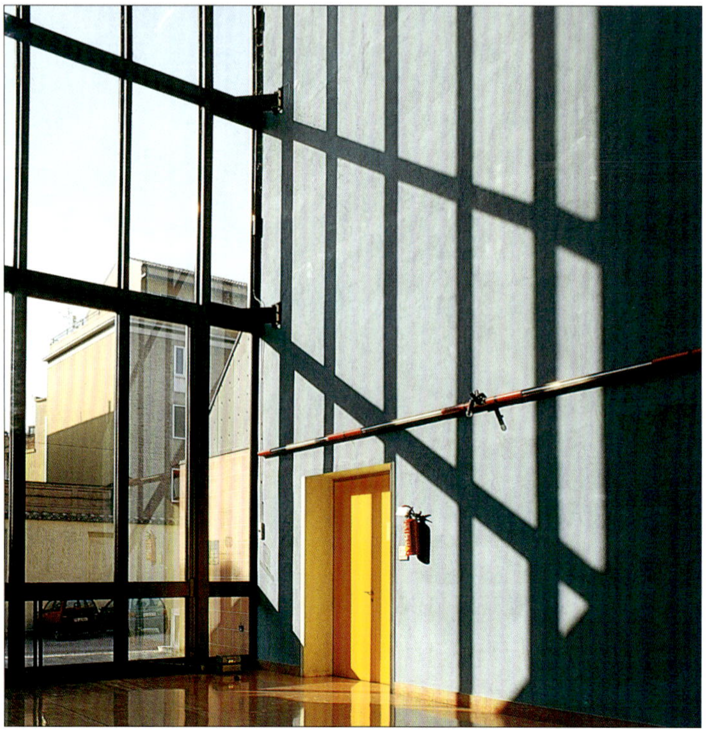

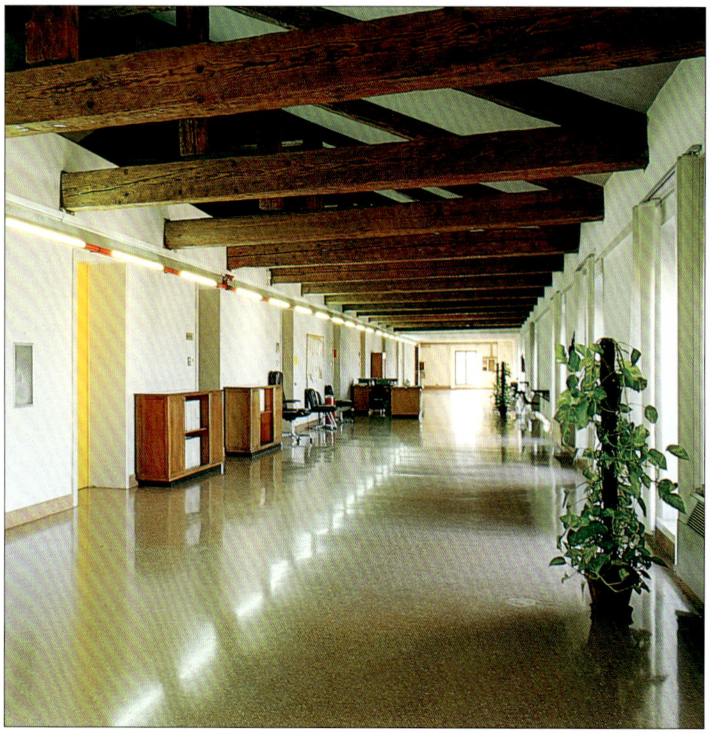

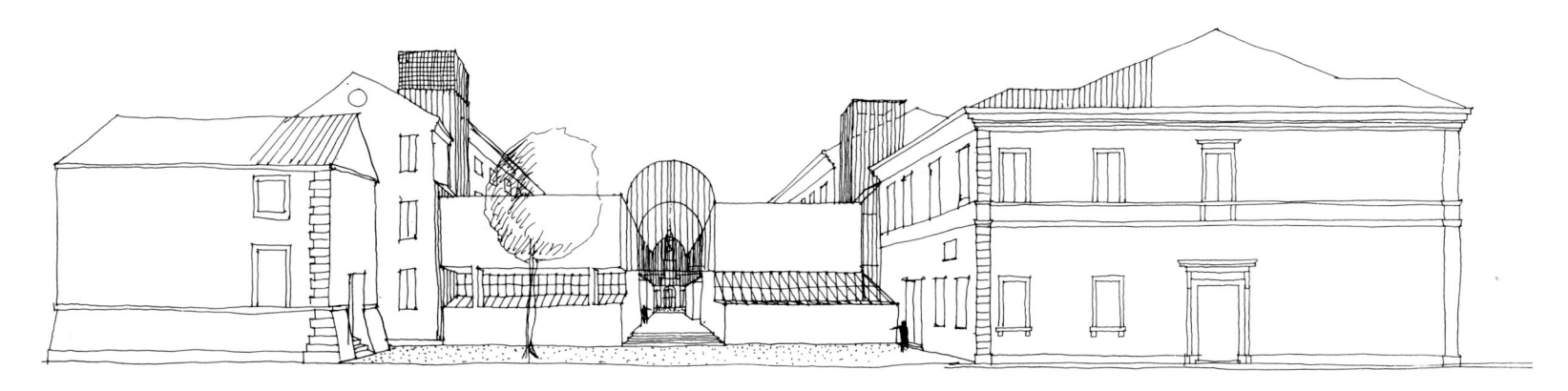

Perspective sketch

PIAZZA DEL POPOLO, PIAZZA SOLFERINO AND PIAZZA EUROPA, TERNI, 1985-90

With Maria Luisa Tugnoli

During the course of the centuries, the 'trace' of an ancient forum, at the junction between the *cardo* and the decuman of the Roman city of Terni, developed into a square. In the Gregorian land register of 1819, this is indicated as a 'public square'; to which is added, with an irregular perimeter, a second 'gymnasium square'. In 1869, the two squares became, respectively, the Piazza Vittorio Emanuele and the Piazza Solferino, maintaining a central location accentuated by a new route from the station to the city centre, Via Tacito.

Later, the ancient structure was destroyed and rendered unrecognisable by bombing. The plan for the reconstruction of the city and the regulatory plan were both designed by Ridolfi, to achieve a defined city centre, based around the three squares: Piazza del Popolo (formerly Piazza Vittorio Emanuele), Piazza Solferino and the new Piazza Europa, where the Palazzo Spada and some of Ridolfi's most handsome buildings were built. At the centre of the plan is the Istituto Nazionale delle Assicurazioni (INA) office block, which competes with the ugliest banking and insurance offices built in the historic centres of many Italian cities.

The design task was to accentuate the 'diversity' of the three squares, while determining their underlying integration as a series of spaces with a central pedestrian system, and, also, to attenuate the negative architectural presence of the INA building. These small-scale interventions are recognisable, as a mark of addition, or, of completion. Each of the various components is distinguishable: the truncated and full-height marble columns between Piazza del Popolo and Piazza Europa, a permeable boundary that divides and connects the two spaces; the corner building, ruined by the bombardments, which completes the Piazza Solferino; and in the Piazza Europa, four architectural 'objects' built in stone (real or false) at a scale that does not compete with the existing volumes, but allows the four objects to be distinct, both individually and as a group. The square is completed by a stone fountain – a cube superimposed by a sphere – echoing the small monument that Goethe had built in his villa in Weimar. A large benched area provides a meeting and resting place.

The most significant intervention of 1985 to Terni's central squares, the wall of four objects, allowed Piazza Solferino to regain a domestic and private dimension, such as it had prior to the second World War. With the decision of the *comune* administration to designate the square for the use of children, pedestrianisation of the square was a fundamental element.

The paving design stems from these principles, integrating a magical dimension that stimulates children's games and fantasies within a rigorous composite structure of focal points, axes and lines. This basic structure takes advantage of the essential elements of the space: a longitudinal axis, which marks the differences between the buildings (including the INA) on the south side and the north (which requires vehicular access for services), and a focal point at the far end of the square.

The perspective of the main axis is broken by a building which houses the children's library on its ground floor, and also, at the end of the square, by a sculptural reclining figure rising from the surface of the piazza, forming a small but perceptible three-dimensional barrier to the Piazza Europa.

Planes, axes, focal points and traces are enriched by figurative and chromatic values evocative of children's imagery, albeit dispersed with formal models, and liberally inspired by Italian painting: in particular, by the fish, sea and extraordinary sun of De Chirico's *Mysterious Spectacle*.

The south and north sides of the new children's square assume different qualities: on the south, alternating bands of basalt and travertine stone zig-zag, like rippled water; whilst the north has simple travertine strips running perpendicular to the building frontages. Against the backdrop of the former, a fish-shaped figure emerges from the ground, an unusual bench with undulating levels which is also a slide for younger children.

The focal point of the square is De Chirico's sun, which extends its rays from this secluded corner of the city. Here, basalt and travertine are substituted with yellow and red cotto tiles, to emphasise the central nucleus and contours of the burning sphere, laid in alternating rows to define surfaces and lines. Cotto tiles, warmer than travertine and basalt, are traditional materials of Terni's squares. A line of street lamps follows the longitudinal axis of the square and illuminates the sun's position.

Each element offers itself to the gradual discoveries of children, who run across the square in all directions, like a story by Collodi.[1]

Notes

1 Carlo Collodi is the author of *Pinocchio*, among other children's stories.

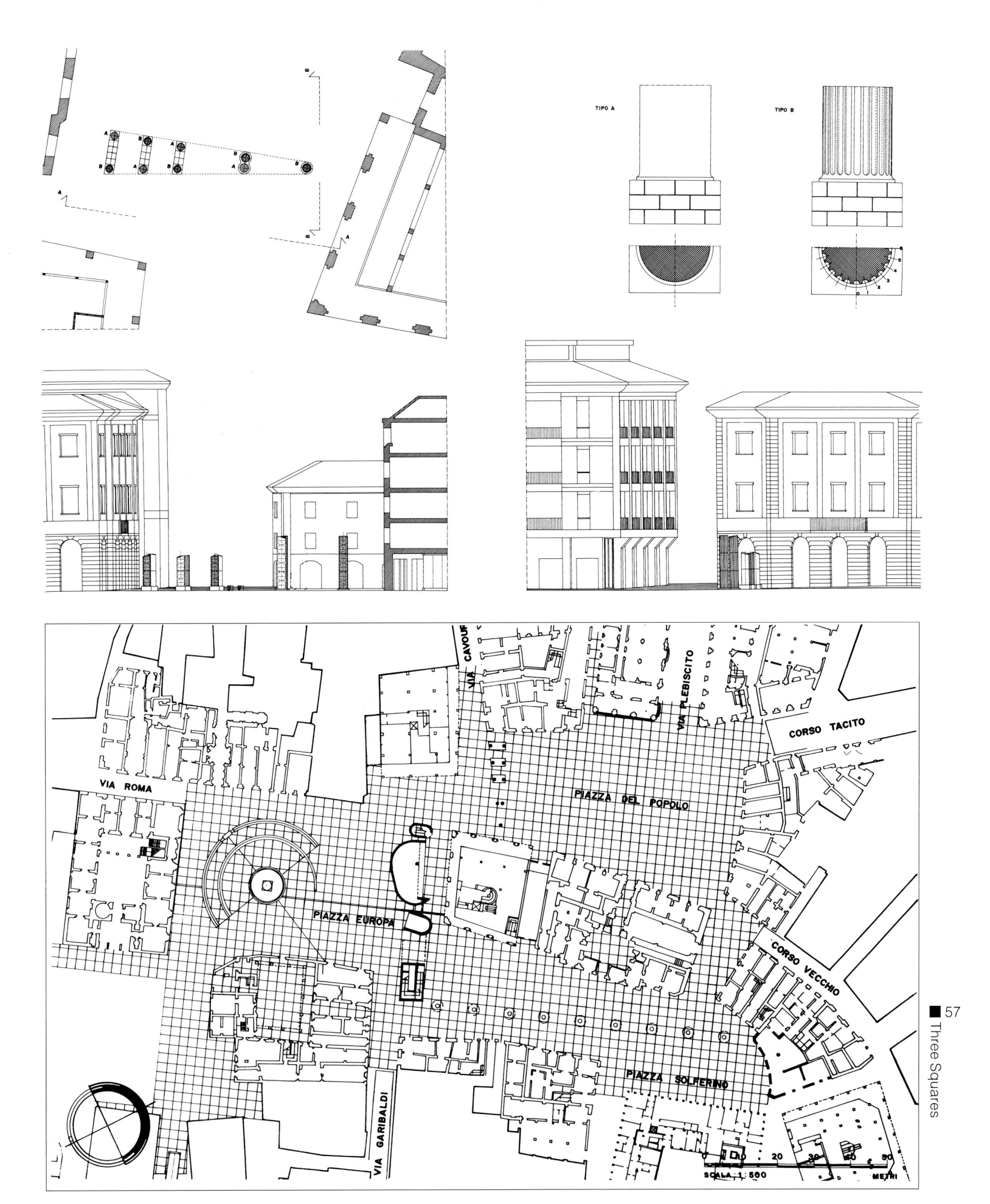

PIAZZA DEL POPOLO
ABOVE LEFT: Plan; ABOVE RIGHT: Plans and elevations of
columns; CENTRE: Elevations of the square entrance; BELOW:
Site plan of the three piazzas

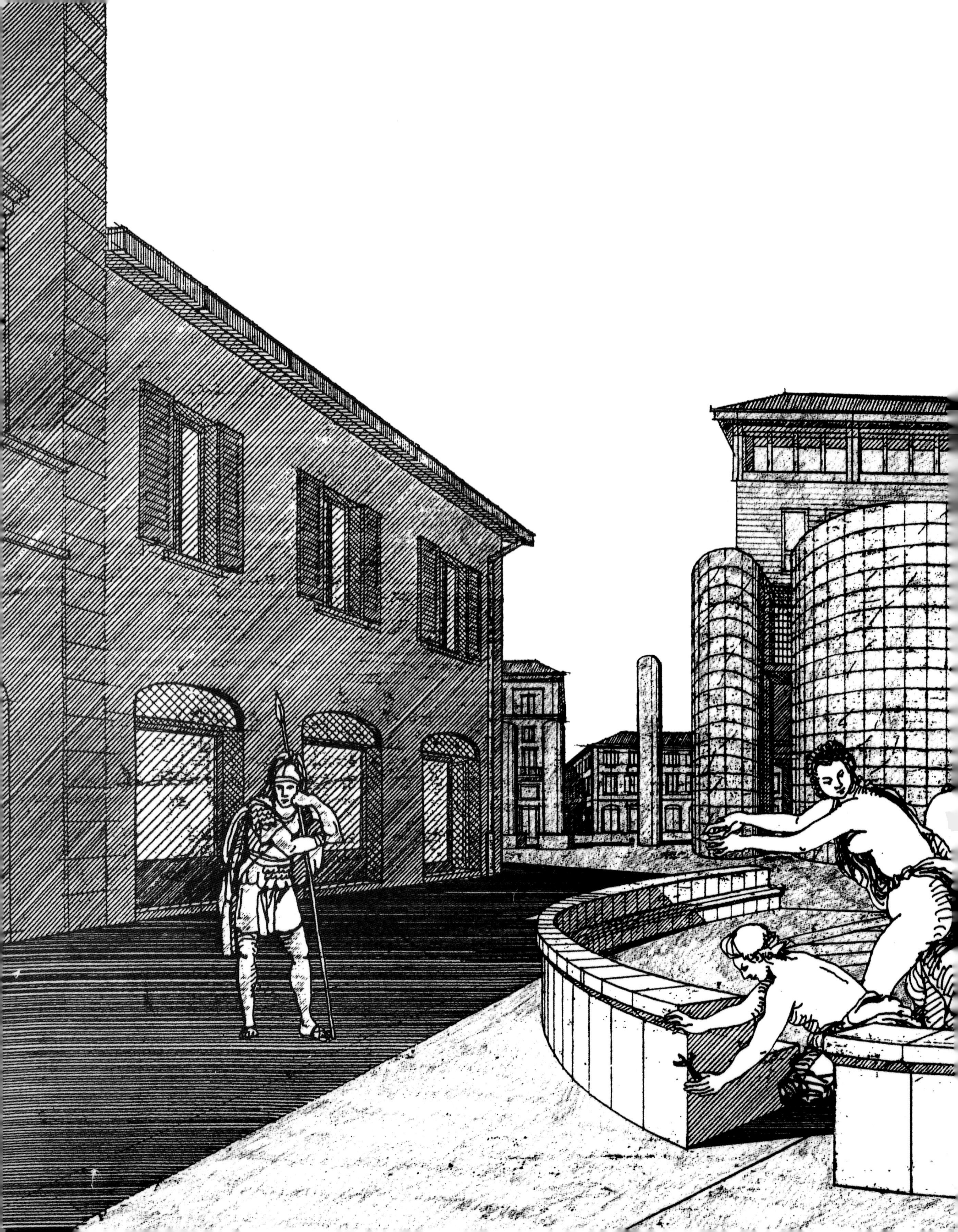

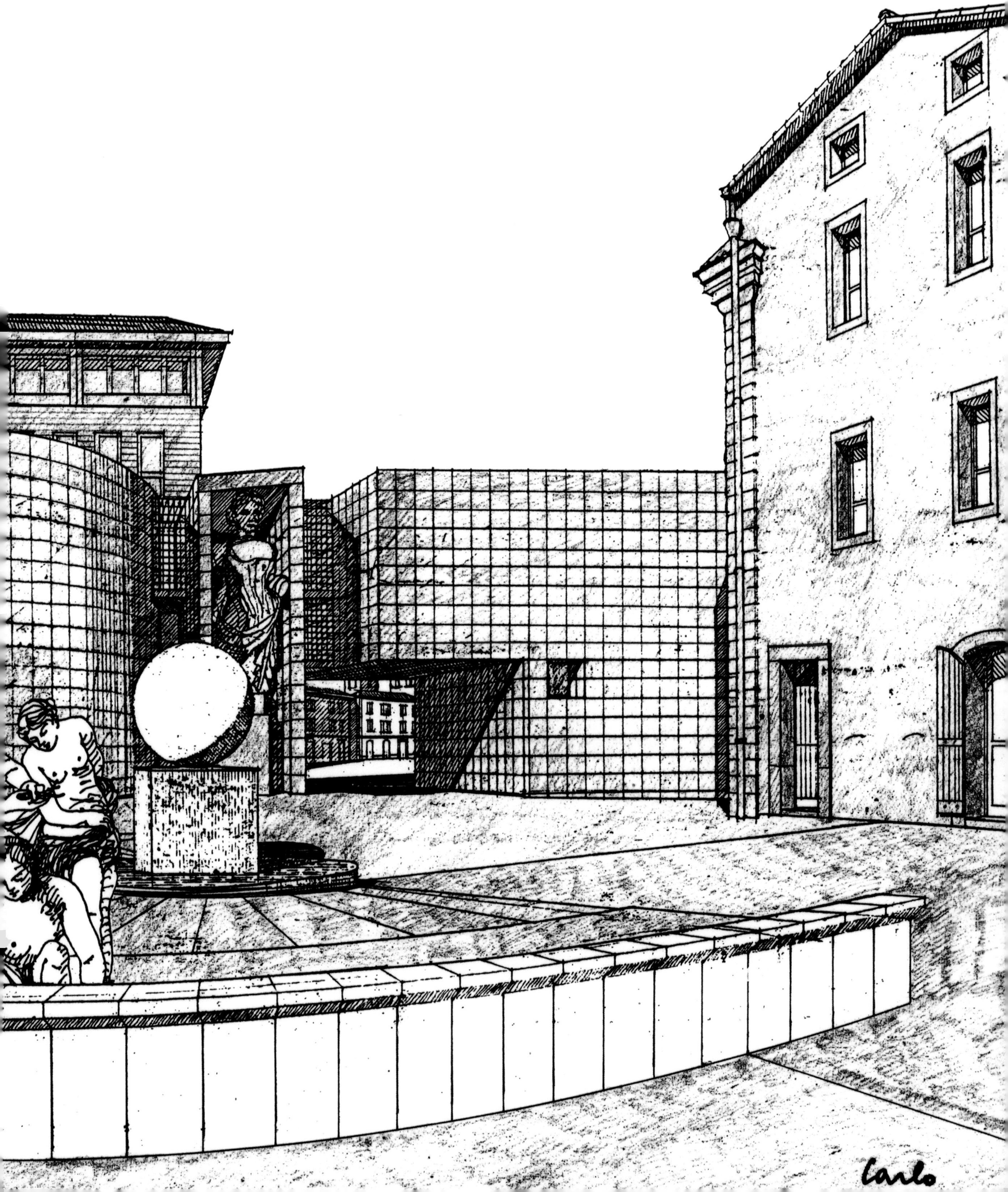
Carlo

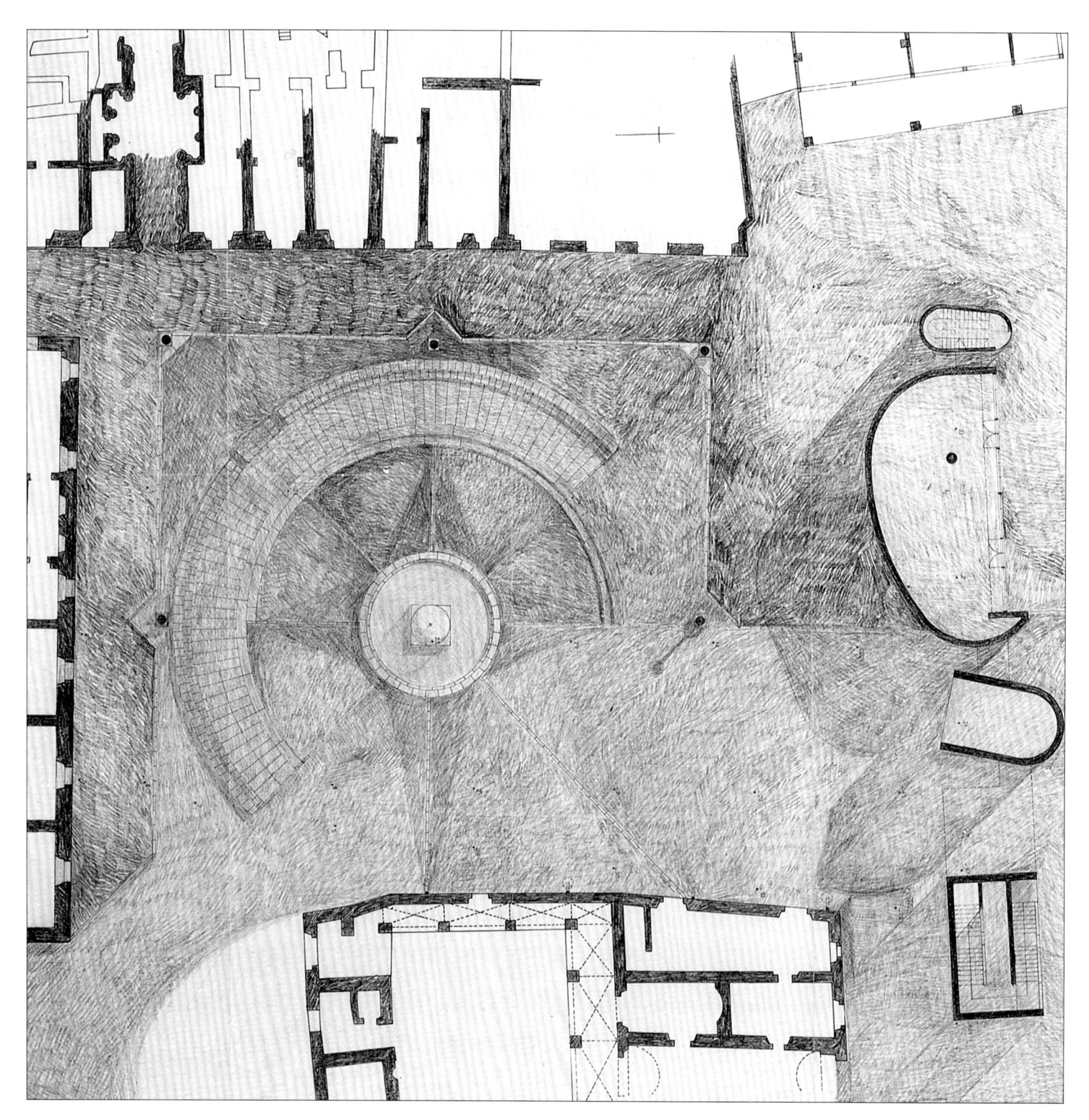

PIAZZA EUROPA
PAGES 58-59: Perspective; ABOVE: Plan

Carlo Aymonino

PIAZZA EUROPA
Axonometric of the entrance to Piazza Popolo and Piazza Solferino

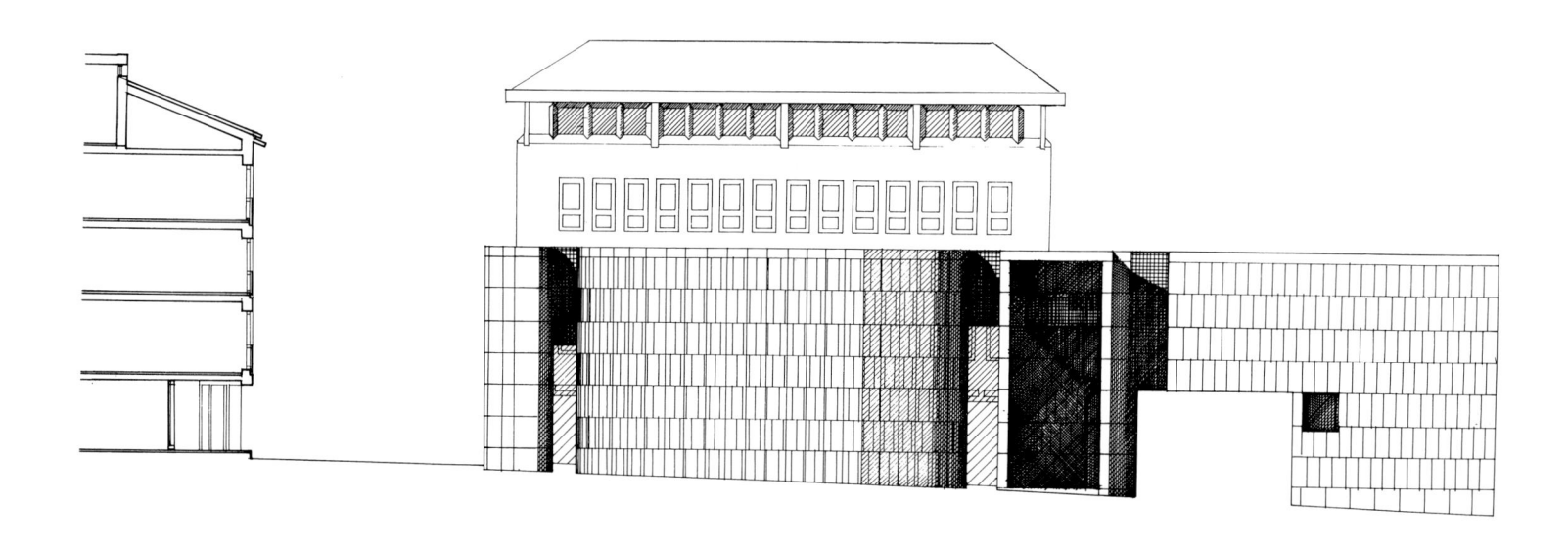

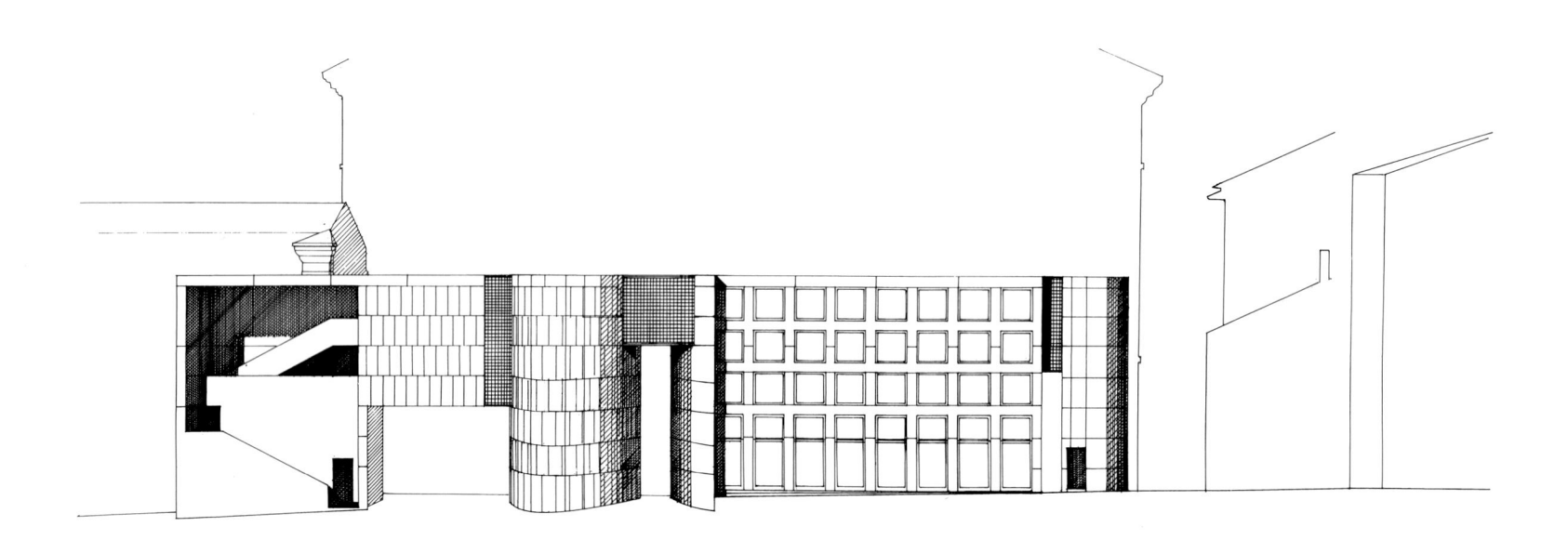

FROM ABOVE: Elevation from Piazza Europa; elevation from Piazza Solferino

PIAZZA SOLFERINO

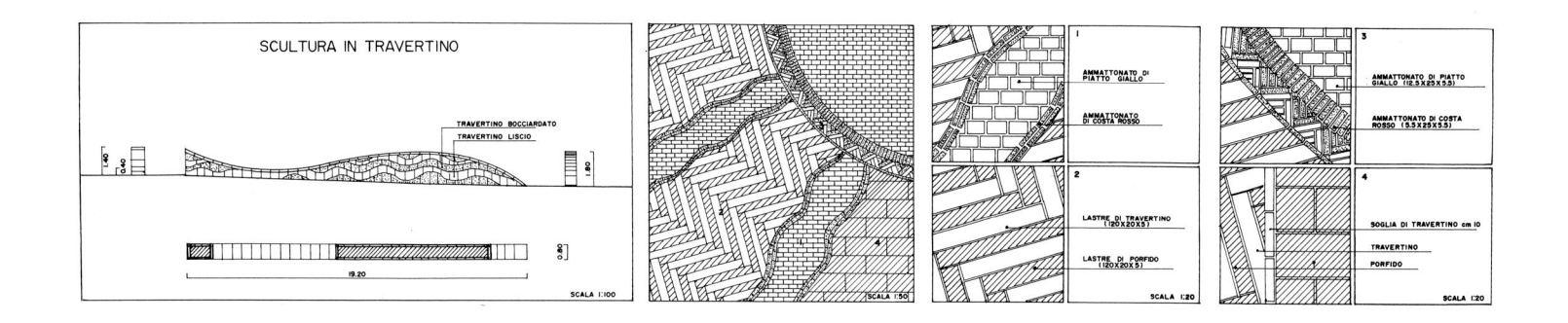

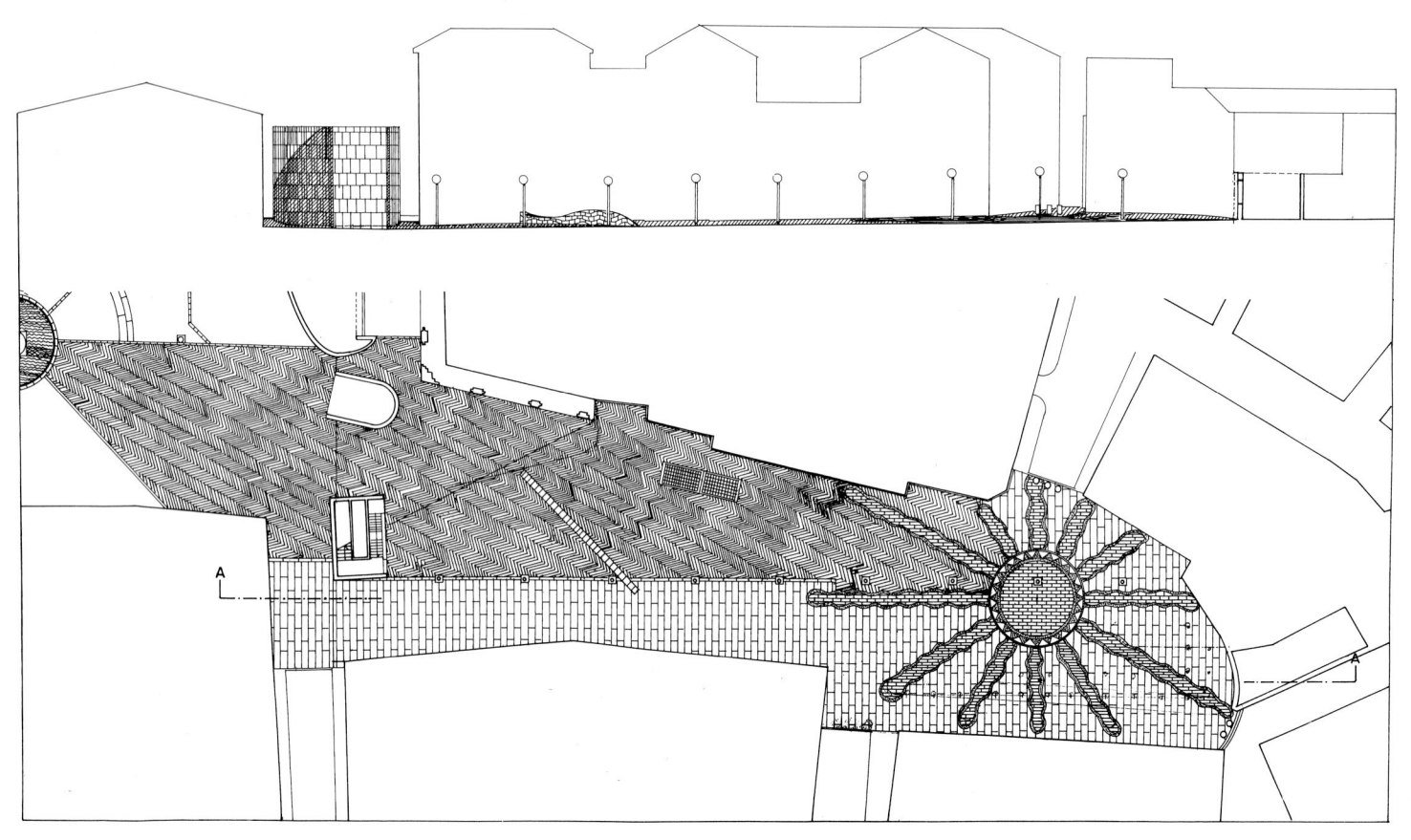

64 ■ PIAZZA SOLFERINO
*FROM ABOVE, L TO R: Elevation and plan of the sculpture;
details of paving; elevation; plan*

Carlo Aymonino

PIAZZA SOLFERINO
FROM ABOVE: Photomontage of pyramid; plan; elevation

THEATRE COMPLEX, AVELLINO, 1987-96
With Gianmichele Aurigemma, Maria Luisa Tugnoli, Aldo Aymonino and Efisio Pitzalis

Part of the restructuring of the city centre – which includes the reconstruction of the buildings along Corso Umberto, renovation of the cathedral and the conversion of Victor Hugo's house as a cultural centre – involves the installation of a new multi-purpose theatre. This facility is currently lacking in the city, and reinforces, along with the rebuilt conservatoire and the planned reconstruction of the castle, the cultural function of the central quarter.

From the earliest studies, the entire theatre complex has been placed to mark the boundary between the pedestrian areas of the hill and the park, and the ring road running along the Acropolis.

This chosen site, with pronounced differences in level, guarantees the maximum civic benefit from the new structure, both as a place for shows and as conference centre and dance school.

There are multiple means of access: pedestrians can approach from the hill and park, and along with cars and service vehicles, also through subways and parking proposed for a new commercial and residential centre, which will in turn lessen the disruption to traffic on the ring road.

The pedestrian circulation, at 348.4 metres (+19.8 metres) allows access to the belvedere above the auditorium and provides a connection with the conference and public service areas (bar and restaurant). Rather than prioritise between either pedestrians or vehicles, a decision made in many historic centres, the solution attempts an architectural integration of both.

The architectural and functional presence of the new complex in Piazza Castello thus acquires a determining role within the city's historical structure. The three cultural facilities (the conservatoire, the castle and the theatre) which face the Piazza help to enrich it as a public place *par excellence*. Ultimately, the relation between the Acropolis and the new Piazza Castello will be architecturally strengthened by the new complex which adds necessary paths and utilities to this strategically important part of the city's reconstruction.

The principal organisational axis – between foyer, auditorium and enclosed and open stages – was rotated by ninety degrees to allow the semicircular portals of the entrance foyer and the pedestrian and vehicular access to the theatre to face on to the Piazza Castello. The open-air theatre follows the contours of the hill, a movement which can also be detected in the terraces and the pathways of the adjacent park.

The theatre presents itself, not as a backdrop to the square, nor as a single building unit within the urban environment, but as an articulated construction, determined by context and function. This represents an appropriate architectural solution for this part of the city, whereby the pre-existing diverse natural elevations are made use of (one has only to think of the splendid construction of the Trajan Market, or that between the Capitol Hill and the Forum in Rome, with the inclusion of streets, stairs and routes within the architecture).

> The diverse appearance of the theatre depends on the natural and artificial differences along its perimeter emphasising its individual parts, each one expressing a function.
> *Friedrich Gilly*

The semicircular *scene* on Piazza Castello and the great portals on the ring road are architectural signals indicating the presence of the theatre. From the former Piazza Maggiore it is just possible to see the *cavea* of the open-air theatre and a *scene* as a backdrop. This architectural element is proportioned to relate to the existing buildings (the cathedral apse and Victor Hugo's former house), and provides a physical and acoustic separation from the buildings behind, without obscuring the panorama of the substantial surroundings.

Perspective

Theatre Complex

67

Carlo Aymonino

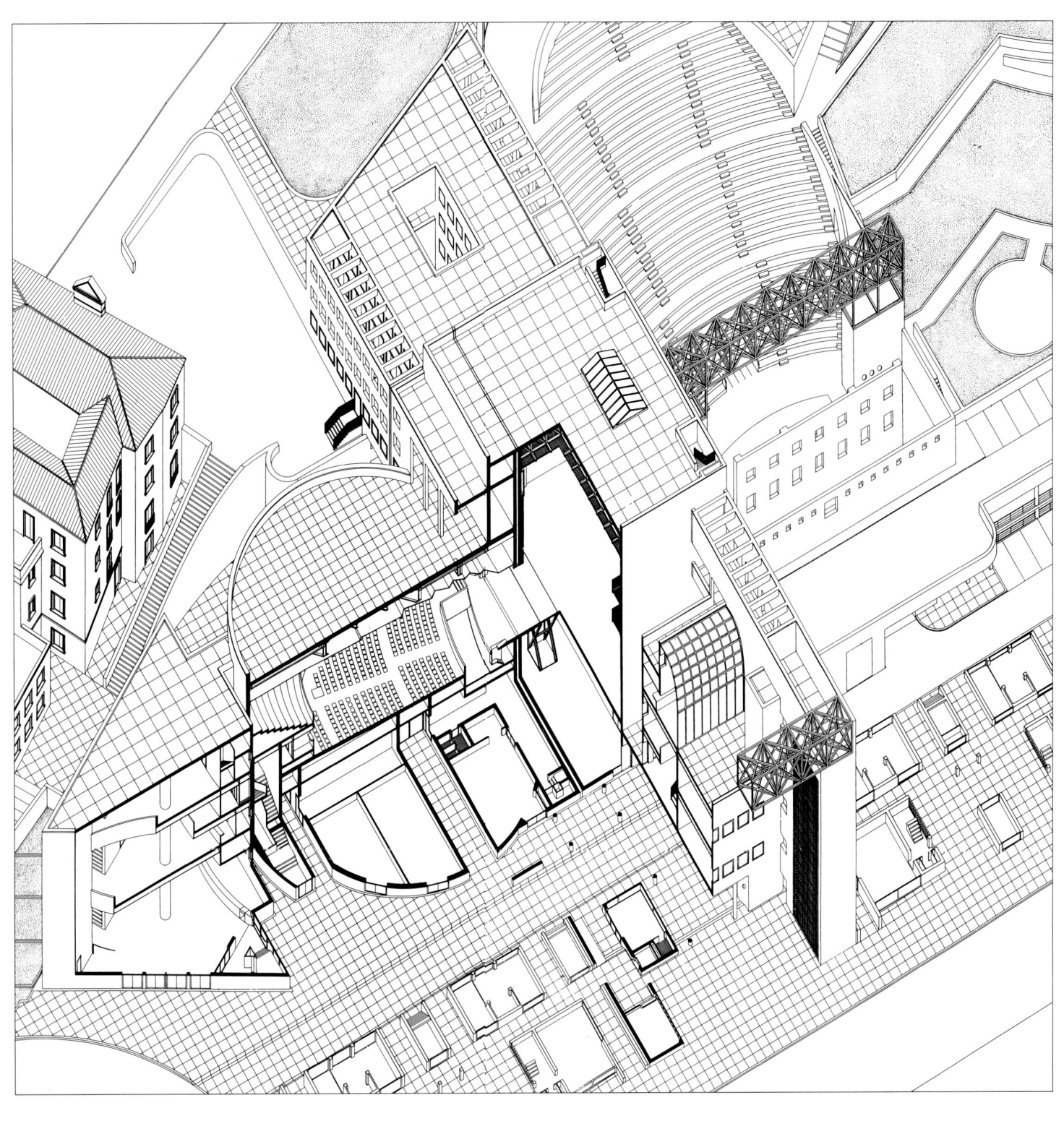

Axonometric

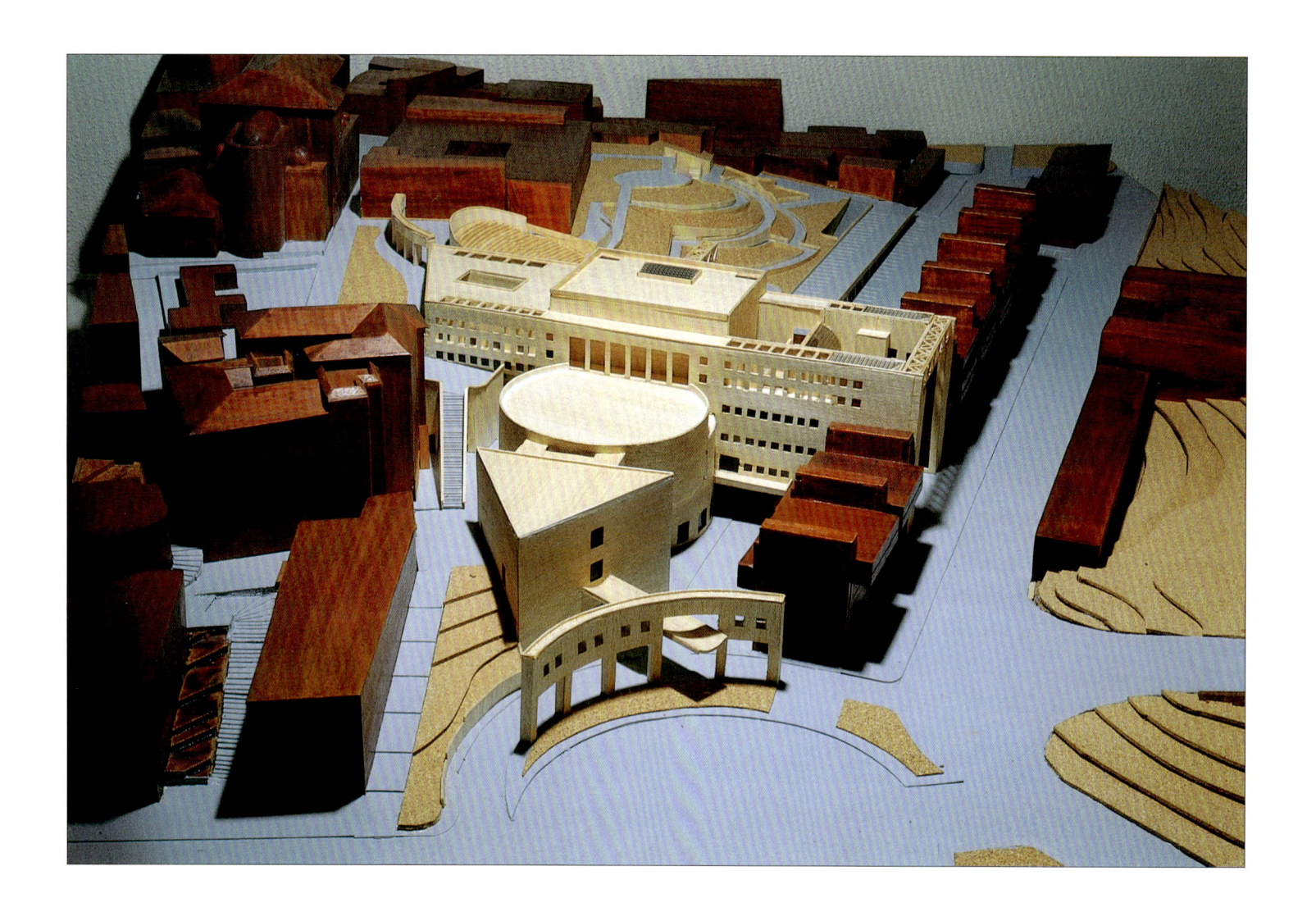

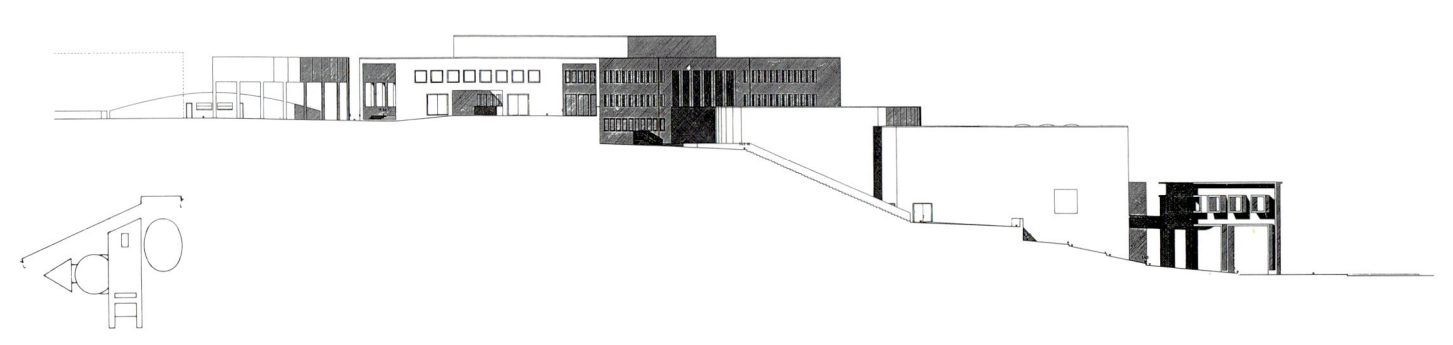

FROM ABOVE: Model; section L-L

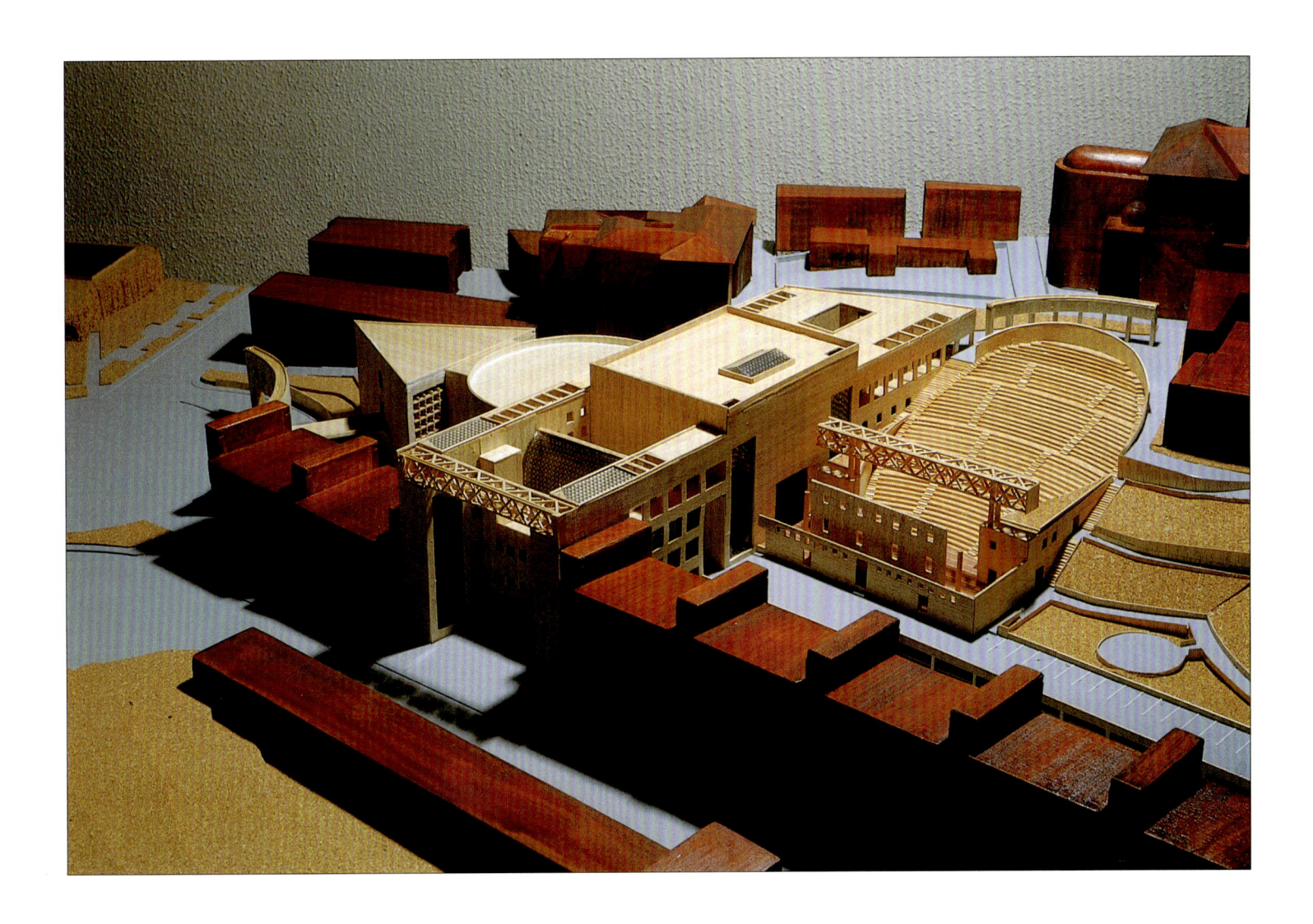

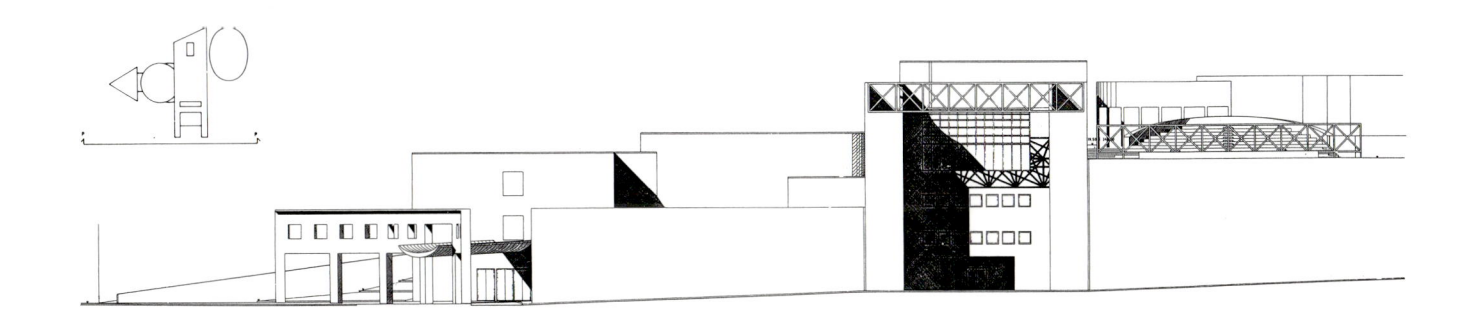

FROM ABOVE: Model; section P-P

Carlo Aymonino

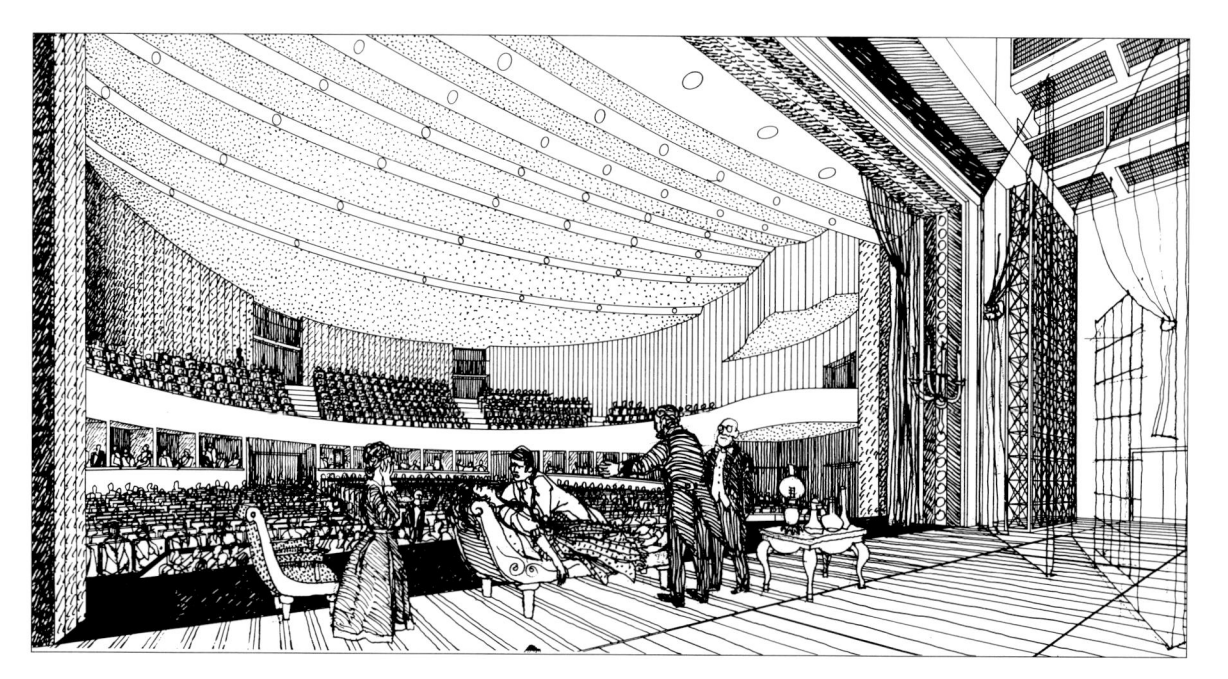

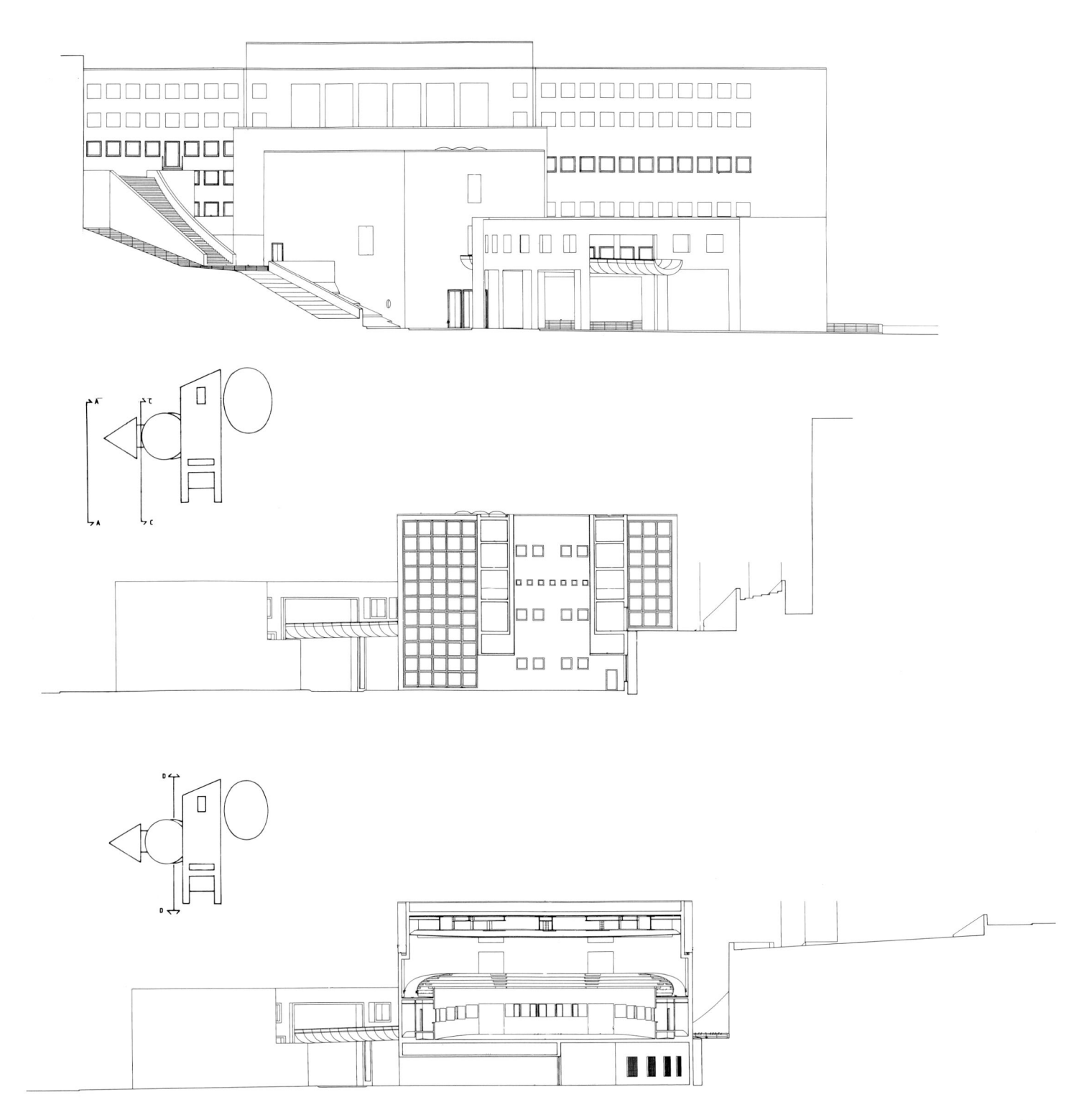

OPPOSITE: Perspectives; FROM ABOVE: Section A-A; section C-C; section D-D

Carlo Aymonino

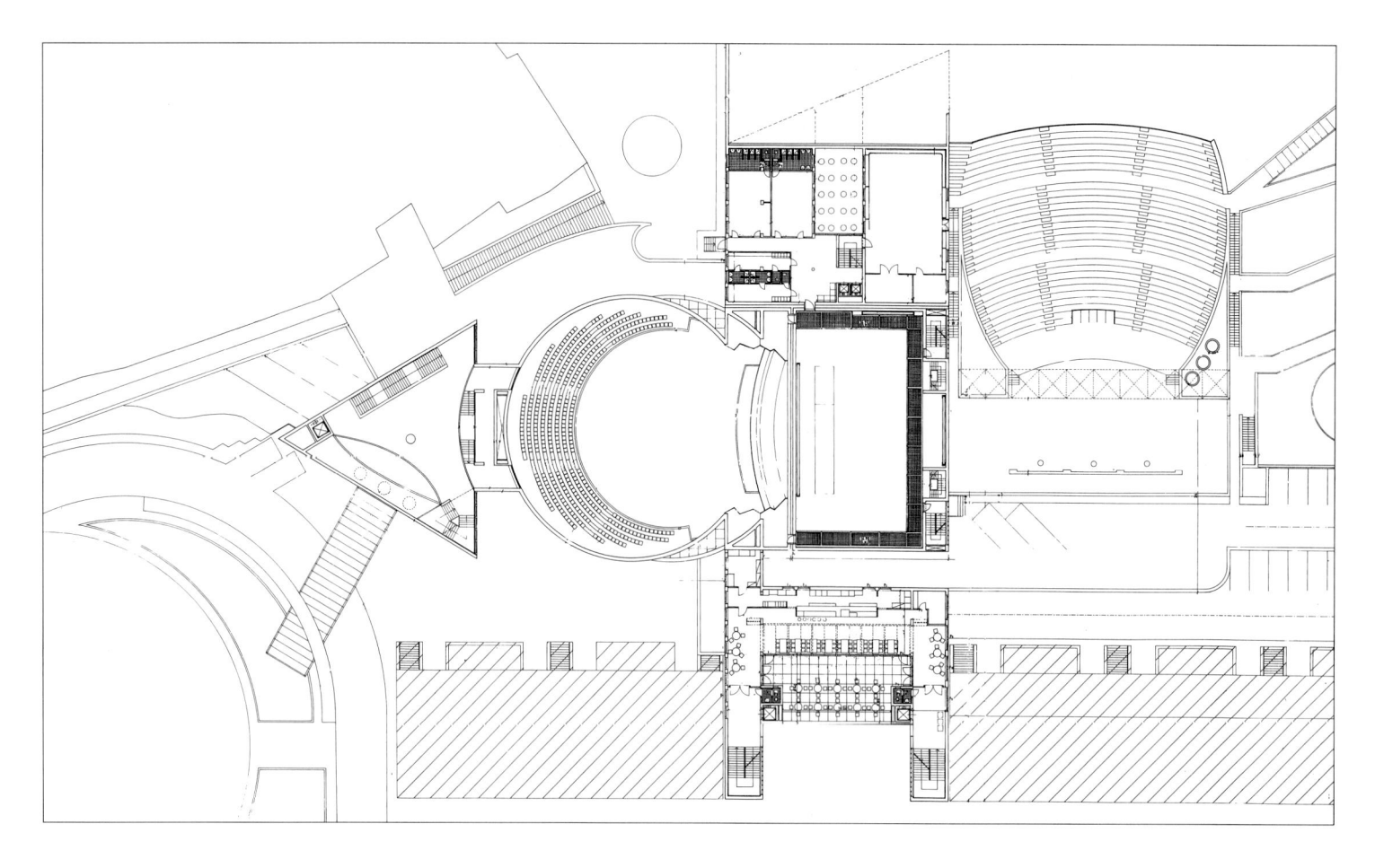

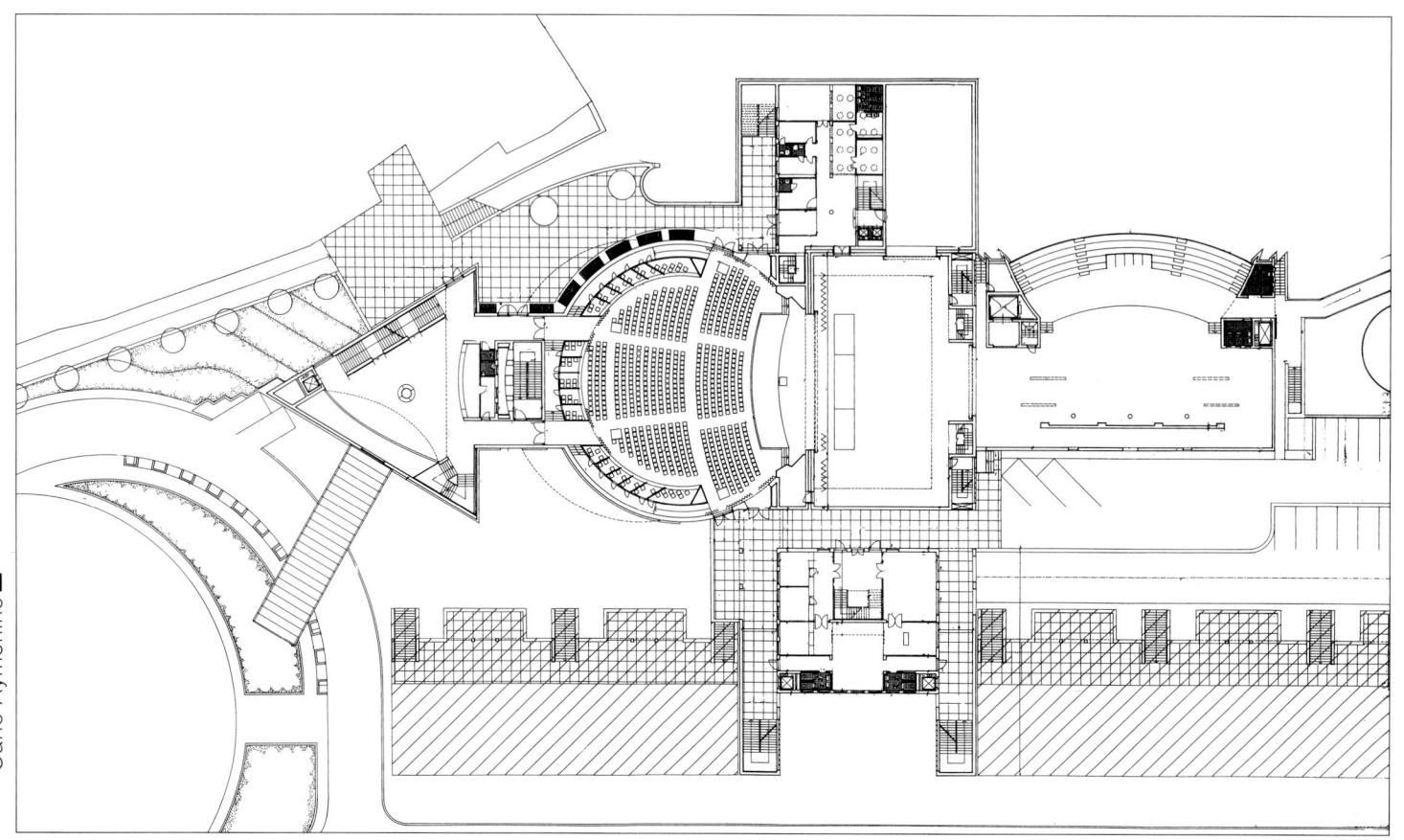

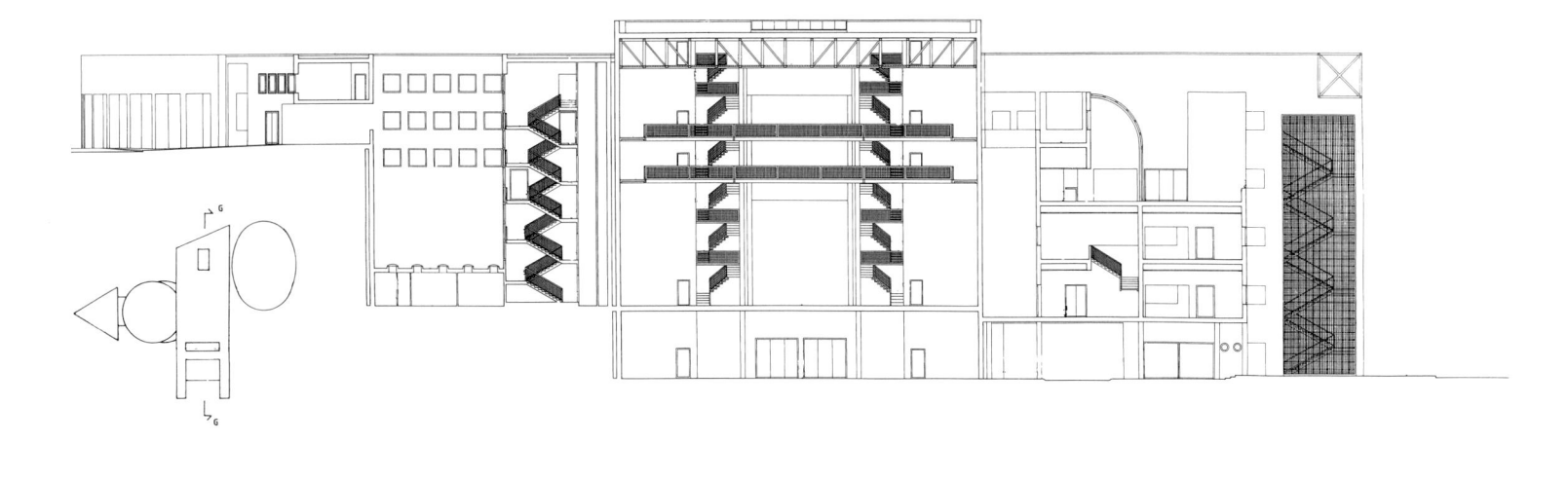

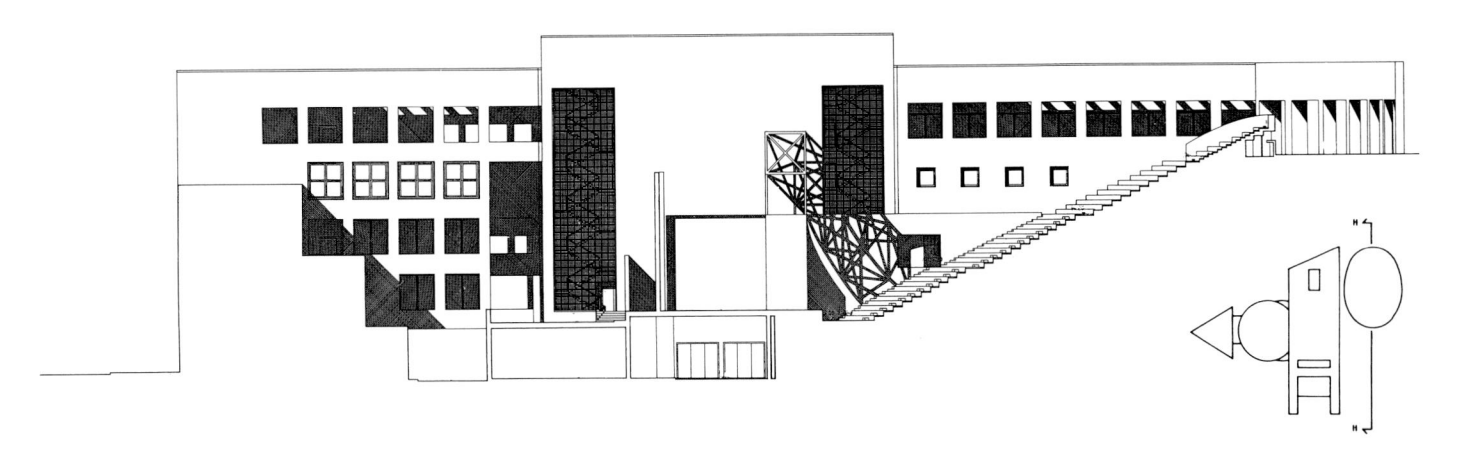

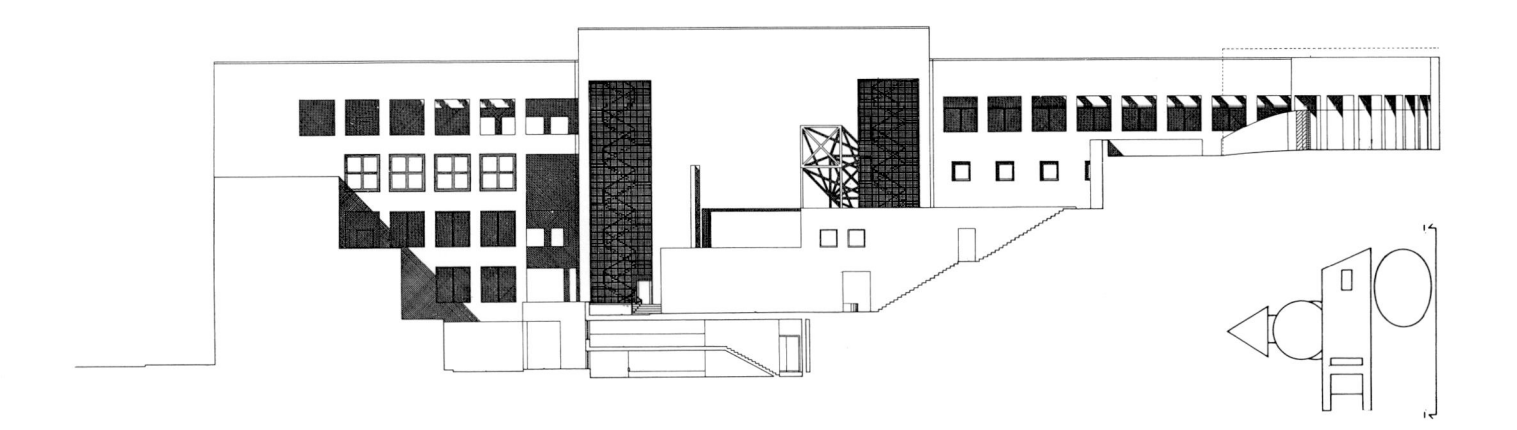

OPPOSITE, FROM ABOVE: Third floor plan; first floor plan;
FROM ABOVE: Section G-G; section H-H; section I-I

76

Carlo Aymonino

PIAZZA DEL MULINO, MATERA, 1988-91

IMPROVEMENTS TO THE AREA OF THE FORMER ANDRISANI MILL

With Raffaele Panella and Piergiorgio Corazza

The building complex is structured by two integrated public circulation spaces: a semicircular porticoed pedestrian square on the Via Lucana, formed by moving the building line back from the street, and an arcade developed at the back of the square, at the foot of Via Passarelli. A route between Via Passarelli and the square, cutting transversely across the first floor of the arcade, connects the square with the gardens of the Tramontano castle.

Thus, the buildings are grouped around these communal spaces and passages according to their function, typology or structural form. There are two main buildings: the first is a linear building, on Via Passarelli, the second, is open-planned, enclosing the semicircular public square. The arcade runs between the two, exploiting the differences in level which exist between Via Passarelli and the southern end of the Mill site, to create a double-height space, with vaulted ceilings, and a perimeter gallery at a level (4.8 metres) that allows access from Via Passarelli. In fact, it is possible to directly access the first floor of the arcade from here and to reach the ground floor (the level of the square) by means of a system of ramps. The development of the spaces and the connecting man-made structures between the square and the arcade, and between the arcade and Via Passarelli was ordered by the axis of the part of Via Lucana to the north, which subsequently assumes a fundamental organising function in the composition.

The portico of the square encompasses this axis, which also directs the 'transverse' line of the pedestrian passage within the block placed between Via Passarelli and Via Castello, which terminates at the Tramontano castle.

Finally, the arcade connects with the area of Palazzo Riccardi, with the market, and also with the system of central squares by an open space on Via Lucana, a veritable 'piazzetta', between the porticoed area and the linear building.

The principal components of the architectural system are complemented by other, more 'secret', spaces: two small courtyards and a small open air amphitheatre which completes the arcade.

The new architectural complex was to be built in stone: the architectural configuration of the new square, of the arcade and the courtyards is that of a boulder carved in various shapes. The wall on Via Passarelli is rendered with the Greek key design of the socle. Within the context of 'the Stones of Matera' the suggestion of the metaphors is very strong. The methods employed in Matera, which incorporate (and therefore preserve) buildings, man-made structures, simple passages or even images from the past in a modern urban situation stem from the notion and the practice of transformation.

Even this is a way 'to refuse the hereditary diseases' cited by Ernest Nathan Rogers, little more than thirty years ago, in the introduction to *Casabella* on the inquest of Southern Italy.

Carlo Aymonino

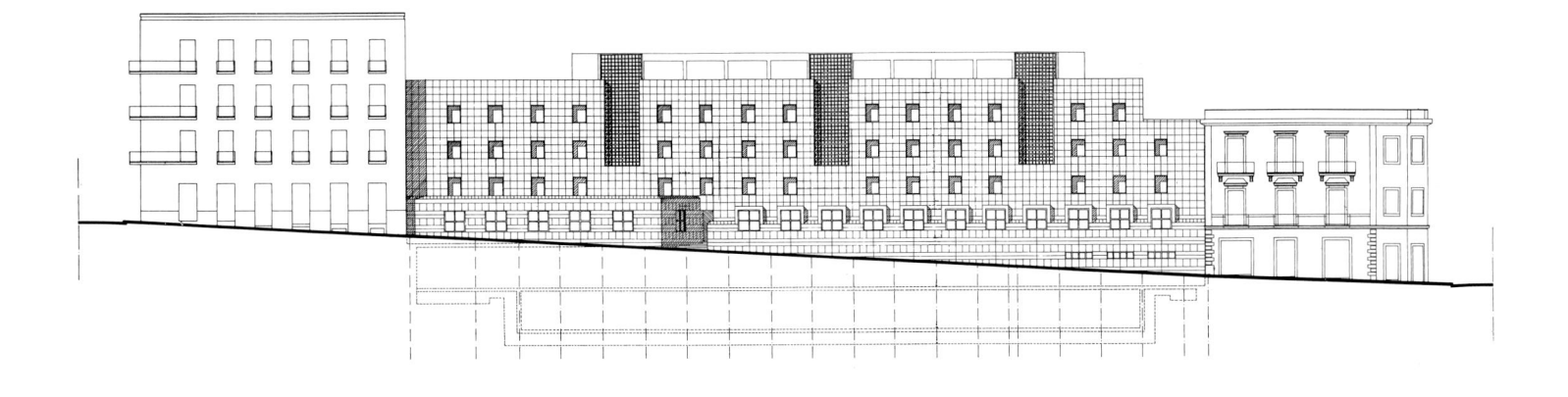

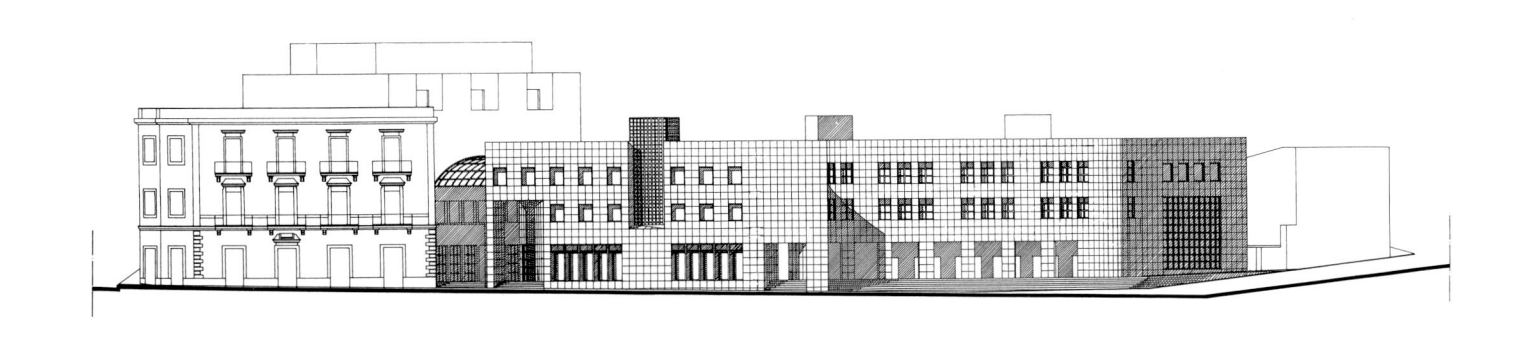

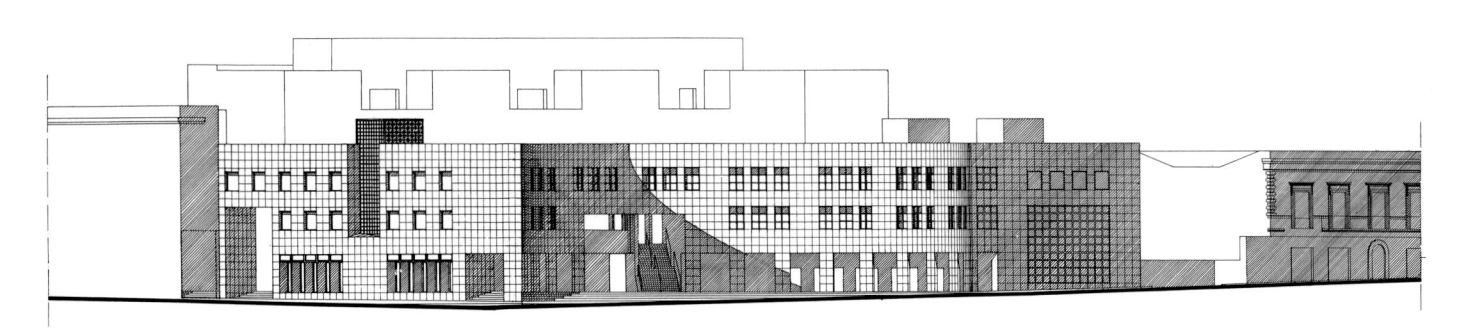

OPPOSITE, ABOVE: Perspective; FROM ABOVE: South-west elevation; north-east elevation; north-west elevation

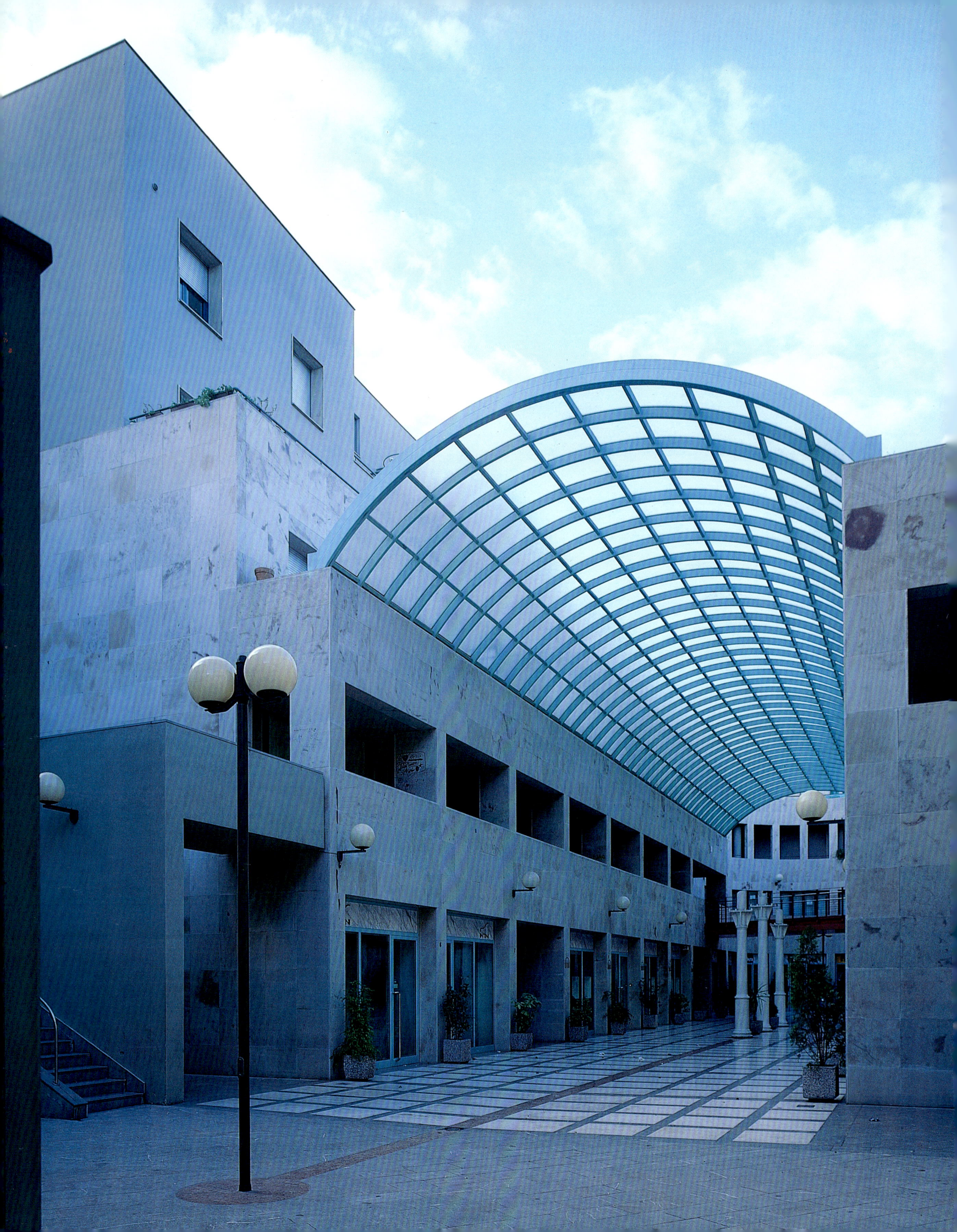

Piazza del Mulino

Sections

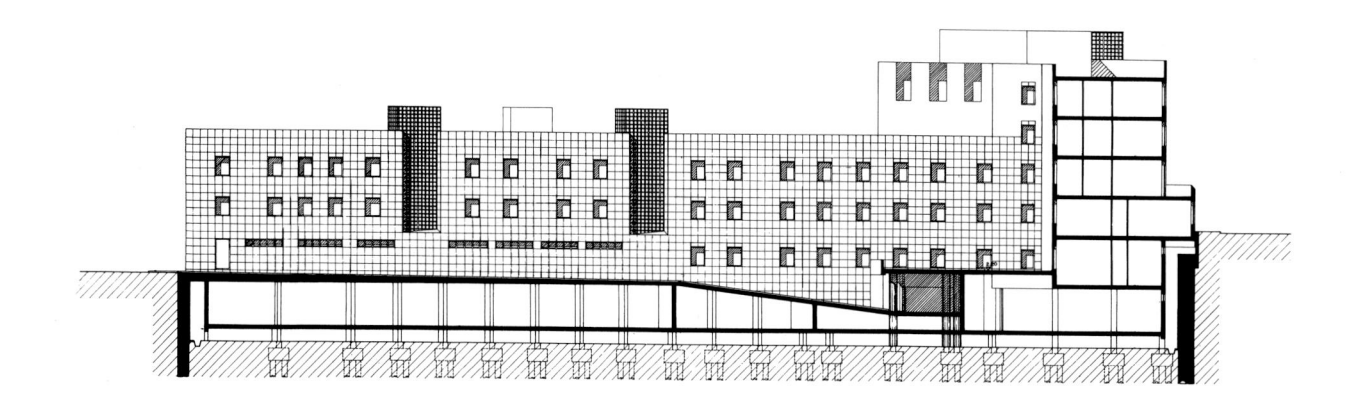

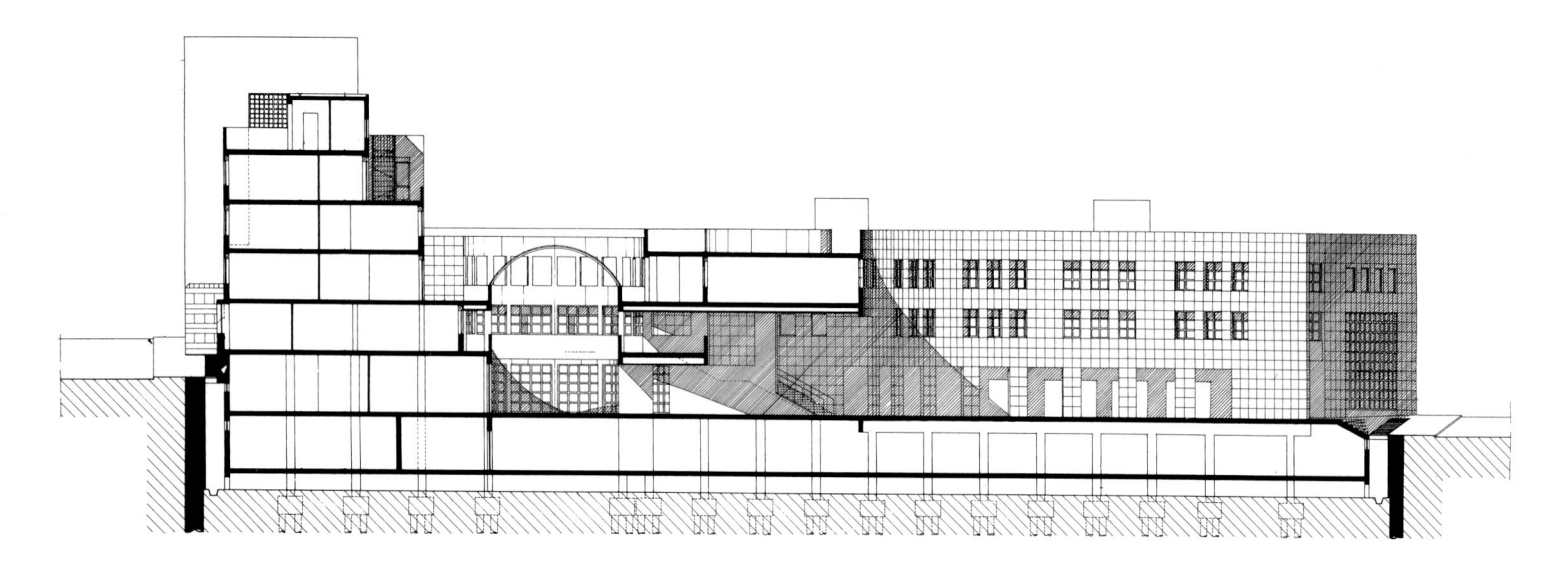

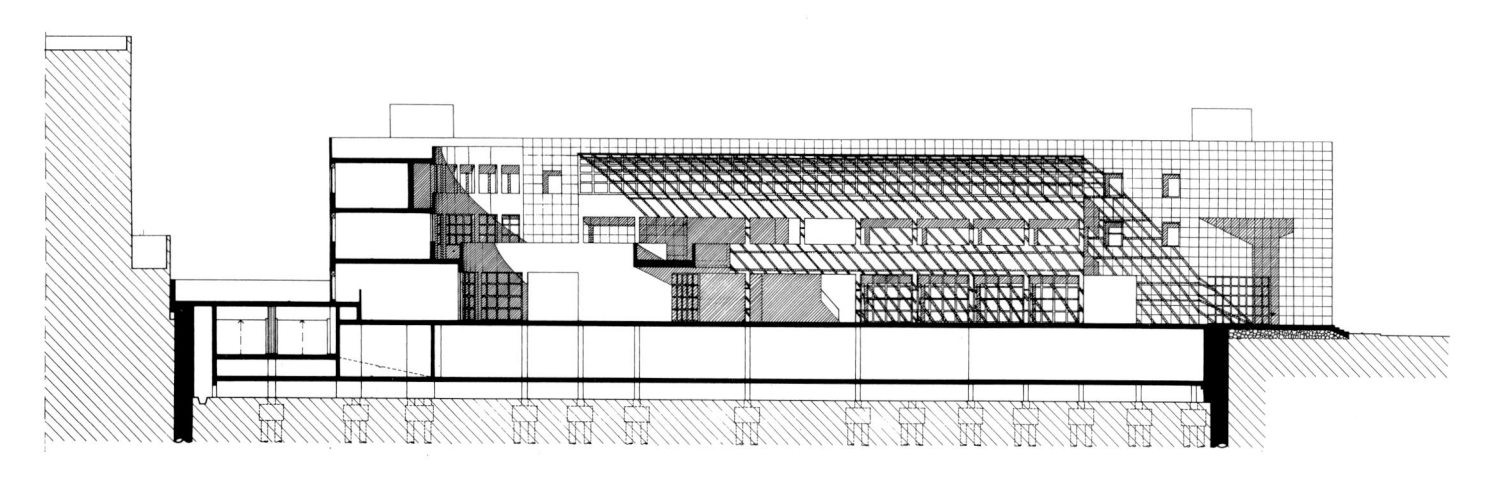

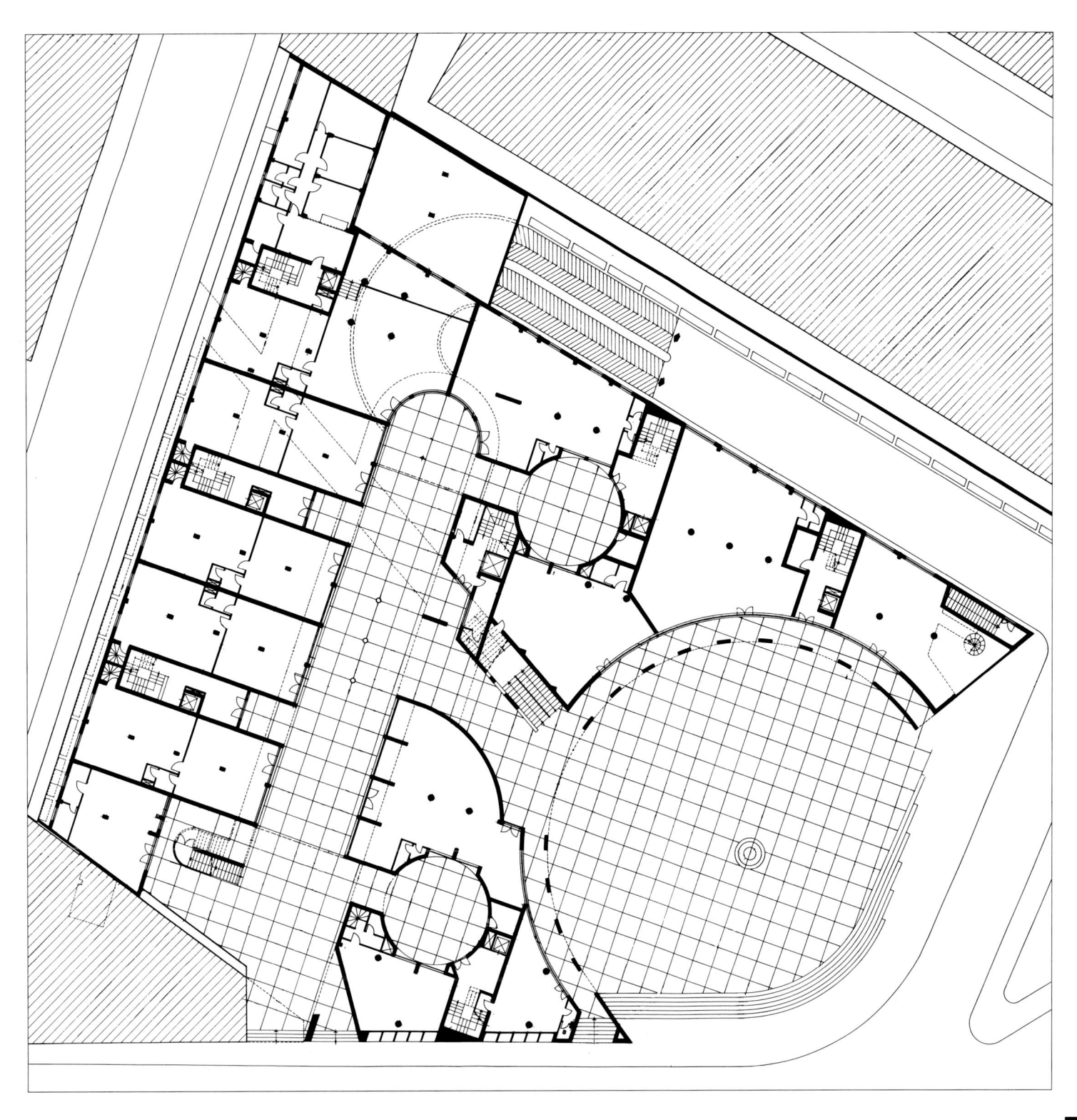

Ground floor plan

84 *Which Venus? Milo's Venus or the Crouched Venus at the Terme Museum in Rome*

Carlo Aymonino

ST MARK'S BASIN, VENICE, 1985

URBAN PROPOSALS

With Gabriella Barbini

One cannot visit Venice and view the Bacino, with its ample spaces and variations of light, without being struck by the positioning of the monuments, that both confirm and highlight the finite and infinite qualities of the space. At the time of its formal completion, it would have represented one of the grandest visible and enjoyable spaces in a European city. The Grand Canal would have been seen – with its built up course and the constant distance between the two banks – as the greatest urban thoroughfare then conceivable: the Giudecca Canal as comparable to the urban section of the estuaries of the great rivers (the Thames in London or the Rhine in Rotterdam), for its mercantile usage.

As with all the great scenographies – whether they are pictorial or theatrical – the spatial planning is certainly determined by the major monuments – the Palazzo Ducale, St Mark's spire, the churches of La Salute and San Giorgio Maggiore – but at the same time it owes its unified character not only to the water but also to minor monuments. These monuments, all built in white Istrian stone, are the boundary 'marks' of the space: the tip of the Dogana, the Coffee House and the lanterns of St George.

After eighteen years as a frequent visitor to Venice, the architect had the distinct feeling that something was missing – some other 'mark' was necessary for its completion – a feeling that was to be confirmed by the publication by Manfredo Tafuri of Alvise Cornaro's project for St Mark's Basin (dated c1560). This project called for the 'completion' of the Marcian Basin with a 'dainty little hill' surmounted by a lodge and an open air theatre 'in stone, large and comfortable', exactly where the two Canals, the Grand and the Giudecca, meet. The only reservation to this was the introduction of greenery to a space already characterised, in nature, by a vast expanse of water. 'The Marcian Basin is interpreted as a vast public space', notes Tafuri.

A competition organised by the Venice Biennale and a request by Aldo Rossi to participate, offered the chance to realise a project around the threads of these loose, sparse thoughts, but in order to do so, it went beyond the extents of the competition.

The St Mark's Basin is certainly not a square, at least not in the canonical sense of the word, but a vast expanse of water, to which splendid architectural structures contribute to a spectacular perspective of the city. A space that is simultaneously commercial and celebratory, of 'service' to the city, its entrance from the sea and the first image for the foreign visitor, is immortalised in the paintings of Canaletto. A space that, with its bustling scenes of boats, gondolas, barges and small ships, is not dissimilar in its physical depth and variety of uses from that of St Peter's Square in Rome – as seen in the view by Gian Paolo Pannini of the visit of Charles the Third to the Basilica, with the crowds of people, horses, coaches and sedans. In this sense it is the most important square in the city.

A space of such magnitude, raises the question of where and how to 'complete' it. The most obvious site lay to the centre of the Basin, at the junction of the two Canals, and towards the east facing the St Elena Gardens and the Lido. At the intersection, a great statue of Istrian stone would emerge from the waters: a Venus.

Several possibilities were looked at and initially a preference was for the crouching Venus in the Terme Museum in Rome. Its beauty, however, did not resolve its centrality nor its physical relationship with high waters. The standing statues considered included the Venus de Milo at the Louvre, the Medici at the Uffizi and the Venus at the Capitoline Museum. In the end, as was the case for the Colossus, the solution was found with Canova: the Venus Hope, twelve metres tall, built in stone blocks, facing the intersection.

Towards the east and the Giardini another dimension is needed to 'mark' the location, a building in the water. What better than to freeze in stone the navigation of Rossi's Teatro del Mondo, to render permanent the memory of its ephemeral passage? The theatre becomes the entrance to the Biennale, the place of information, of possible spectacle, and the completion of the 'minor' triangulation of the Basin; two very simple and comprehensible symbols, like the lanterns, the tip of the Dogana, the Coffee House. As part of the city, the Basin thus becomes formally completed.

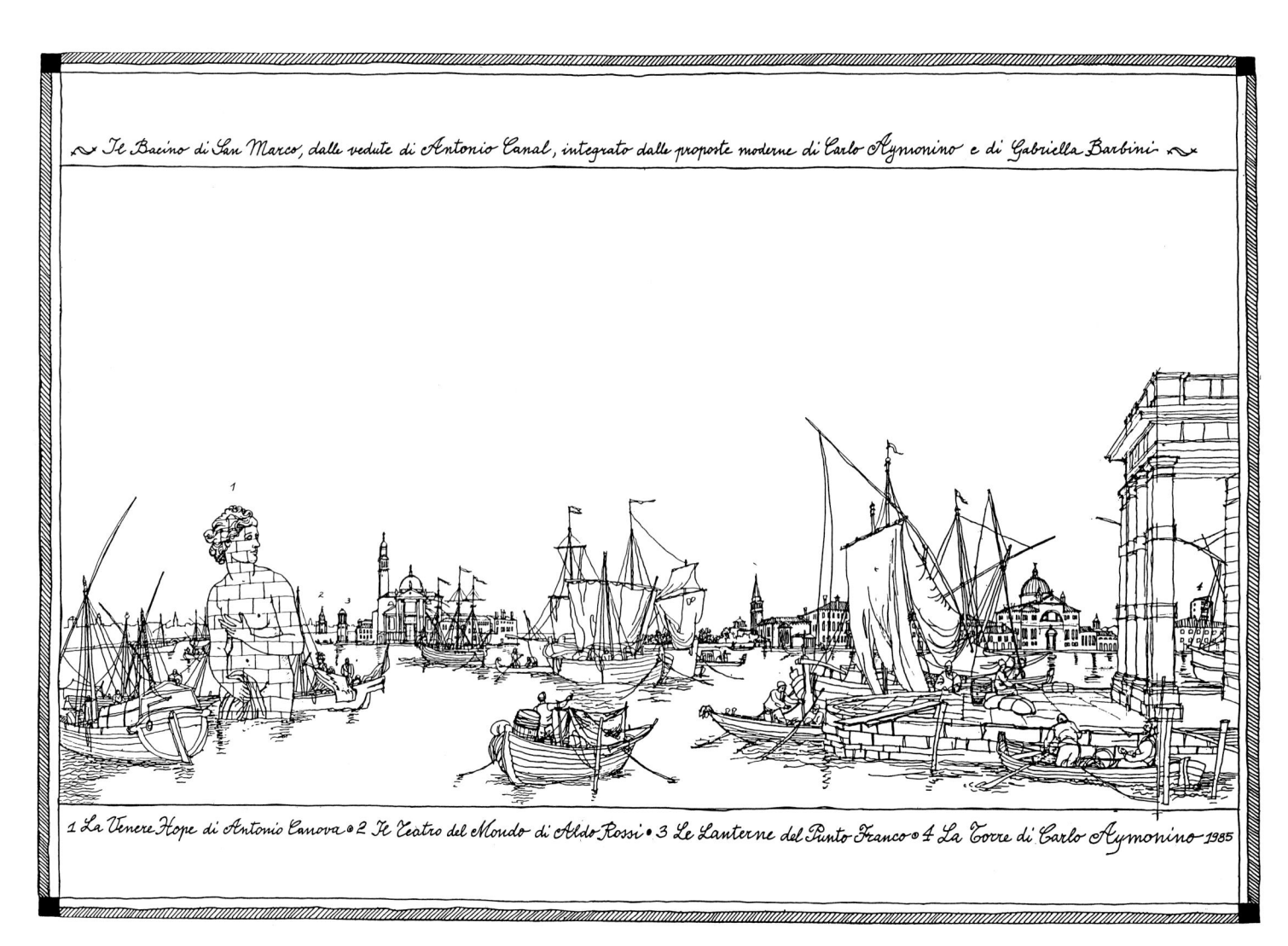

View of St Mark's Basin from a view by Canaletto, with proposals integrated. Key: 1 Hope Venus by Antonio Canova; 2 The 'Teatro del Mondo' by Aldo Rossi; 3 The lighthouse at Punto Franco; 4 The tower by Carlo Aymonino

Carlo Aymonino

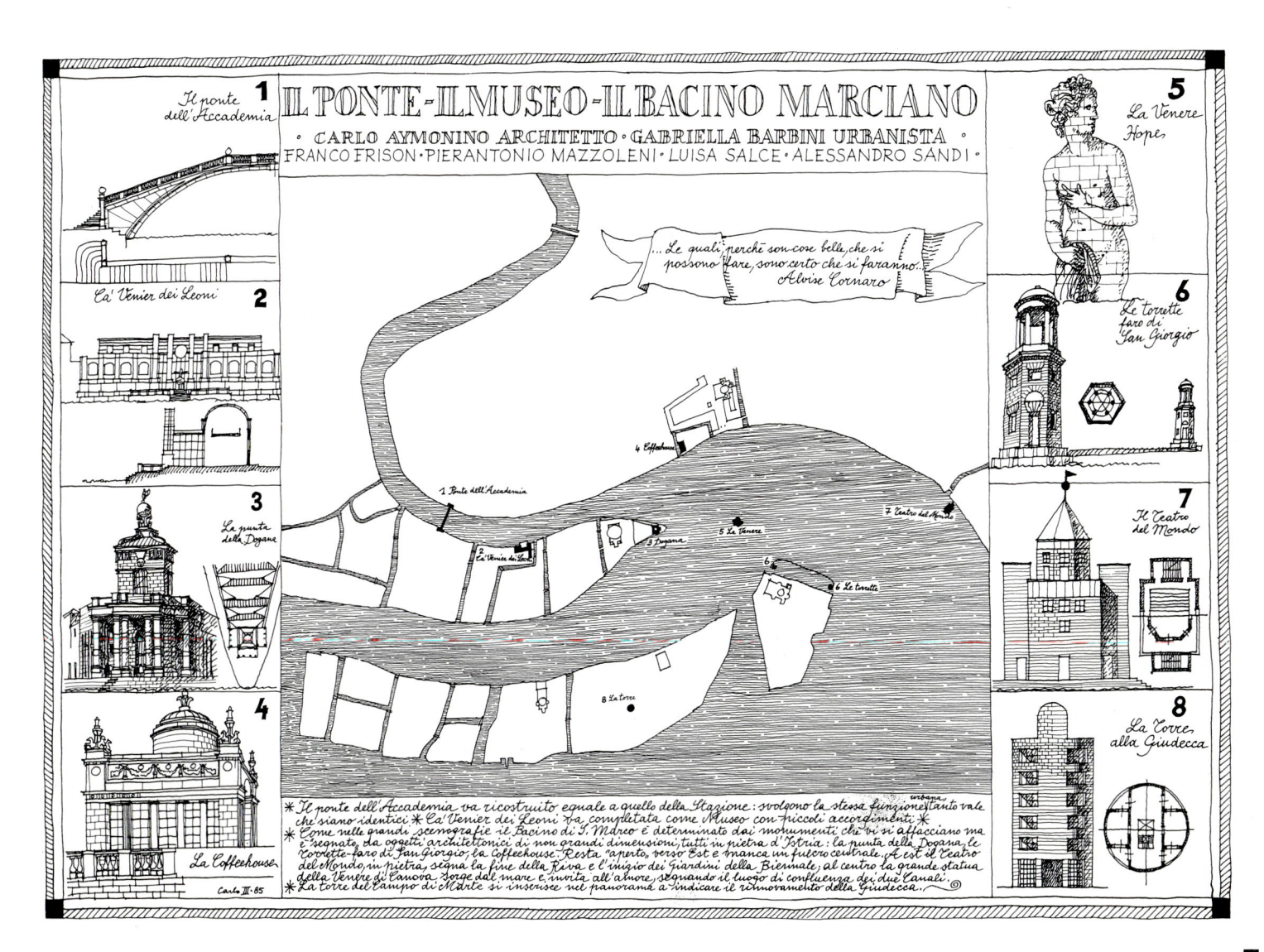

The landmarks which form the stage set for the designs for St Mark's Basin

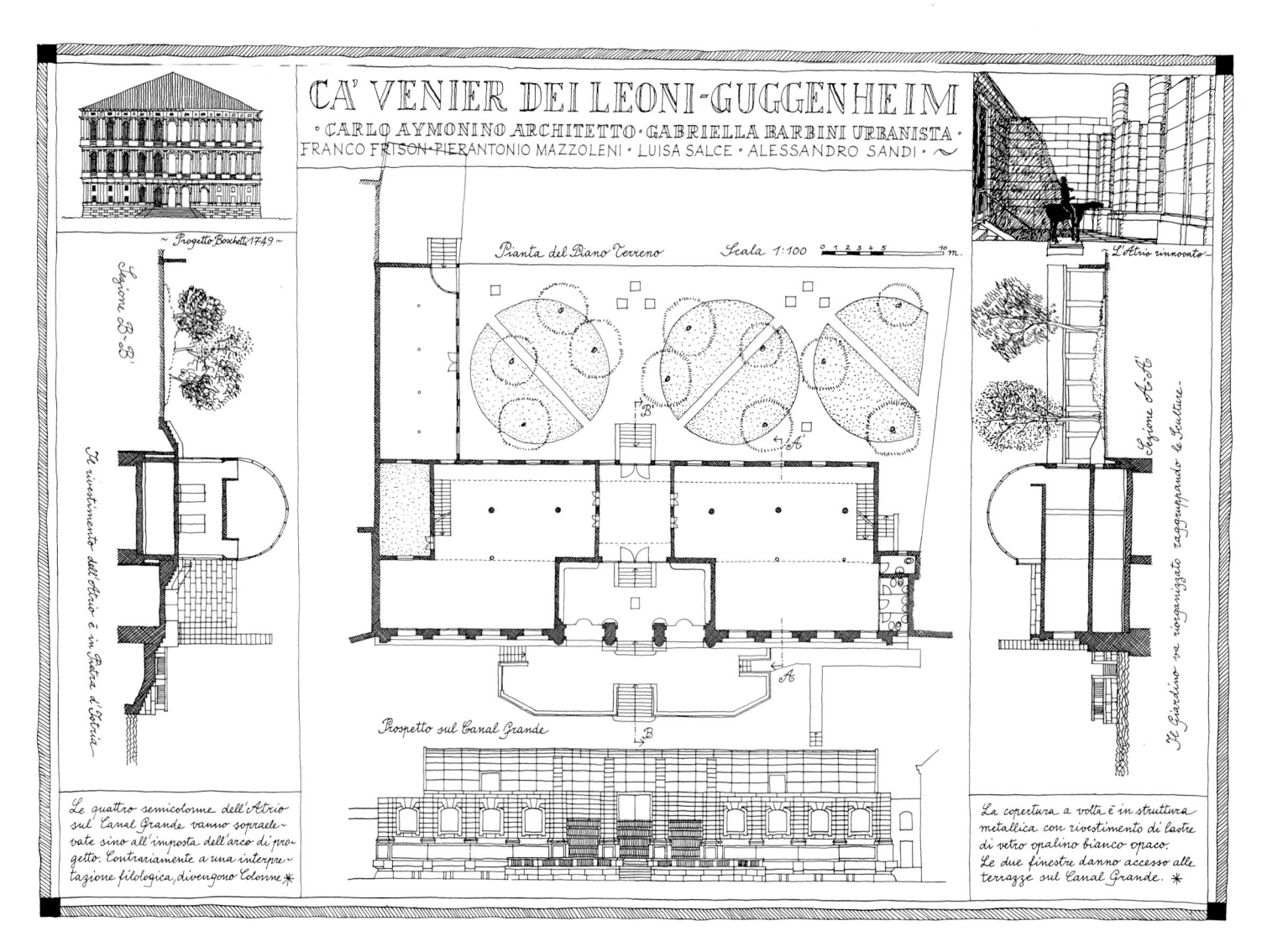

PEGGY GUGGENHEIM MUSEUM
The Peggy Guggenheim Museum was one area designated for redevelopment in the Biennale competition. LEFT, FROM ABOVE: Elevation of Boschetti Project in 1749; section B-B showing the atrium; CENTRE: Ground floor plan; elevation on the Grand Canal; RIGHT: View of atrium; section A-A showing the garden

PEGGY GUGGENHEIM MUSEUM
View from the Grand Canal

Elevations, plans and sections over site plan

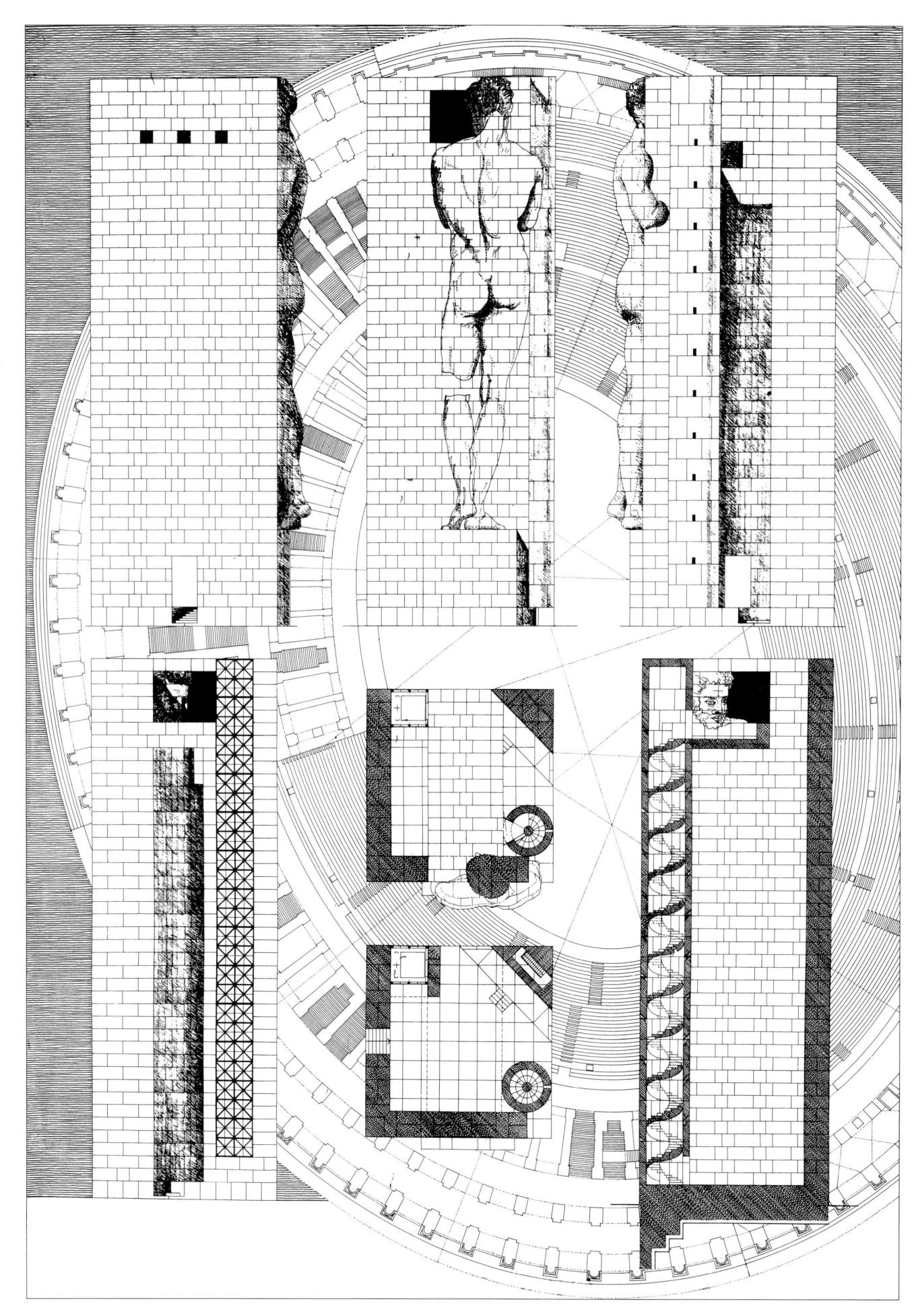

THE COLOSSUS, ROME, 1982-84

With Aldo Aymonino, Sandro Giulianelli and Maria Luisa Tugnoli

The idea for this project was first proposed to Carlo Aymonino by Adriano La Regina, the archaeologist supervising the Forum restoration during one of their many unofficial meetings. At this time there was great interest in developing the area around the Forum – reintegrating the buildings with Rome, providing the necessary amenities and re-establishing the original architectural relationships. To facilitate this process it seemed prudent to construct a monument on the foundations of the Colossus; a recovered site 15 metres square. The proposal was particularly challenging because, as Regina observed, the new construction would complete the original Roman composition connecting the Colosseum, the Temple of Venus and Rome.

However, the main problem with this proposition was the lack of information available on the original Colossus. No one is even certain how high the original was, and the only records that exist today are images pressed on coins and literary descriptions. Unfortunately, these methods are particularly subjective and have been open to a number of interpretations over the centuries; one only has to consider the disparity between the work produced by Canina and Coquart. One such description, by Canina in his book *Ancient Rome*, describes the Colossus in the following terms:

On the same site was then discovered where Nero's great Colossus stood, after it was moved by Hadrian, under the direction of the architect Demetrianus and by the means of twenty-four elephants, from the position where Vespasian had placed it. On this site the Colossus elevated itself by means of a great brickwork pedestal, evidently clad in marble . . . The height of the Colossus was, according to the general consensus, 120 feet and had on its head seven rays measuring 12 feet each . . . it turned continuously with a movement concurrent to the sun maintaining its gaze fixed on the star.

The initial proposals involved a 36-metre tall marble monolith – the supposed height of the original – on a square base containing a staircase leading up to the belvedere from where it would be possible to admire the Forum, the Colosseum and the remains of the Colle Oppio. This monolith was then broken down into separate units to reduce its visual mass. As a result the monument is now composed of two walls to the south and west, constructed from 2-metre thick marble blocks, and a triangular monolith – of the same dimensions as the Trajan column – positioned at the north-west corner creating an internal courtyard.

Within this space Aymonino placed the staircase and the lift, both of which were now separately articulated elements, providing access to the original belvedere. This viewing platform is cut into the top of the building's south face, projects into the central void and provides views to the north and south.

Originally there was to be an image of the Colossus carved into the blocks of the south facing wall, but this was rejected as the architects felt that it resembled Corbusier's Modulor. Surprisingly the solution to this problem was discovered by Aymonino at an exhibition of drawings by Canova for the Campidoglio: a male nude facing away from the viewer; a giant who could be none other than the Colossus.

This image was superimposed onto the south wall in bas-relief, with the face and arm revealed in full relief within the courtyard as a tribute to Savinius. This Colossus is a prisoner contained within the south wall and is partially exposed by the process of erosion reflecting the passage of history. Like the Trevi Fountain this monument manages to fuse art and architecture.

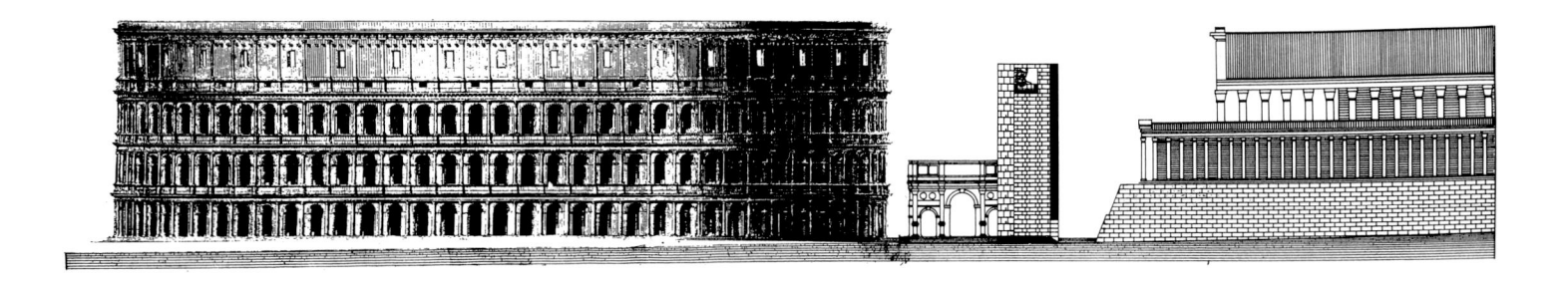

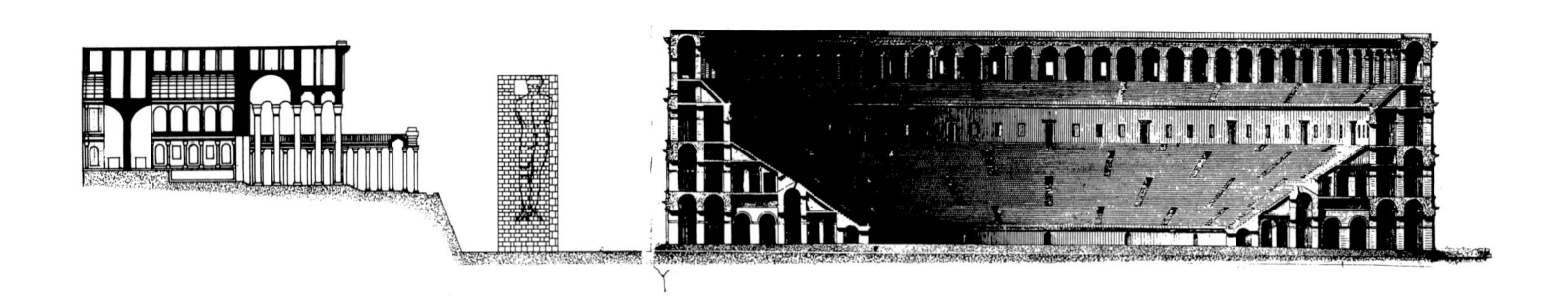

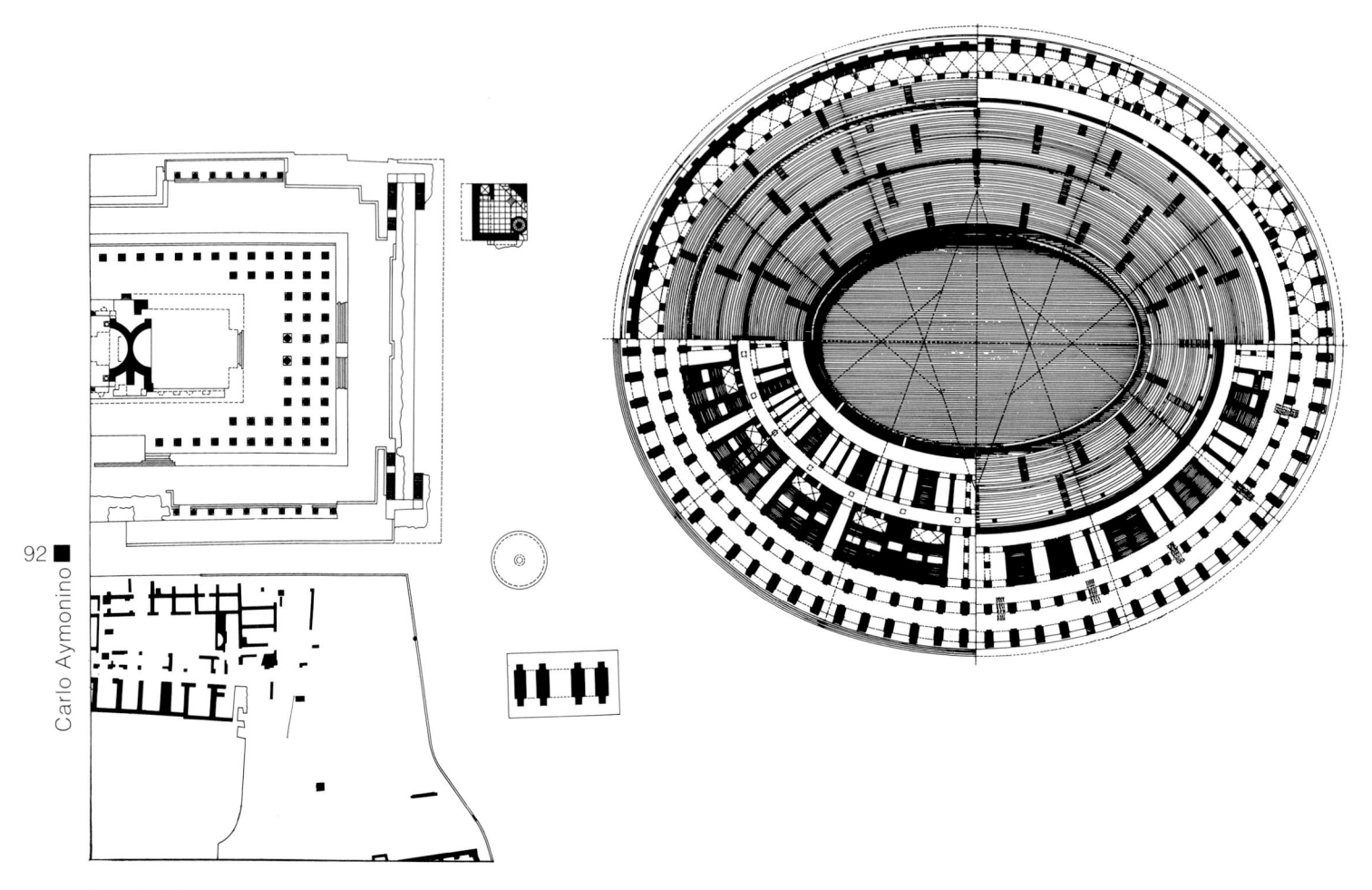

FROM ABOVE: Elevation; section; site plan;
OPPOSITE: Rendered studies

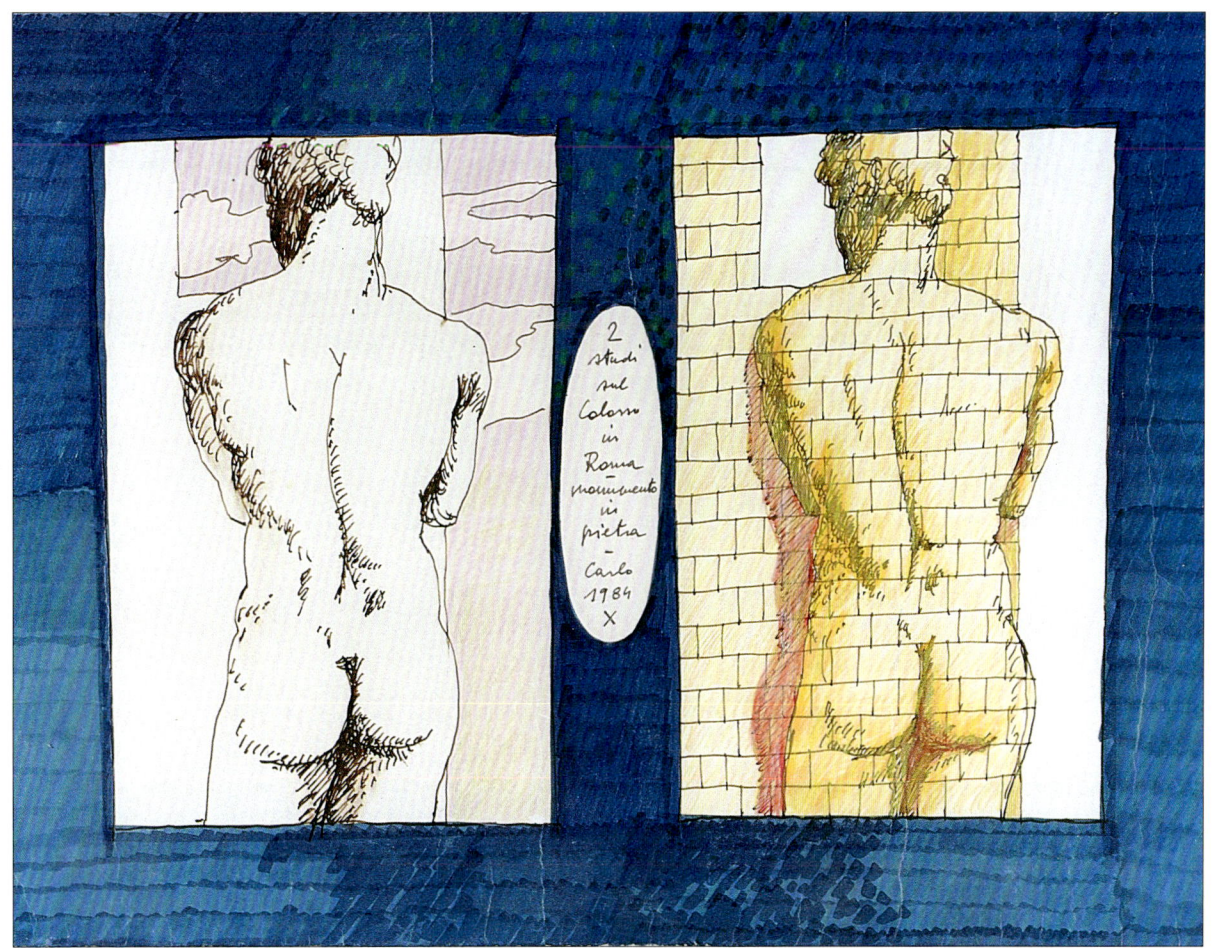

The Colossus

94

Carlo Aymonino

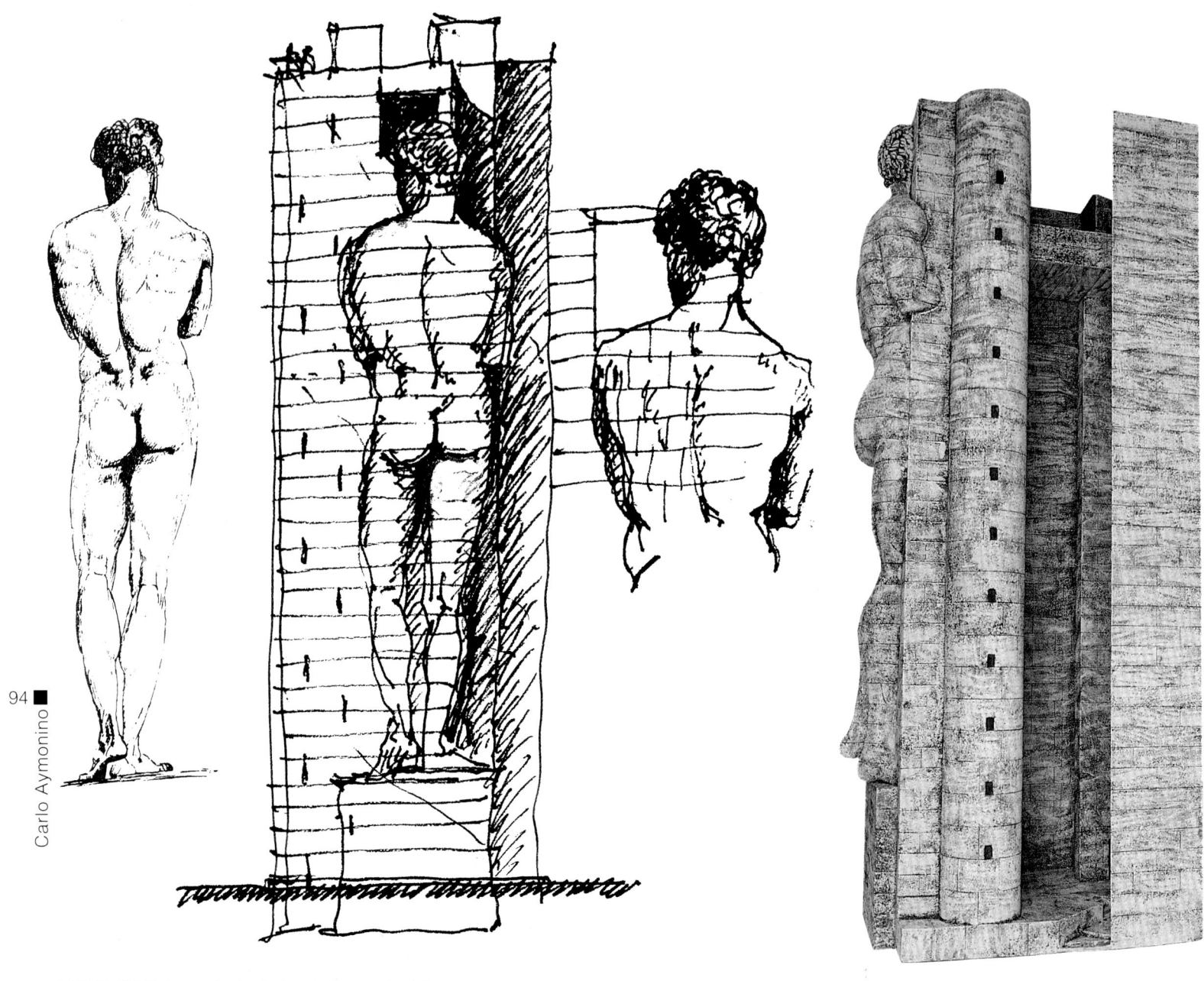

LEFT TO RIGHT: From a drawing by Antonio Canova; sketch by
Carlo Aymonino; model; OPPOSITE: Perspective

The Colossus

Carlo Aymonino

SOTTO NAPOLI, NAPLES, 1988
PROJECT FOR THE MONTE NECHIA AREA

The caves and catacombs beneath Naples have provided a variety of functions for the city's inhabitants over the last two thousand years: in the sixth century BC this area was used for burials and pagan ceremonies; the Romans and Carmignano constructed aqueducts that utilised the numerous springs and abandoned wells. From the sixteenth century onwards quarries were even excavated to provide the tufa stone required for repairs to the city's buildings, and during the last war it was used for air raid shelters.

The aqueducts that remain are very complex and vary from awkward narrow channels, that a person can barely squeeze through, to enormous caves some 30 metres across. This succession of palatial spaces and claustrophobic passages is a spatial experience that has no equivalent on the surface. Similarly, the tufa quarries, either domed or conical depending on how they were excavated, create another unusual environment, compounded by the great supporting structures that prevented collapse. Furthermore, there are natural caves, a mute testimony to entirely different processes, which provide yet another unique subterranean experience.

This project, commonly referred to as 'The Statues Beneath the City', involves the restoration of these catacombs with the intention of creating a gallery that is not only unique but also of immense archeological value. Consequently, the major problem presented by this project was how to incorporate sculptural and constructional elements within these spaces during and after their reconstruction. Typically Aymonino treated this challenge as an opportunity to experiment with a variety of exhibition styles and architectural integrations; providing dramatic installations without disrupting these valuable archaeological sites whilst challenging the visitors' perception of container and contained, new and old.

The Monte Echia system (Table 1) will be used as a gallery for artists concerned with antiquity – Kounellis, Paolini and the Poiriers – and reconstructions of famous monuments – the chariot racer at the Esquilino in Rome or the Domitian Nerva equestrian group. These works will be displayed with the minimum amount of alteration, paving and illumination restricted to those areas where it is absolutely necessary, to engender a sense of antiquity. The exhibits may be arranged either singularly, the gilded Cartoceto group with the totally reconstructed Knight, or in a sequence illustrating the various stages of reconstruction.

In a similar vein Mitra's Grotto (Table 2) will be used to house a permanent installation of statues from the Archaeological Museum of Naples. This is particularly useful as it will allow the museum to display exhibits that are presently in storage, and which account for over half of its total collection. The exhibition design involves crowding the statues into the grotto in an attempt to communicate the wealth of knowledge we have learnt about Greek and Roman societies from these treasures.

Interestingly there are alternative plans for Monte Echia and Mitra's Grotto that involve a permanent exhibition of chronologically arranged artifacts contained within free-standing architectural pavilions. This arrangement (Table 3) differs from the preceding proposals in that the visitors' attention will be concentrated entirely on the exhibits rather than their relationship to the environs. The pavilions will be constructed from valuable materials, including marble and ebony, alluding to the treasures that are concealed within the earth, and the entire display will be strongly illuminated. The exhibitions will include busts and portraits from the Farnese Collection and the Vesuvius region and be arranged in a similar fashion to the gallery in the Palazzo dei Conservatori in Rome.

Finally, there are plans to use the aqueducts in the Carita quarter for the temporary exhibition of regional and national sculpture of archaeological value. (Table 4) Like the first two schemes this will involve the eventual restoration of the areas where the original architecture is evident. When complete this area will be utilised to explain the caves' origins, the reasons for their development, the functions they fulfilled and their eventual decline. The architects are also evaluating the possibility of reintroducing water into these areas providing that it does not affect the delicate micro-climate that exists today.

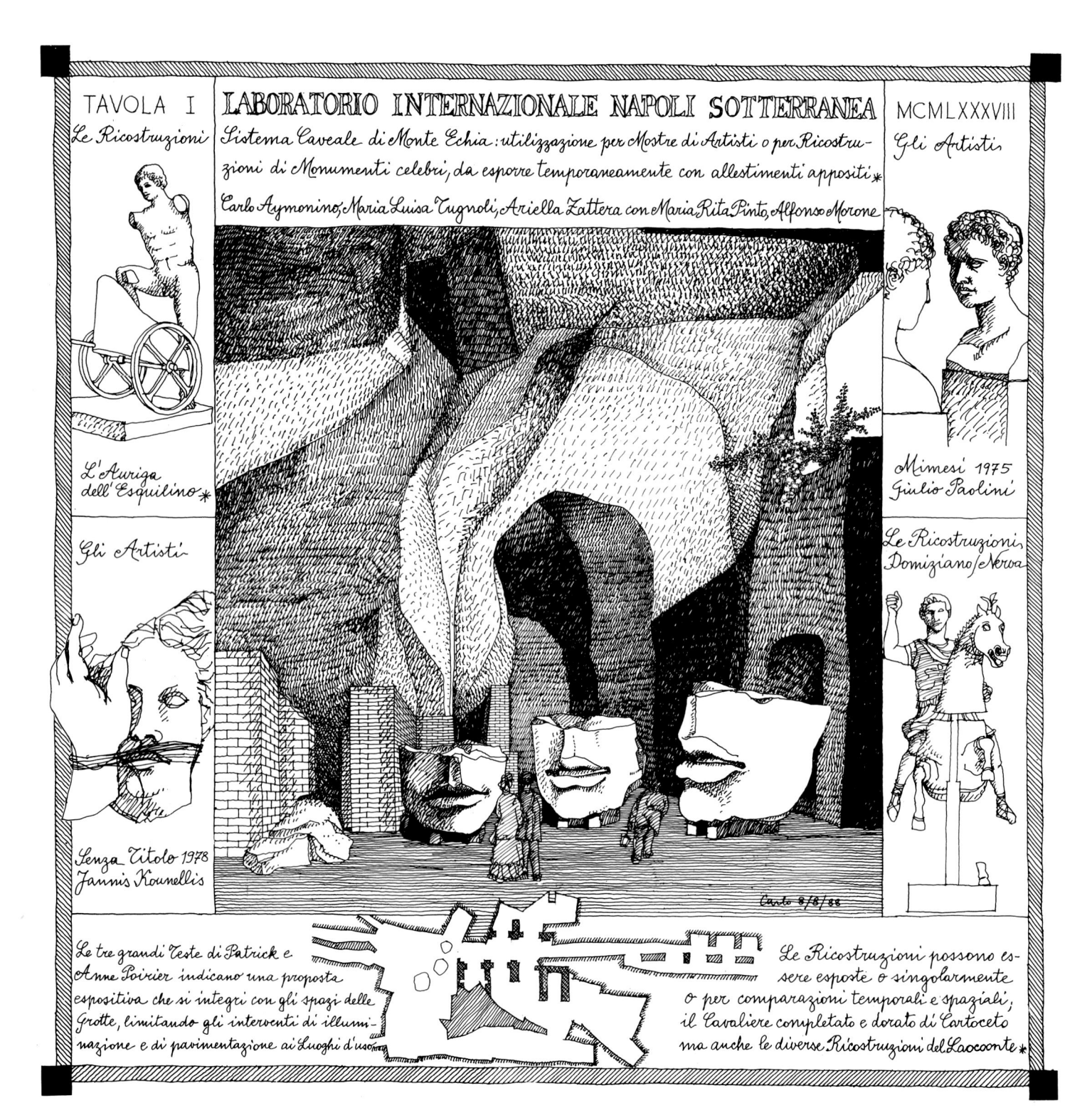

TABLE I
Suggested use of the cave area for exhibition of classical and contemporary sculptures

TABLE II
The Cave of Mitra has been the area most used in time, as is indicated by a considerable wall system

TABLE III

This uses architectural elements which explain the former use, but do not transform the structure of the caves

Carlo Aymonino

TABLE IV
The architectural intervention is more visible in part of the caves once used for the water system of Carmignano, which could be used again with the water reinstated in the pools

CAMPO DI MARTE, GIUDECCA ISLAND, VENICE, 1984
URBAN RENEWAL PROJECT FOR THE INTERNATIONAL INVITED COMPETITION

With Gabriella Barbini

The island of Giudecca is isolated enough not to be physically connected to its neighbours in the Venice lagoon, but not to be considered an independent and autonomous structure. As a result it has remained an urban periphery, possessing both the negative and positive associations of such transitional zones. The Campo di Marte is the area that has the greatest social problems.

An accurate and specific analysis of the site indicated to the architects that the only viable approach was a mixed-use development. This entailed dismantling the existing and highly defined districts and replacing them with more integrated proposals; areas of commercial and residential use where the boundary between public and private is less distinct. The scheme includes plans to improve the island's infrastructure, connecting it with the other islands and reducing its isolation.

A new residential area is planned, starting at the Rio della Croce and continuing past the bridge, that will help to define the proposed public square focused around the old church. As this building is currently abandoned its old spire will be replaced with a residential tower whilst the rest, including the convent and walled garden, will be restored and utilised as a cultural centre. Similarly the old State Archive, also including the proposed square, will be converted into a further education facility. Another residential block is planned that completes the square's sense of enclosure and is integrated into the commercial activities to the rear; comprised mainly of warehouses. The park will be transformed partly into a botanical garden, for educational purposes, and partly into a sports area including two tennis courts requested by the residents.

This square will be the new urban focus for the island and is located in close proximity to the original civic centre and fruit market. To ensure that this development is incorporated into the existing urban fabric, with old and new forging a symbiotic relationship, the new square is connected to the civic centre by two thoroughfares; one direct and the other via the proposed housing and Aspasia Park.

The old convent of St John, the Guardia di Finanza, is to become a museum; a conversion that will retain the existing facades, due to their architectural value, despite the fact that the majority of the interior will be altered. When completed it will contain an analytical study of the island, from its genesis to the present day, in order to promote civic research and study. A general market is also planned to complement the existing fruit and vegetable one. This proposal is also intended to strengthen the development's boundary; a canal that abuts the site, separating it from the neighbouring light industry. No proposals were outlined for the primary school or property owned by the IRE as it is unlikely that they will ever be acquired for development.

The design of this suburb was defined by the following criteria: to maintain a high residential density, typical of an historical city like Venice; to ensure that every dwelling had either a balcony or a garden; to connect the proposed development with the civic centre, fruit market and park, and, with the exception of the market, residential and commercial areas were to be integrated.

The building methodologies that will be employed here have been designed in order to ensure maximum comfort within every unit whilst providing the maximum uniformity. This standardisation will enable the majority of the architectural components to be prefabricated, a process that will reduce both the cost of the development and the construction period. To further facilitate this process the entire development has been planned according to a 2.4-metre module. The only exception to this was the circular tower that replaced the church spire and will be used as an architectural feature to locate the development within the existing urban structure.

Perspective

104 ■ *Axonometric*

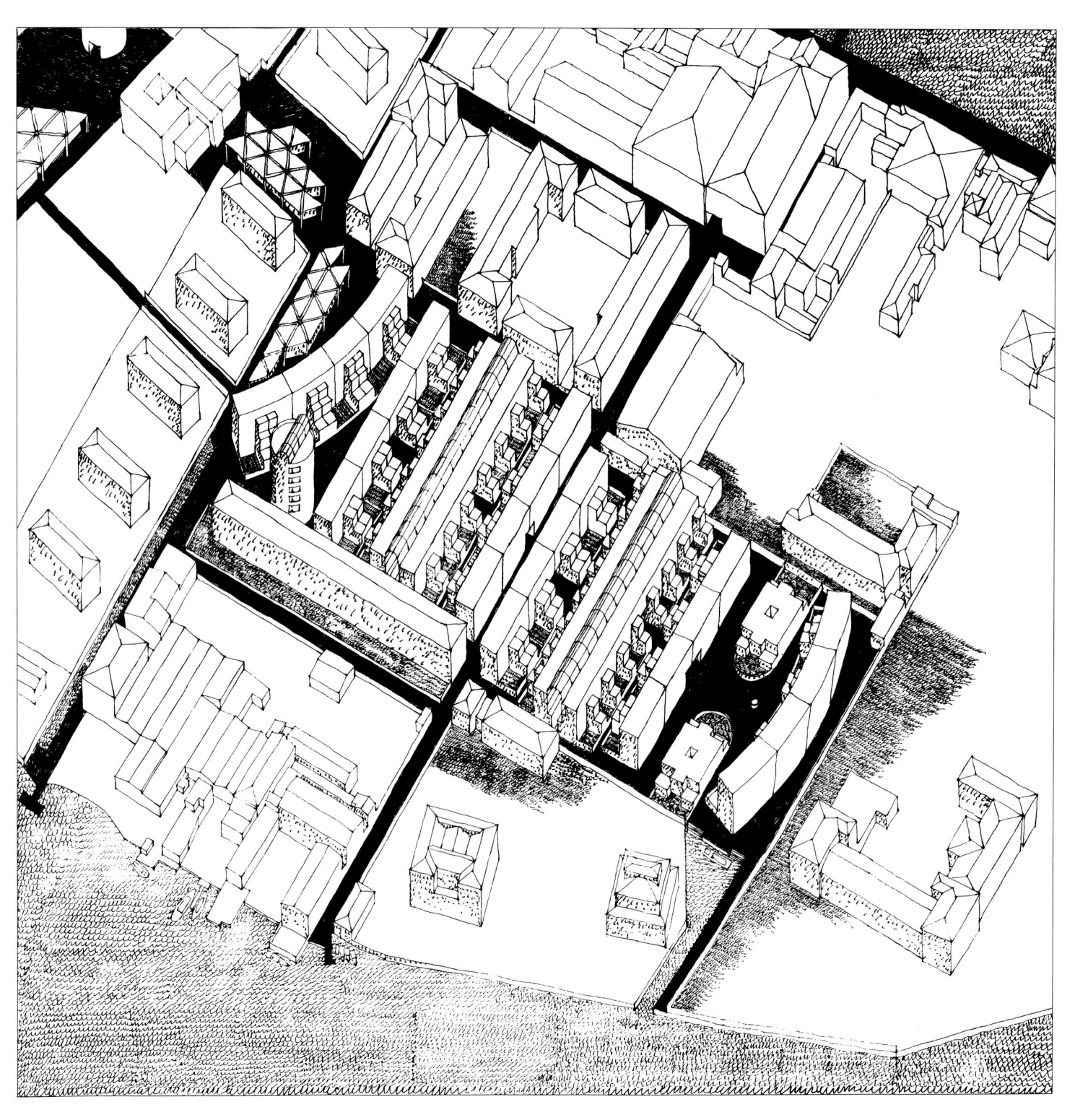

Carlo Aymonino

BLOCK 1
ABOVE, L TO R: Ground floor plan of block; ground floor plans of individual flats; first floor plan of block; first floor plan of individual flats; section A-A of individual flats

BLOCK 2
CENTRE, L TO R: Ground floor plan of block; ground floor plans of individual flats; first floor plan of block; first floor plan of individual flats; section B-B of individual flats; BELOW: Elevation of buildings C and E

Campo di Marte

BLOCK 1
ABOVE, L TO R: Second floor plan of block; second floor plan of individual flats; third floor plan of block; section A-A of individual flats
BLOCK 2
CENTRE, L TO R: Second floor plan of block; second floor plan of individual flats; third floor plan of block; section of individual flats; BELOW: Side elevation of buildings C, D, and E

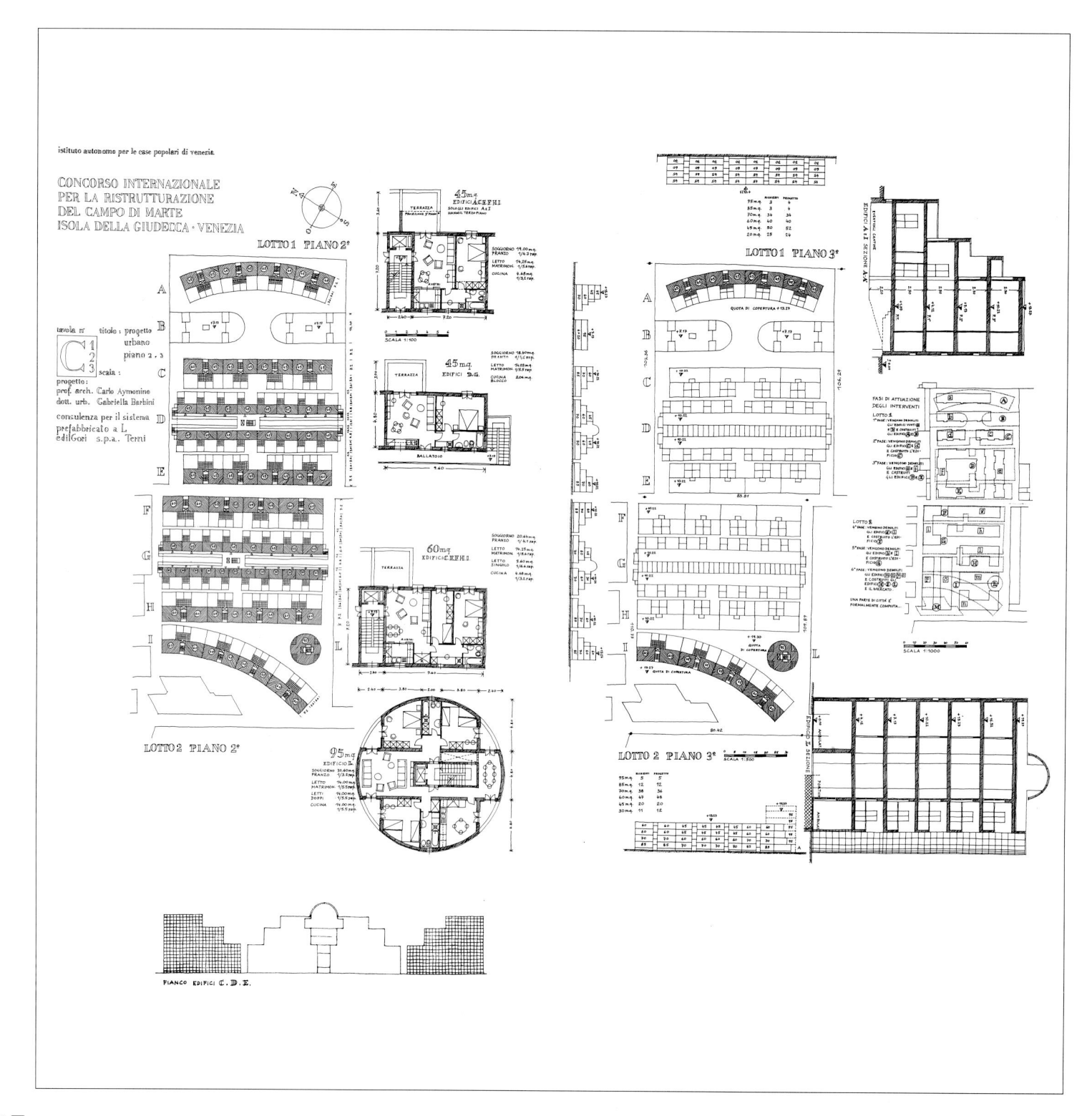

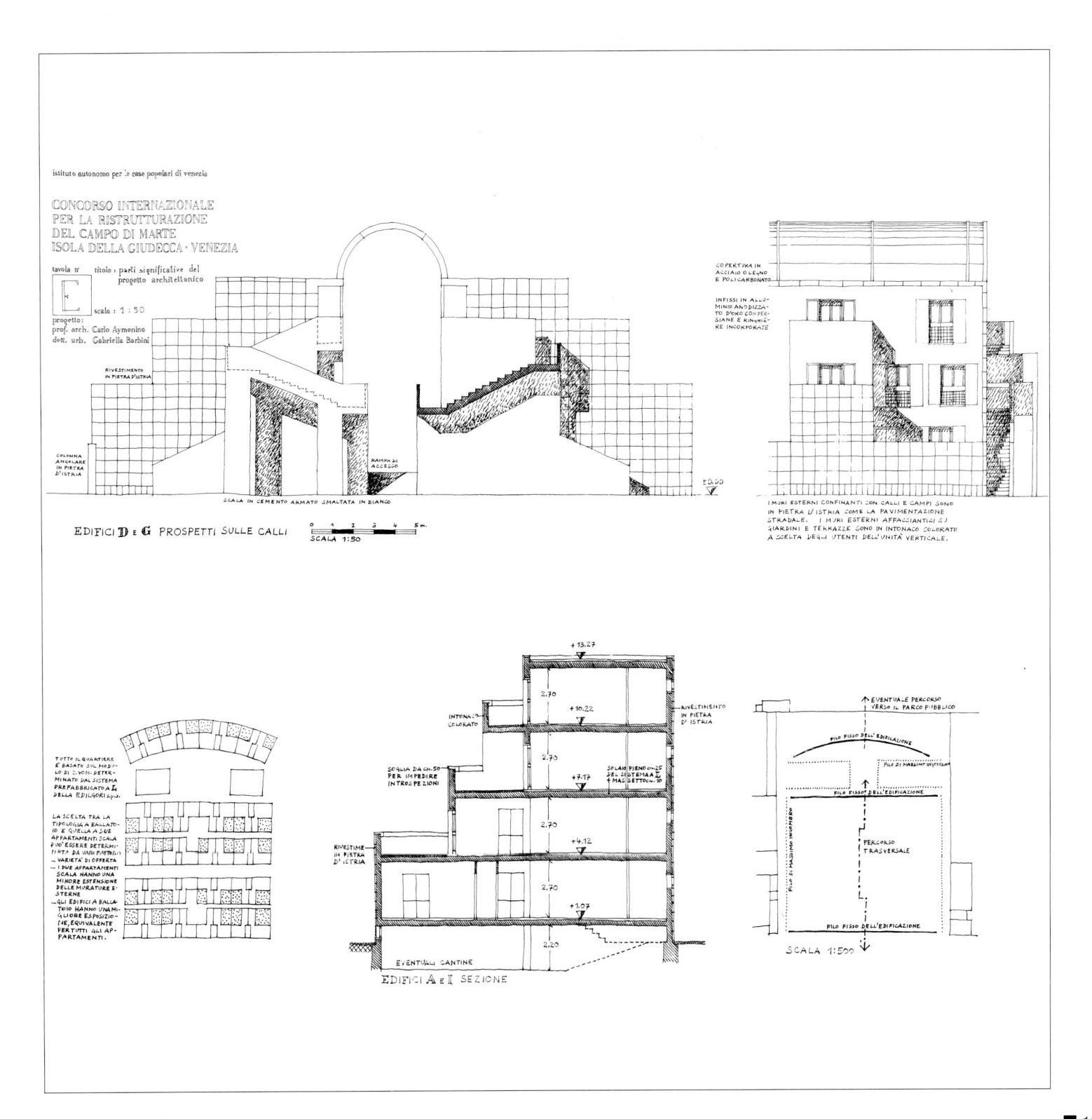

FROM ABOVE, L TO R: Elevations of buildings D and G; diagram of the module system; section of buildings A and I; circulation diagram

Campo di Marte

PALAZZO DEL CINEMA, THE LIDO, VENICE, 1990

With Gabriella Barbini, Giulio Paolini and Giovanni Morabito

Initially this project was arranged around a central axis intended to unify the two existing auditoriums and the proposed waterfront extension, as well as accommodating the cinema's increased demands. However, the design was subsequently altered so that the activities were organised around a central nucleus providing a more compact, but irregular, solution.

The building and site are defined along the road by the existing portico and wall presenting a homogenous facade to the public. However, behind this element the new additions are easily identifiable due to their individual articulation. These are based primarily on function, and create the impression of a varied urban landscape.

As a result of the numerous activities contained in this complex, the cinema does not have a single foyer or entrance but an ensemble of external and internal anterooms providing access to individual functions. This area terminates on the outside reception terrace with its views of the sea. All waterborne approaches have been provided with separate entrances, including one for heavy vessels with direct access to the theatre's backstage. Moorings are also available for the public allowing patrons to alight under the covered walkway and proceed into the foyers.

The existing theatre, normally used for concerts and operas, has been preserved in its entirety, although the stage has been altered to accommodate a more diverse range of musical and theatrical styles. The remaining three auditoriums are of varying sizes and seating capacities to increase the complex's potential repertoire.

The facades are clad in stone, including the arches of the walkway, with the major activities of the building articulated through the use of different marbles: Istrian marble for the portico; grey Carrara marble for the theatres, and Serena for the office complex. The interiors, including those facing the street like the entrance halls, are decorated in yellow, red and blue. The whole of the design is an homage to the beauty of black and white cinema.

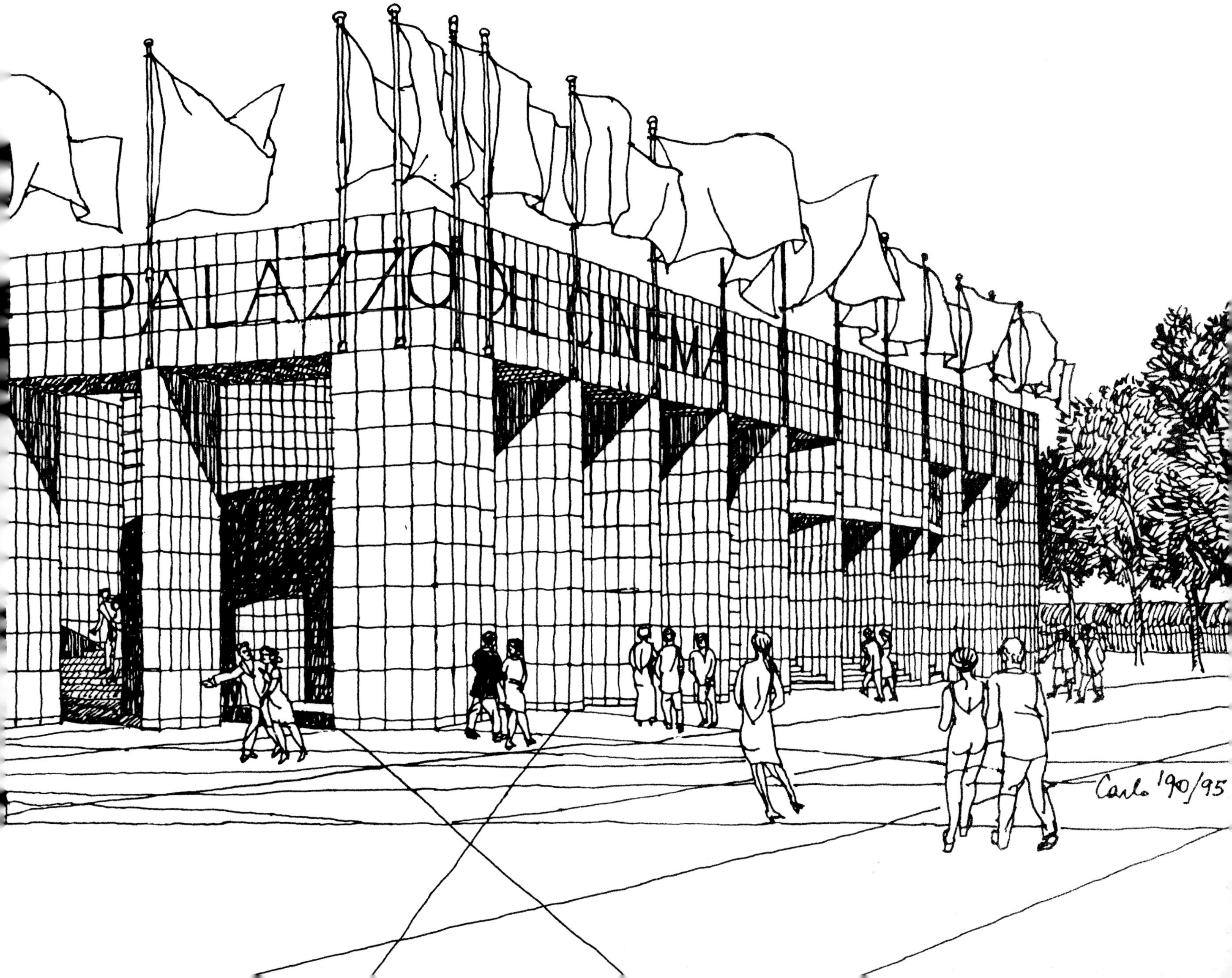
PALAZZO DEL CINEMA
Carlo '90/'95

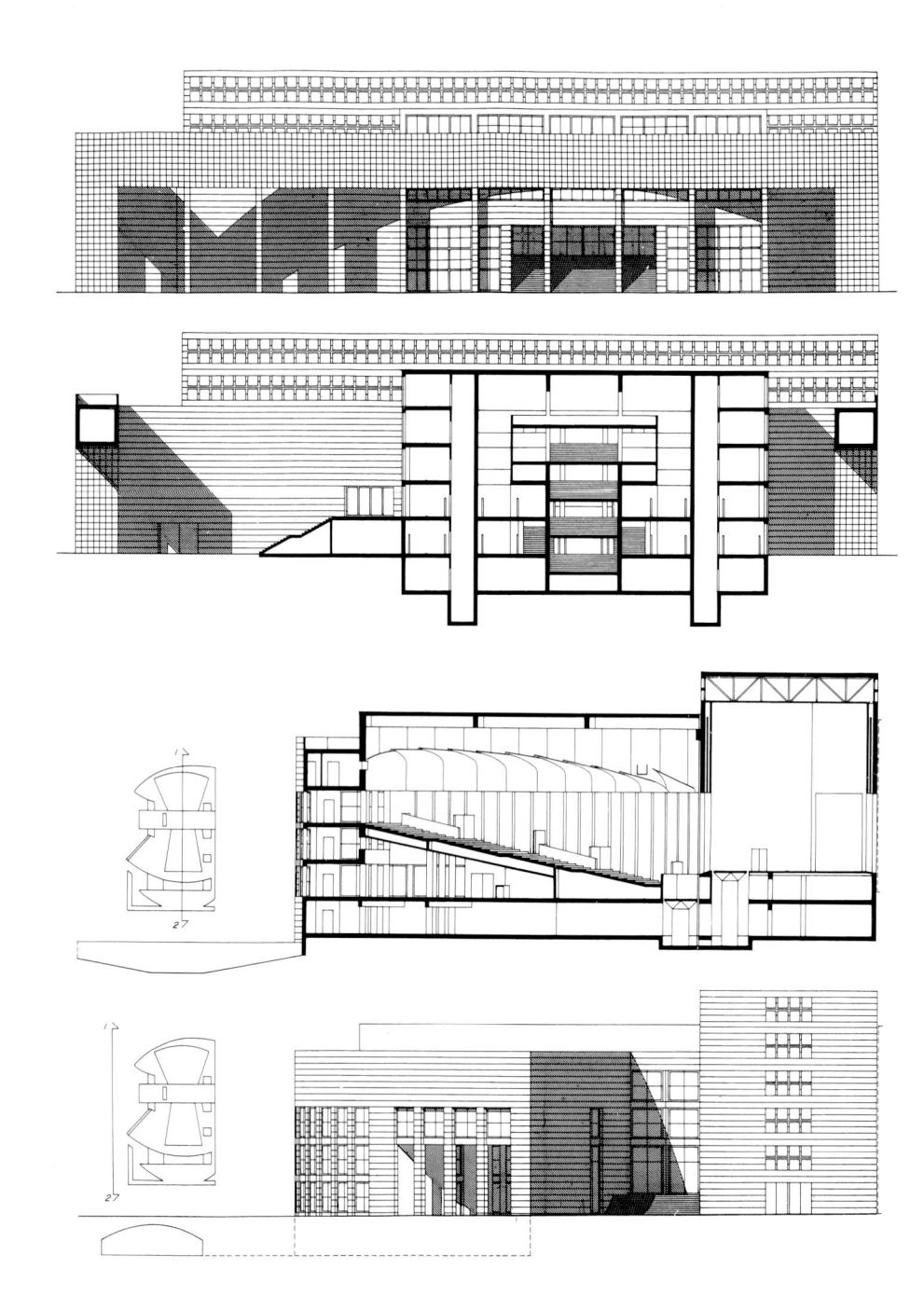

FROM ABOVE: South-east elevation; section A-A; section B-B; south-west elevation; north-east elevation; OPPOSITE, FROM ABOVE: First floor plan; ground floor plan

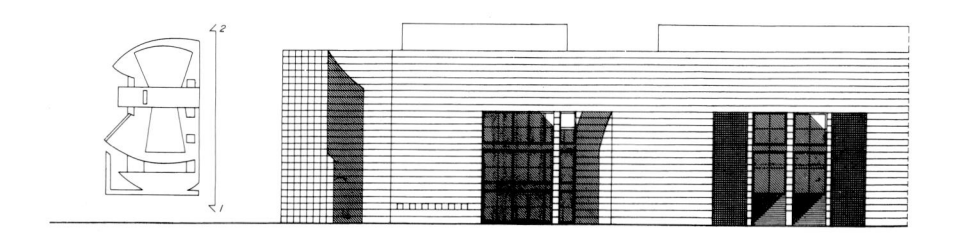

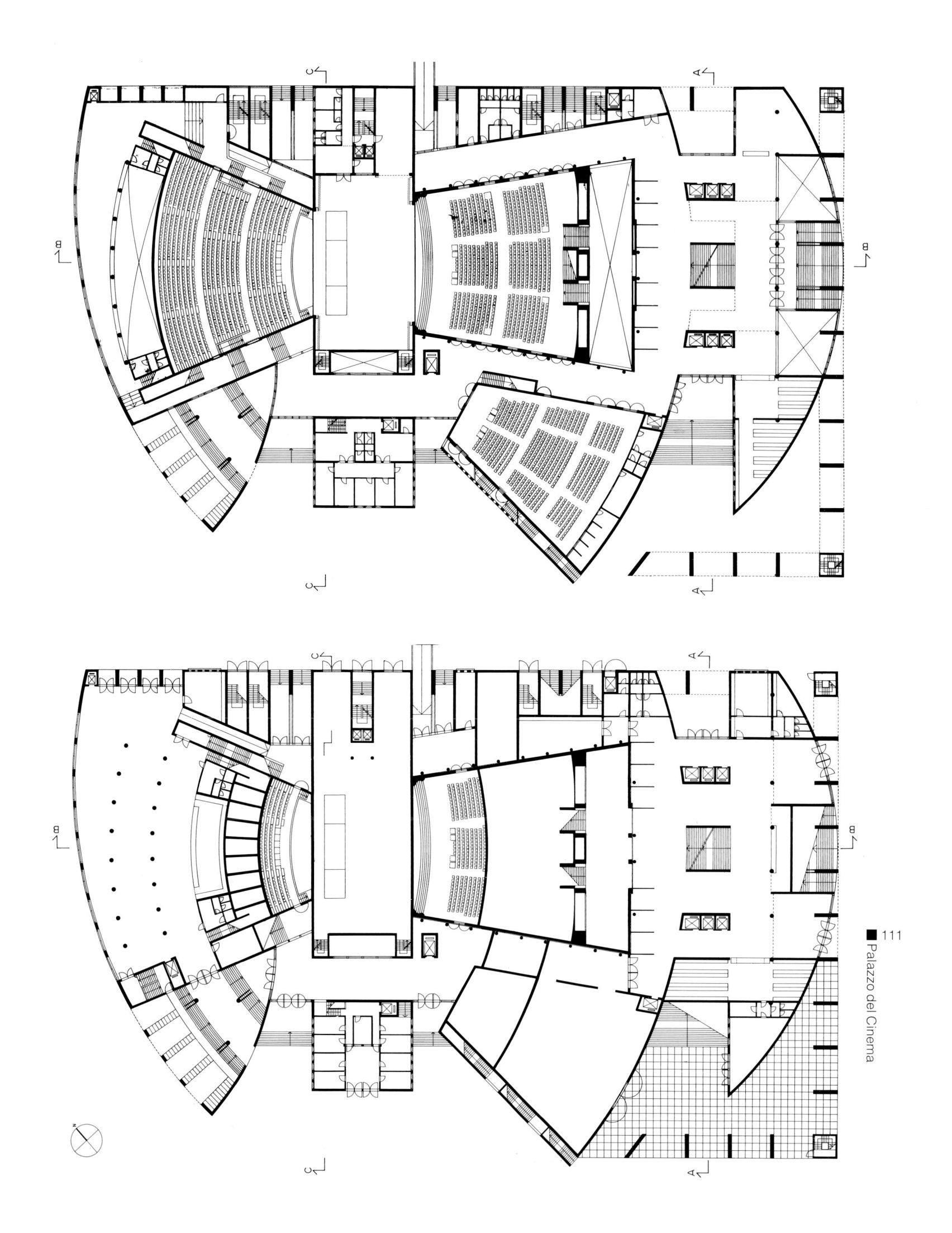

Palazzo del Cinema

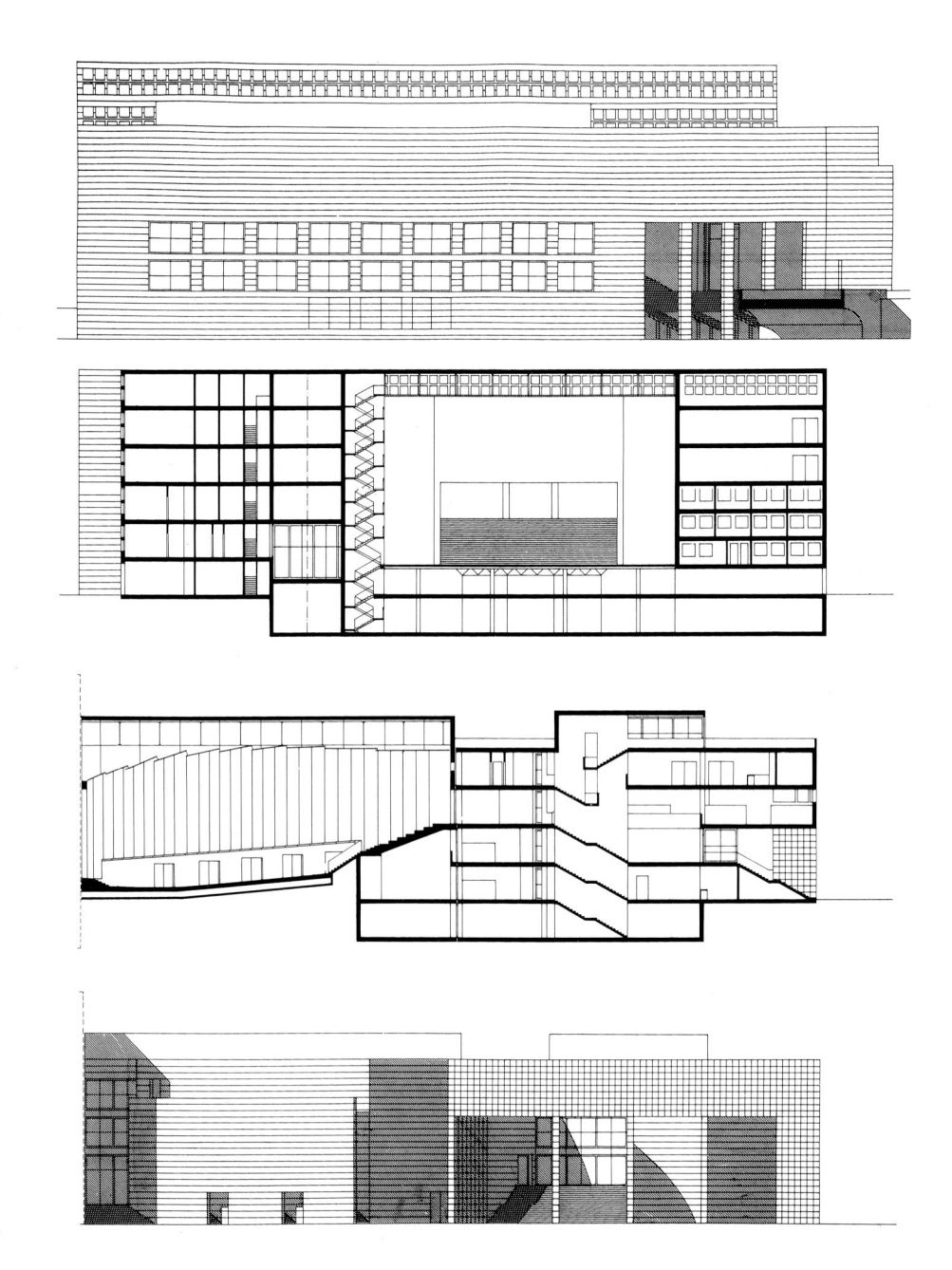

FROM ABOVE: North-west elevation; section C-C; section B-B; south-west elevation; north-east elevation; OPPOSITE, FROM ABOVE: Third floor plan; second floor plan

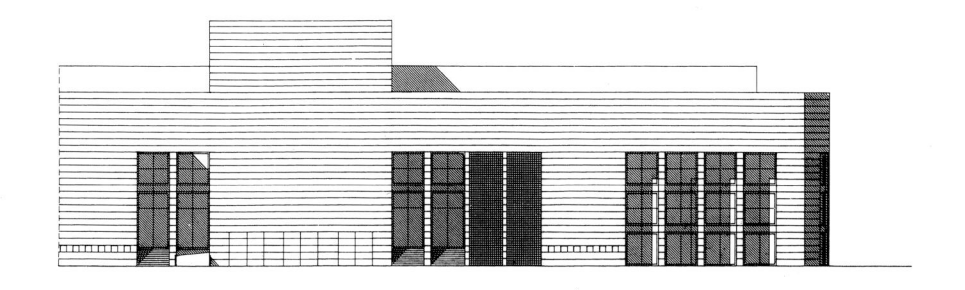

Carlo Aymonino

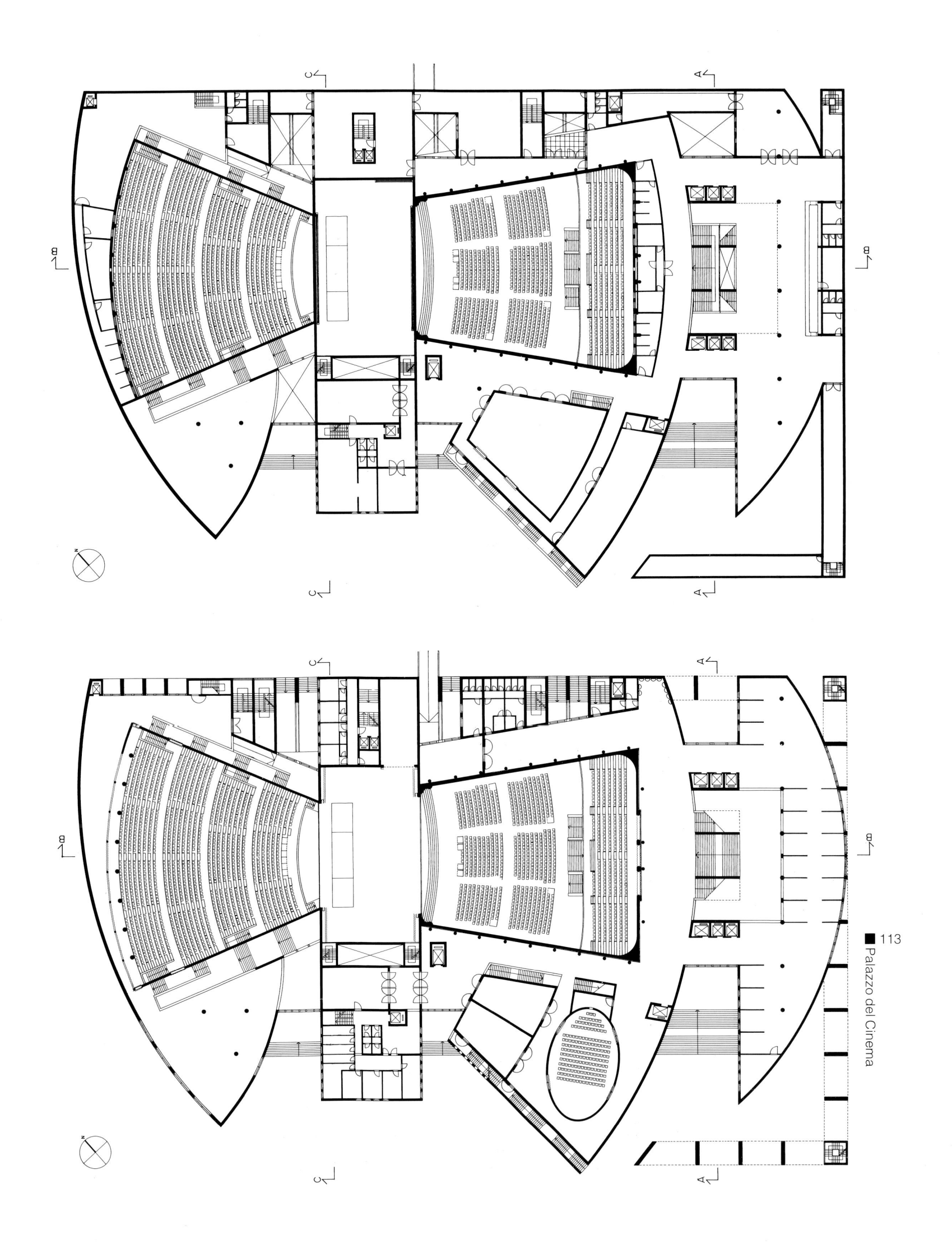

113 Palazzo del Cinema

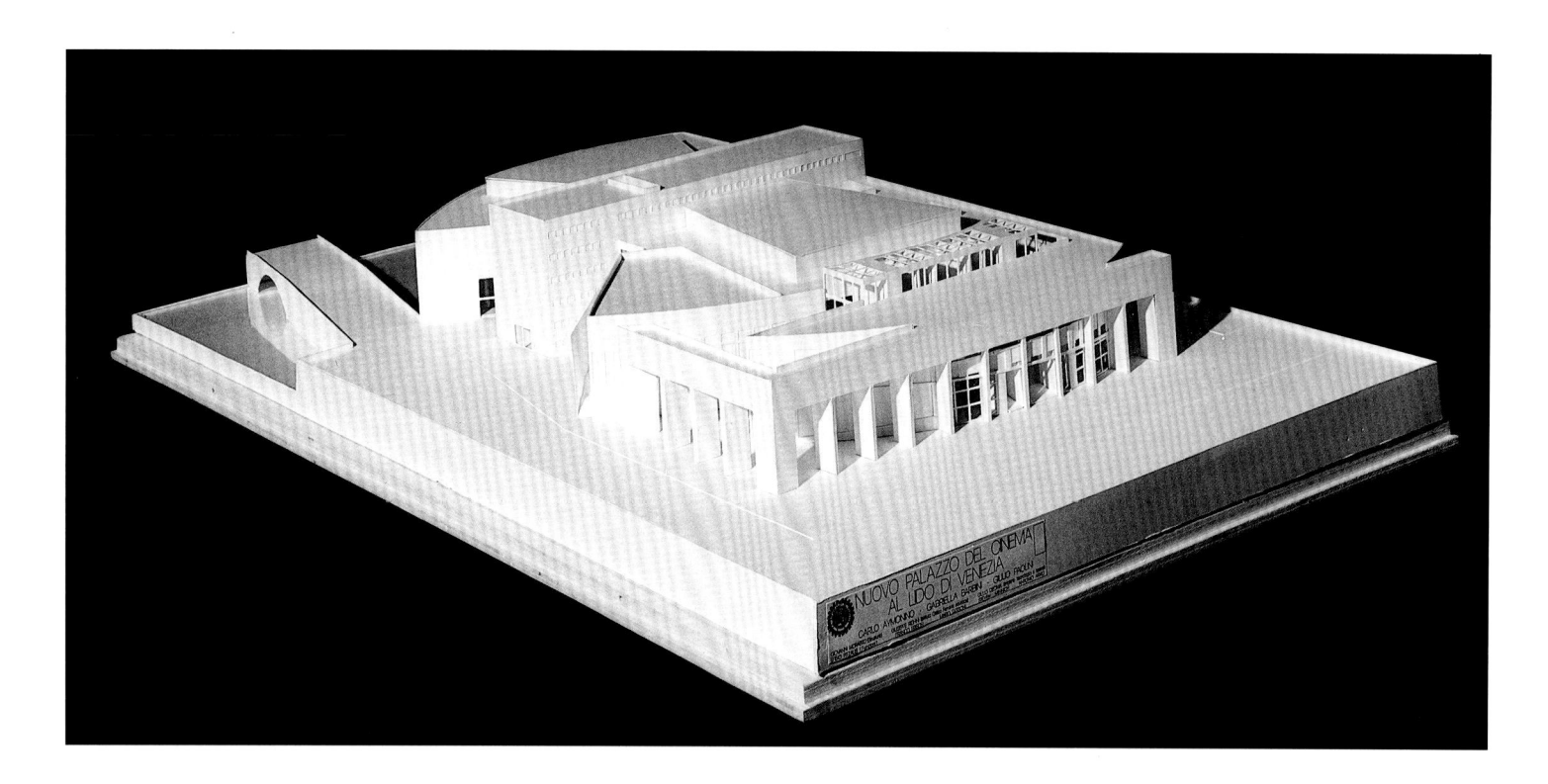

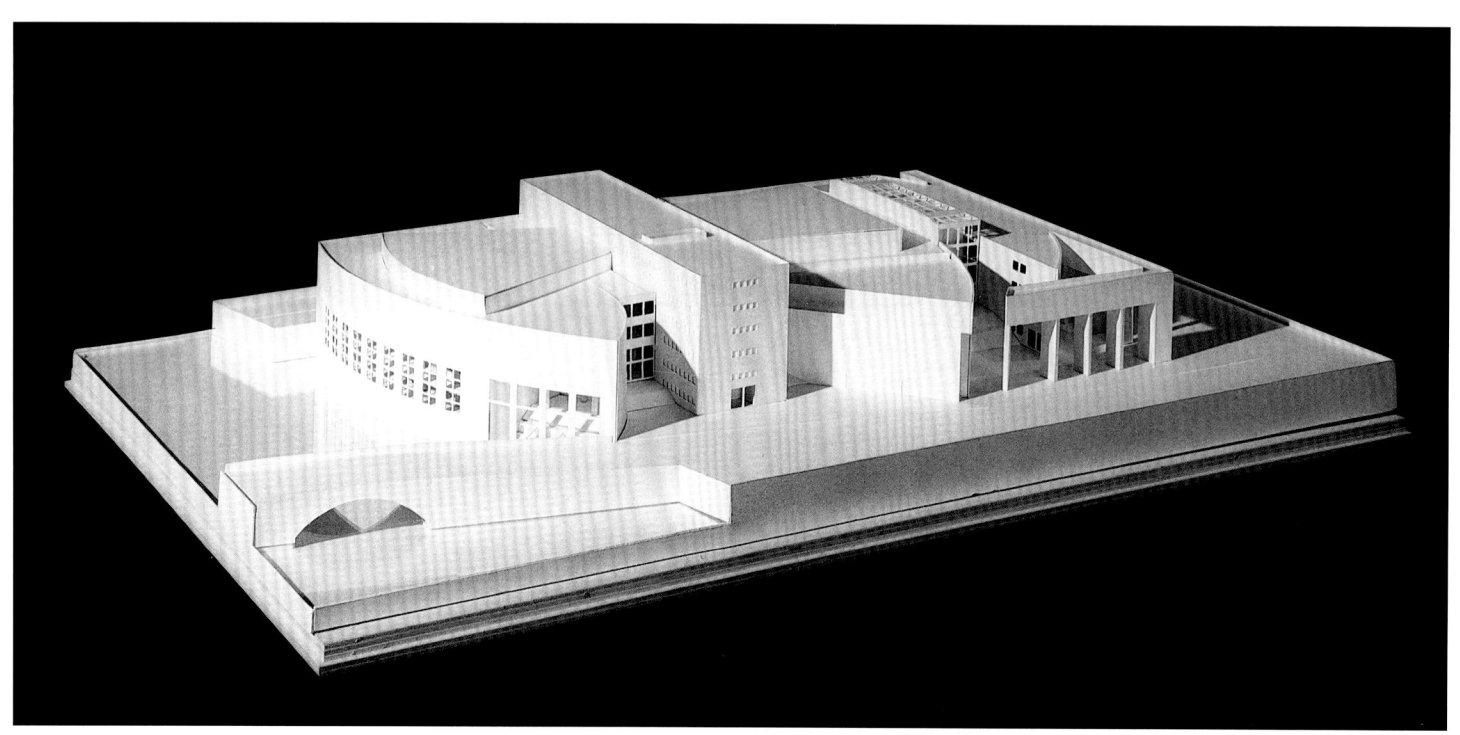

OPPOSITE: Perspective views; PAGES 116-17: Development studies

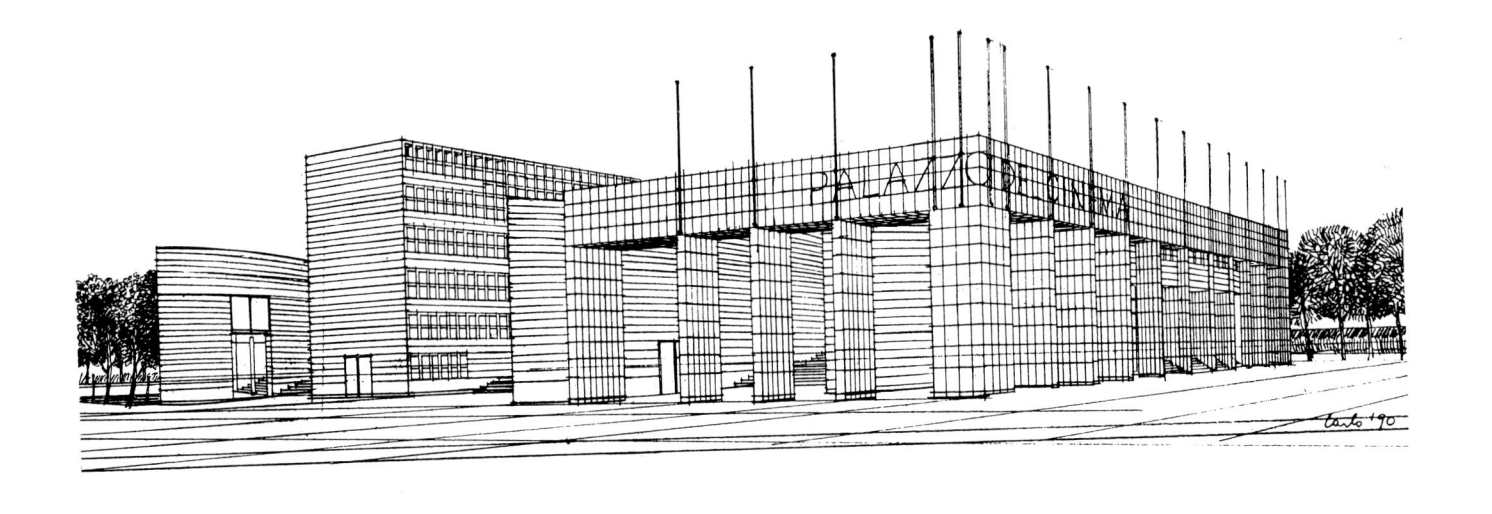

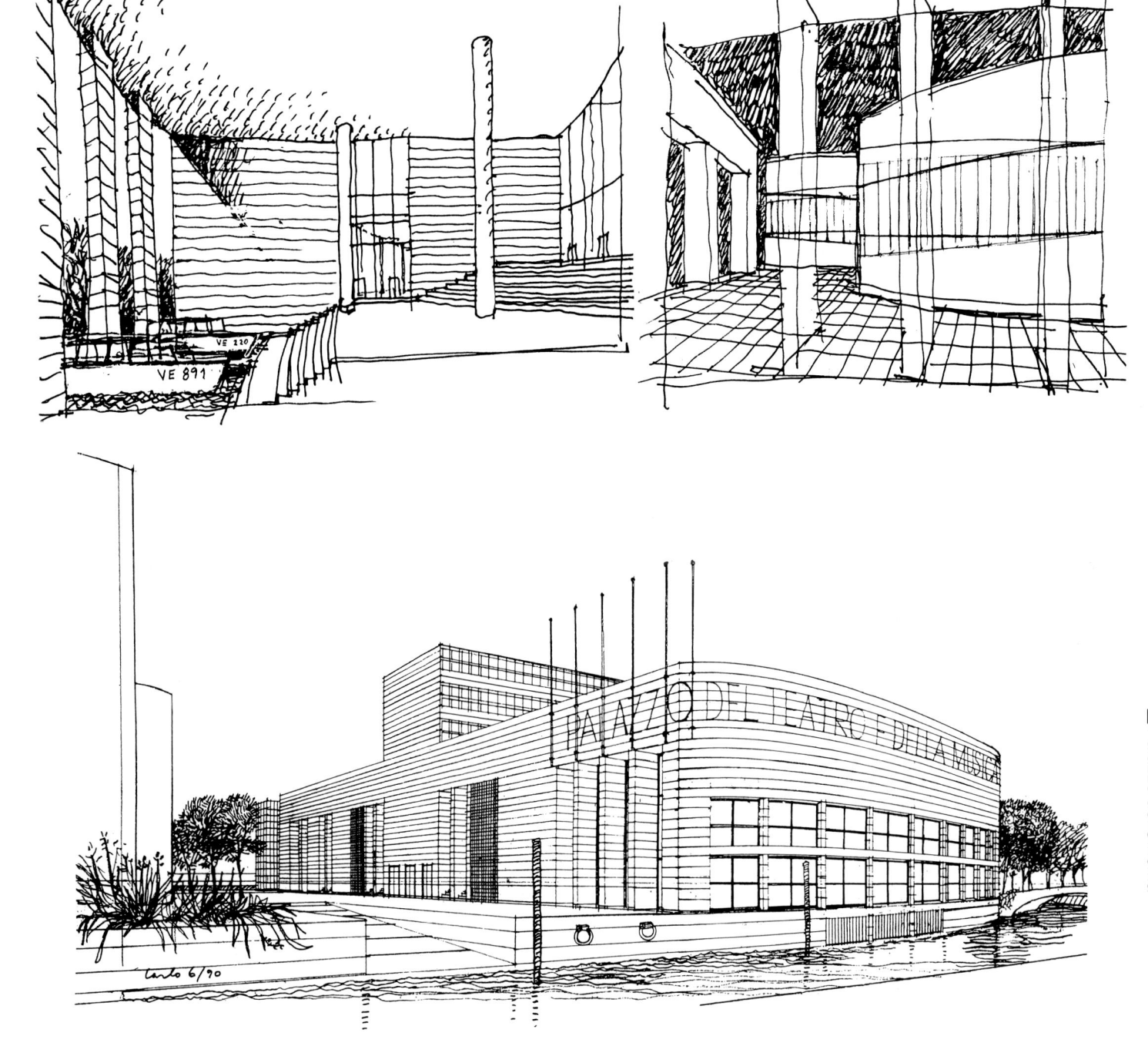

Palazzo del Cinema

*Venezia non mi lascia mai
e la mia vita sarà la sua fine*
Corto Maltese

Relazione

"Il concorso ha per oggetto la ristrutturazione del Palazzo del Cinema al fine di renderlo pienamente funzionale allo svolgimento delle attività della Biennale di Venezia (Festival del Cinema, Festival della Musica, Festival del Teatro, ecc.) e di altre attività culturali e artistiche in qualsiasi periodo dell'anno." (art. 4 del Bando).

Le prime idee, non avendo ancora tenuto conto dei confini del lotto, erano impostate su un asse centrale unificante le due sale e un eventuale prolungamento sulla riva del mare, sul quale attestare le nuove richieste di sale e di servizi.

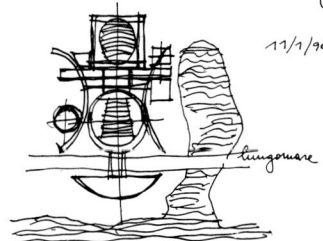

Lo stesso impianto è stato poi adattato in una soluzione più compatta, ma sempre simmetrica, rispetto all'asse principale, nel tentativo di organizzare un nucleo centrale intorno al quale aggregare le varie diversità funzionali.

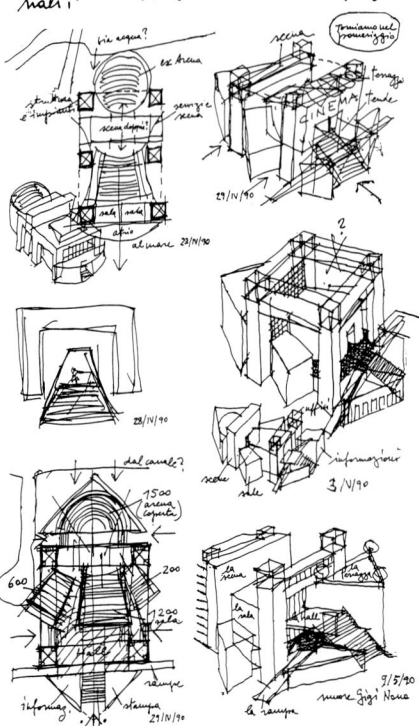

Ripresi in considerazione i confini reali e tenuto conto del vincolo di H=22 m (ma i volumi tecnici sono al di fuori?) l'impostazione assiale è stata modificata da simmetrica ad asimmetrica.

A tale decisione si è arrivati anche per conservare l'attuale Sala Cinema, sia come memoria storica del Festival sia per consultazione dei produttori, registi, tecnici e gestori della Biennale che hanno confermato tutte le qualità di spettacolo (visibilità, dimensioni, illuminazione, acustica) della stessa. Condizionando ulteriormente l'impianto generale che, da assiale e relativamente simmetrico quale era si è trasformato in un impianto "aglientino" con caratteristiche altrettanto precise ma diverse.

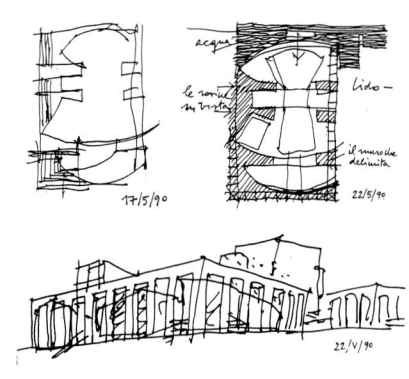

Da queste premesse il portico e il muro – in facciata e della strada di distacco dal Casinò – definiscono il lotto là dove si presenta regolare, confermando le misure e quantità esistenti o sostitutive delle esistenti. Le nuove, notevoli, quantità aggiuntive sono leggibili nella loro legge aggregativa dalla strada in modo da formare quasi un paesaggio urbano variato.

Grande attenzione è stata prestata ai servizi per il pubblico che, dato il carattere di attività multiple previsto dal bando, non ha un unico accesso ma un insieme di spazi esterni e interni integrati tra loro che culminano nella terrazza per ricevimenti dalla parte del mare e nella darsena per motoscafi dalla parte del canale.

I flussi di pubblico possono così essere concentrati e molto suddivisi a seconda del tipo di manifestazioni; in entrambi i casi particolare cura è stata posta nella distribuzione degli ingressi – a loro volta passibili di differenziazione; personalità, VIP, giornalisti, pubblico pagante – e nella differenziazione delle aree di sosta e di incontro, assicurando anche all'interno del Palazzo, oltre che all'Excelsior, una terrazza per ricevimenti, un bar con relativo ristorante, un caffè all'aperto utilizzando la piazzetta risultante dal risvolto del portico di delimitazione.

Anche per quanto riguarda gli arrivi via acqua, fermo restando gli attuali attracchi in corrispondenza del Casinò sono stati previsti accessi differenziati; un attacco per mezzi pesanti in corrispondenza della rampa d'accesso alla via di distacco del Casinò; vari attracchi in corrispondenza dei fornici del magazzino affacciantisi sul canale; infine gli attracchi per il pubblico si corrispondenza della grande darsena coperta, con una capienza di tre motoscafi alla volta, col accesso alla hall della sala Teatro e Musica, all'ingresso degli uffici, al lungo foyer da cui è possibile accedere alla sala Cinema, alla sala Stampa, ecc.

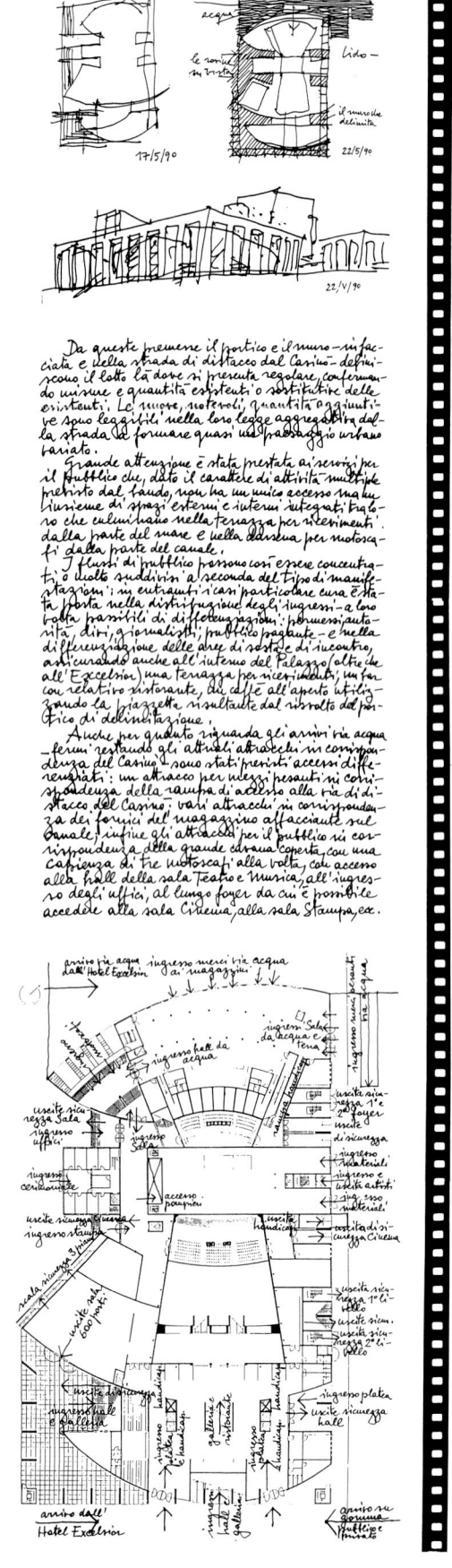

La presenza delle tre sale – di dimensioni e numero dei posti molto diversificati – permette di ipotizzare un loro uso differenziato.

L'attuale sala cinema, conservata nel suo insieme ma con il palcoscenico ristrutturato, può essere destinata a proiezioni cinematografiche mantenendo la sorgente sonora nello stesso luogo, e a rappresentazioni teatrali, con l'eventuale riduzione dei posti a 700, isolando la galleria con una supertenda ed aggiungendo ai lati del palcoscenico due elementi forati-fondenti per rinforzo sonoro "naturale".

La nuova sala grande può essere destinata a spettacoli di varietà teatrale e musicale ma soprattutto a manifestazioni musicali di tipo concertistico o parzialmente operistico. Nel caso di esecuzioni sinfoniche va alzato il tempo di riverberazione con sistemi artificiali con l'aggiunta di una camera d'orchestra (conchiglia e simili). La parete di fondo della sala è chiusa da una serie di tende a fini acustici, mentre nel caso di congressi o convegni può essere interamente aperta sul foyer superiore.

Nella sala da 600 posti per attività collaterali, convegni, in alcuni casi le conferenze stampa, dal punto di vista acustico è prevista una riverberazione variabile "naturale".

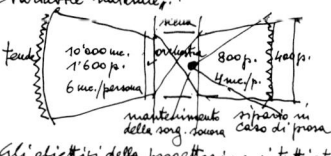

Gli obiettivi della progettazione, in tutti e tre i casi sono l'assenza di "difetti acustici"; l'uniforme distribuzione del livello sonoro; la distribuzione spaziale del campo sonoro; una riverberazione ottimale.

In considerazione delle caratteristiche strutturali (ampi spazi, elevate altezze) e della necessità di notevole quantità d'aria di rinnovo, gli impianti sono ad aria. In particolare si è tenuto conto:
- sovrapressione delle sale principali rispetto ai corridoi o agli atrii.
- eliminazione diretta del calore prodotto dalle lampade.
- individuazione dei livelli di occupazione del pubblico e valutazione delle sacche di stratificazione.

Onde evitare movimenti d'aria e garantire una velocità bassissima si è scelto per le sale il sistema del microclima con distribuzione dal basso. La mandata pertanto è sottostante le poltrone a mezzo di bocchette anemostatiche o bocchette predisposte sulle poltrone stesse anche con possibilità di induzione d'aria; la ripresa è prevalentemente dall'alto anche se non diffusamente ($V = 0,8 \, m/s$).

La mandata dell'aria dal basso, o direttamente dalla poltrona, è un'applicazione innovativa che sfrutta inoltre l'elevato rapporto indotto e di turbolenza dell'aria. Adatta particolarmente per grandi sale ove la velocità di lancio influirebbe negativamente sia per la diffusione che per la rumorosità.

— mandata e ripresa d'aria da sotto la poltrona con possibilità di interruzione del flusso a seduta con poltrona verticale od orizzontale —

In tutti gli altri ambienti del Palazzo il condizionamento d'aria sarà realizzato con sistema misto a canali o a ventilconvettori.

Per garantire la massima libertà nell'uso e nella gestione delle sale sarà prevista tre centrali per il trattamento dell'aria, complete di caldaie, di gruppo frigo adacqua e di torri evaporative sul tetto. Il sistema di riscaldamento sarà invece prodotto da una unica centrale a gasolio o a gas metano, in quest'ultimo caso la centrale sarà collocata fuori del fabbricato.

La scena è unica – sia per la Sala Cinema che per quella Musica e Teatro – per consentire una notevole economia di allestimento e di gestione mandata di tutte le attrezzature necessarie, anche per la lirica, e le riprese televisive. Il graticciato della torre scenica, e i soffitti tecnici sono a servizio differenziato delle due Sale, per gli apparecchi di illuminazione scenica e la loro movimentazione, compresi i portali di boccascena, i fronti di luci mobili, gli impianti televisivi (monitoraggio, video proiezione, riprese).

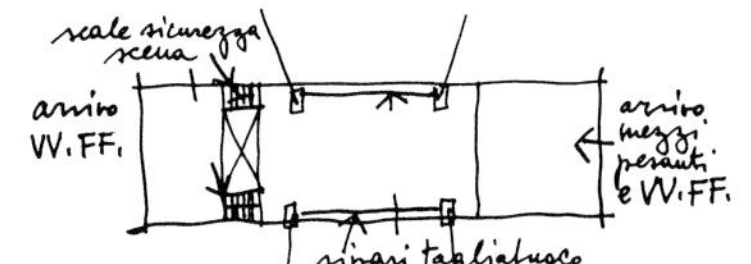

In ogni caso tutte e tre le sale sono dotate di schermo cinematografico "a scomparsa", e della relativa cabina di proiezione adeguata agli apparecchi installati; nelle due sale grandi sono installati anche un impianto di traduzione e conferenze e uno di registrazione sonora, oltre la cabina di regia delle luci sceniche.

Gli impianti sono completati da sistemi antifurto, di prevenzione incendi e di rilevazioni fumi e da sensori per la verifica dell'affluenza di pubblico.

La struttura dell'intero edificio è prevista in cemento armato. Le tipologie costruttive prescelte derivano dalle soluzioni morfologiche adottate nella definizione dell'impianto edilizio complessivo e delle singole parti che lo compongono.

Ampliando in tal modo lo spettro delle soluzioni possibili, pur nell'impiego di tecniche sufficientemente semplici e di materiali ampiamente verificati, si è affrontato in termini unitari il problema delle piastre che, realizzando gli orizzontamenti dei diversi corpi di fabbrica, costituiscono gli elementi strutturalmente più rilevanti.

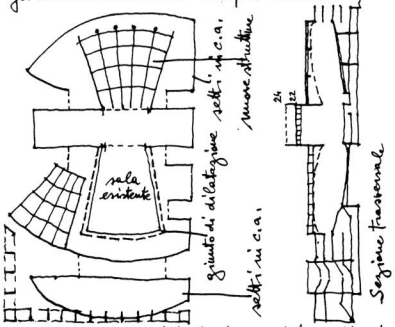

Queste sono costituite da un sistema discreto di travi in cemento armato irrigidite trasversalmente e disposte radialmente lungo l'asse longitudinale dei settori circolari che inviluppano le due nuove sale previste, per consentire una organizzazione strutturale planimetricamente priva di elementi verticali se non in corrispondenza del perimetro esterno delle sale.

In particolare nella sala da 600 posti tale soluzione offre una libertà spaziale che consente di realizzare una diversificata utilizzazione, ai diversi livelli, con possibilità di disporre dell'intera superficie o di frazionarla in sale più piccole per le diverse esigenze da soddisfare.

Nella nuova sala da 1600 posti la soluzione adottata si ritrova nella grande copertura dove le travi radiali, collegate tra loro nel senso trasversale, vengono sorrette sul lato posteriore dalla lastra cilindrica che racchiude la sala e, sul lato opposto, da la grande scatola parallelepipeda in cemento armato, costituita da due grandi lastre a portale collegate sui fianchi e in sommità che consentono l'apertura del fronte scena sulle due sale con doppia fruibilità del palcoscenico.

Al perimetro della Sala Cinema da conservare la soluzione strutturale precede l'innesto dei nuovi fabbricati attraverso un giunto continuo, ottenuto mediante il semplice raddoppio delle strutture verticali che l'adozione di prefabbricati discreti in fondazione consente di realizzare.

La zona dei vestiboli di ingresso infine non presenta particolari problemi strutturali, per i moduli dei setti, di passo modulare collegati a portale in sommità e nelle zone interne, per le lastre curvilinee, resistenti per forma e controventate ai vari livelli attraverso i solai di piano.

Tutte le facciate sono rivestite in materiale lapideo, compresi le rientranze nel "muro" e le pareti della caverna. Le tre "componenti" il complesso sono differenziate di poco, nelle pietre e nei marmi, a sottolineare la diversità compositiva delle stesse. Il portico, per il suo ruolo urbano di confine, è previsto in pietra d'Istria; tutto il complesso dello Spettacolo (Foyer, Sale, servizi, stampa ecc.) è previsto in marmo grigio chiaro tipo Carrara, la grande scatola degli uffici e della scena è prevista in pietra serena; il tutto a conferma della bellezza del cinema in bianco e nero.

Tutti gli interni, compresi quelli che si affacciano su strada come gli ingressi, saranno colorati utilizzando il giallo, il rosso e il blu.

I rivestimenti ora descritti sono sistemati in facciate sospese e ventilate per il miglioramento dell'isolamento termico e acustico.

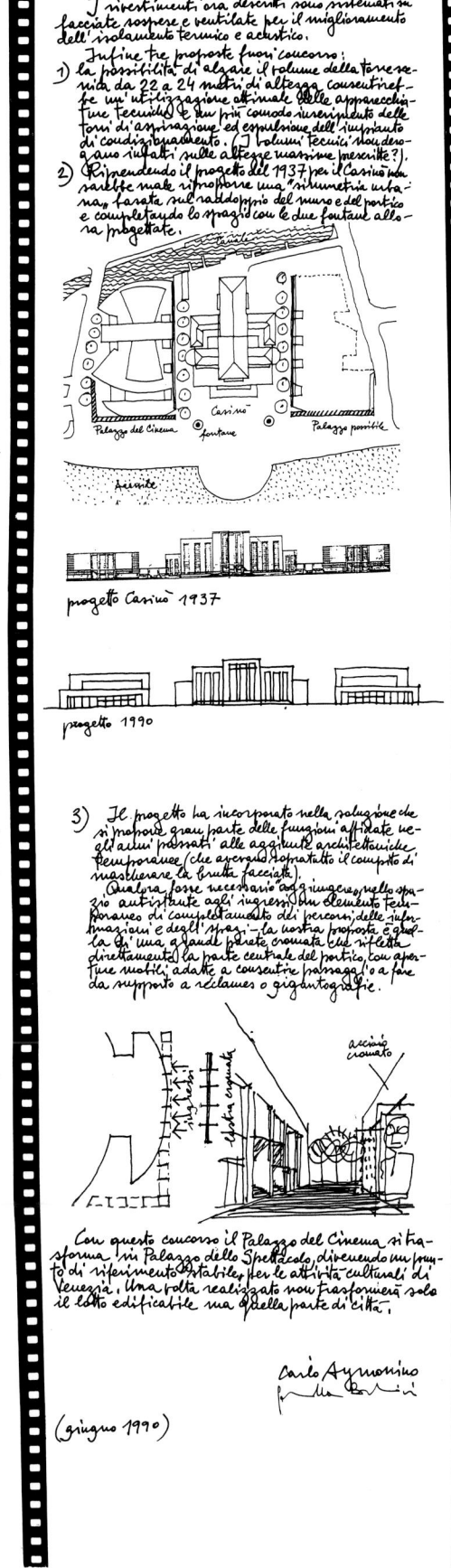

Infine tre proposte fuori concorso:

1) la possibilità di alzare il volume della torre scenica da 22 a 24 metri di altezza consentirebbe un'utilizzazione ottimale delle apparecchiature tecniche e due più comodo inserimento delle torri di aspirazione ed espulsione dell'impianto di condizionamento. (I volumi tecnici non devono infatti sulle altezze massime previste?).

2) Riprendendo il progetto del 1937 per il Casinò non sarebbe male riproporre una "simmetria urbana", basata sul raddoppio del muro e del portico e completando lo spazio con le due fontane allora progettate.

progetto Casinò 1937

progetto 1990

3) Il progetto ha incorporato nella soluzione che si propone gran parte delle funzioni affidate negli anni passati alle aggiunte architettoniche temporanee (che avevano soprattutto il compito di mascherare la brutta facciata).

Qualora fosse necessario aggiungere nello spazio antistante agli ingressi un elemento temporaneo di completamento dei percorsi, delle informazioni e degli spazi, la nostra proposta è quella di una grande parete cromata che riflette direttamente la parte centrale del portico, con aperture mobili adatte a consentire passaggi o a fare da supporto a réclames o gigantografie.

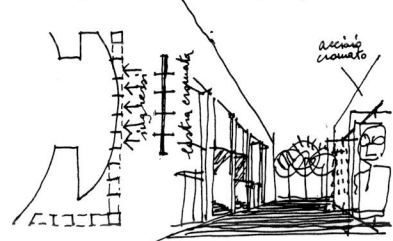

Con questo concorso il Palazzo del Cinema si trasforma in Palazzo dello Spettacolo, divenendo un punto di riferimento stabile per le attività culturali di Venezia. Una volta realizzato non trasformerà solo il lotto edificabile ma quella parte di città.

Carlo Aymonino
[firma]

(giugno 1990)

Sono a Venezia (come non esserci?) ospite del progetto al quale Carlo e Gabriella mi chiesero di collaborare. Nomi propri, scrittura a mano, sono già di per sé denominatori comuni (ma allo stesso tempo singolari).

Mi trovo di fronte a due grandi pareti curve, interrotte, appena dopo aver oltrepassato il colonnato che ci ha accolti. Le due superfici sono teatro di due "proiezioni" contrapposte: dal punto di origine, il tracciato si rovescia su se stesso e dà luogo alla prospettiva del colonnato esterno che compie la ripetizione, in grandezza al vero, della soglia appena attraversata.

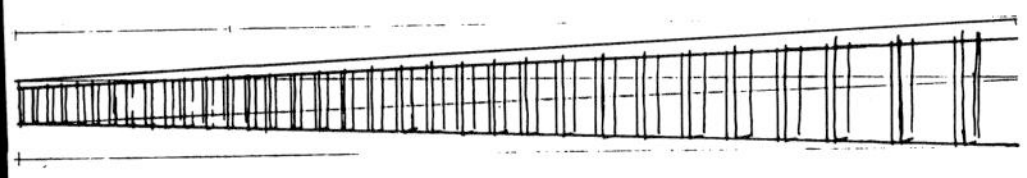

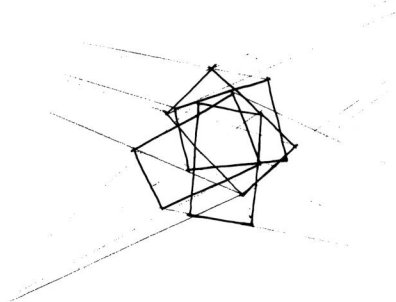

Una versione alternativa è prevista in esterno, sulla sommità centrale dell'edificio. Una struttura costituita da 4 telai rettangolari vuoti (schermi, luoghi della rappresentazione?) è sorpresa da 16 (ai 4 vertici di ciascuno) cavi fosforescenti in tensione: dai 4 punti di tenuta, 4 riflettori di rigore le luce verso il centro...

Giulio Carlini
[firma]

(giugno 1990)

Palazzo del Cinema

118 ■ *Sketch studies*

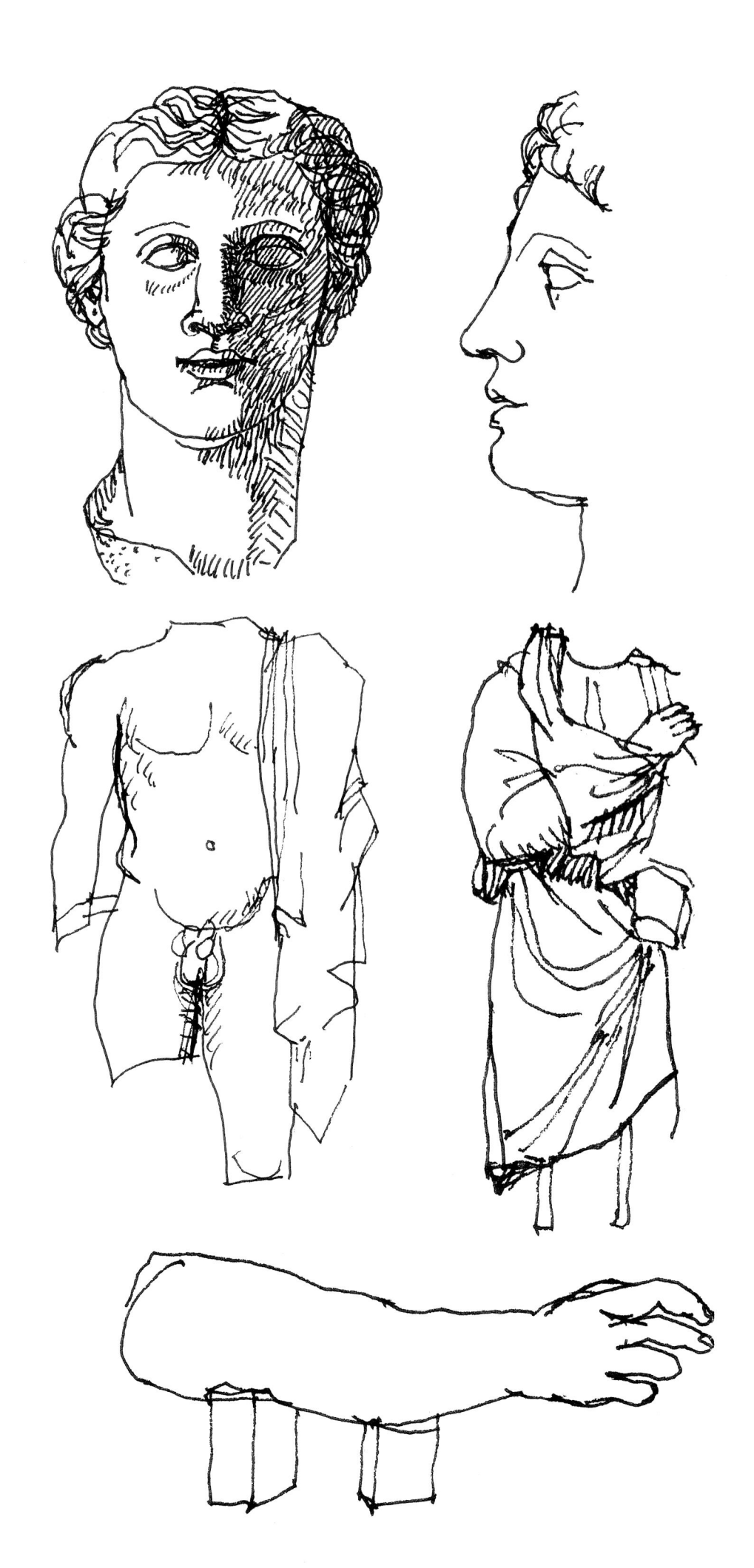

Carlo Aymonino

THE ROMAN GARDEN, PALAZZO DEI CONSERVATORI, ROME, 1993

DEVELOPMENT OF A NEW EXHIBITION SPACE

With Maria Luisa Tugnoli and Geneviève Hanssen

The aim of this project for the Roman gardens at the Palazzo dei Conservatori is to provide new exhibition space for the Capitoline Museum complex. The new hall, which is part of the museum's current expansion and rearrangement, is intended to house exhibits of extraordinary artistic merit in a setting that reflects their value. The majority of these pieces has never been seen by the public.

Conceived in April 1993, the initial proposals involved positioning a number of statues next to the Temple of Apollo's pediment within the circular space directly accessible from the Orti Lamiani Gallery. This courtyard was originally occupied by Virginio Vespignani's Octagonal Hall that was demolished in 1902. Like the permanent gallery that was soon to follow, these figures were intended to provide a suitable contrast to the temple's statues despite being carved contemporaneously.

The design for the permanent gallery was finalised by December that same year and involved turning the courtyard into a vast atrium. The glazed roof was constructed of a filagree steel frame – approximately 1 centimetre in diameter and arranged on a 1 metre grid – whilst a glazed wall, of similar construction, completed the enclosure without hindering access to the Caffarelli Gardens. Within this atrium the existing exhibits – the pediment and chamber of the Temple of Apollo and the remains of the Temple of Jupiter – were arranged to complement the layout of the new exhibition.

The design of this gallery reinforces the museum's commitment to providing informative interactive exhibitions rather than just displaying the exhibits. The emphasis is on a didactic, rather than aesthetic, experience which reflects contemporary changes in international museum design. The exhibits are positioned along a route that traverses the Roman gardens. The display includes original artefacts – fragments rather than reconstructions – from throughout Italy – including the sacred area of Largo Argentina, the Theatre of Pompeius and the Piazza Campitelli – that are arranged chronologically, although the regions are mixed to allow the visitors to compare concurrent designs from different regions. Similarly, the scale of the various exhibits is varied – alternating between large and small pieces – to illustrate the full spectrum of sculptural arts practised by the Romans. This approach enables the embossed seal to be compared with a statue or pediment. The route also includes the existing elements within the courtyard so that they establish a rapport with the rest of the works exhibited. This is particularly evident in the arrangement of the remnants of the Apollo Temple next to a scale model of the complete building, allowing them to be compared to the whole, and stimulating an intriguing dialogue between large and small, object and representation. As an exhibition, the Roman gardens strikes a comfortable balance between a rarefied collection of artefacts and a presentation dedicated to stimulating the civil and educational function of the museum.

Finally, the architects have utilised the ruined walls of the Temple of Jupiter – now separated from its portico – to create an exquisite feature that symbolises the marriage between the archaeological and architectural. This has been achieved by removing the plaster from the temple's walls so that the mixture of Roman and medieval masonry is exposed as a reminder of the numerous constructional strata that are the remains of centuries of Italian history. The meticulous restoration of these features has been so successful that the walls – once decaying – now have a similar patina to marbled marquetry.

La copertura del Giardino Romano consente di organizzare in un' unica grande Sala i resti del Tempi...

Carlo Aymonino

e Capitolino e quelli del Tempio di Apollo Sosiano in Roma,

LEFT: Perspective; ABOVE: Model view

121

The Roman Garden

MUSEI CAPITOLINI · PROGETTO D

In primo piano il muro di fondazione del Tempio di Giove Capitolino e resti di sculture

GIARDINO ROMANO

repubblicana e augustea della Fides e di Mens, 1993

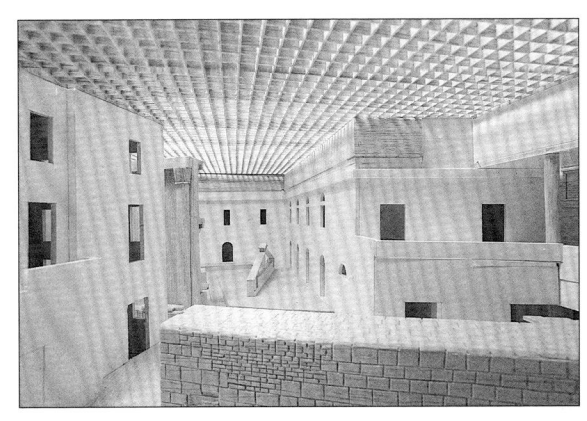

LEFT: Perspective; ABOVE: Model view

The Roman Garden

Carlo Aymonino

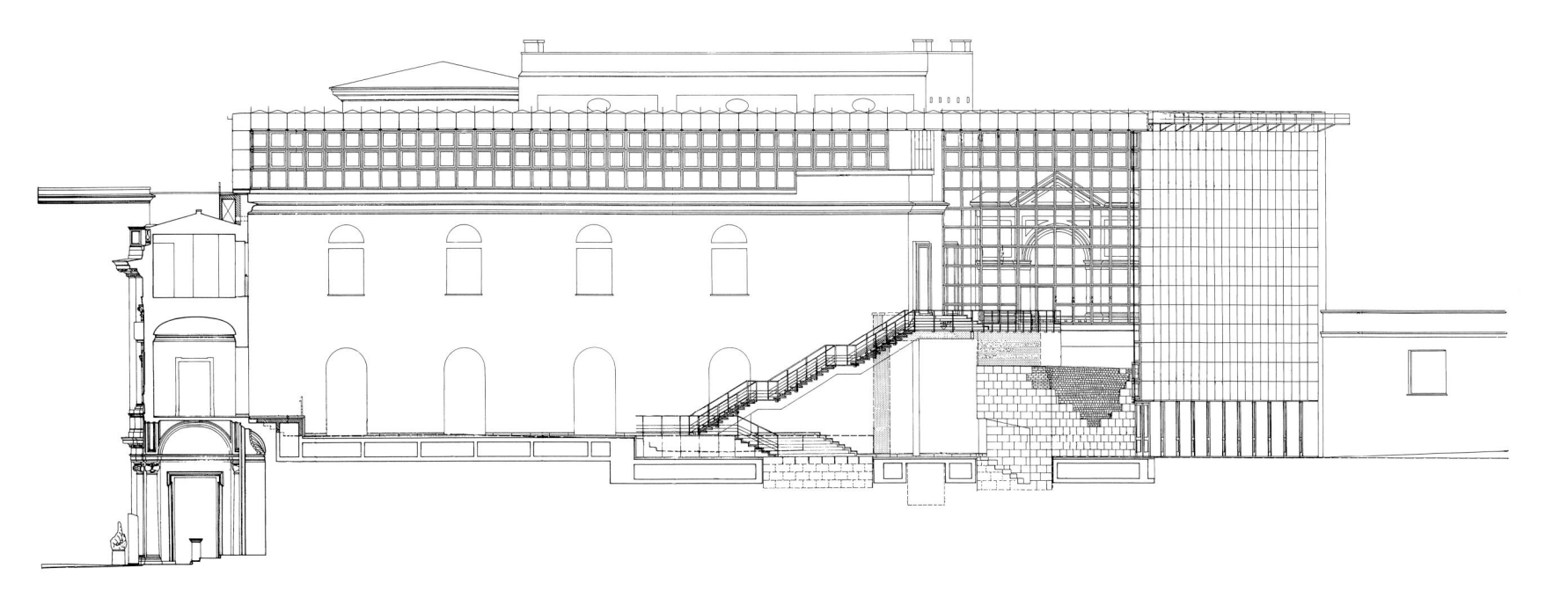

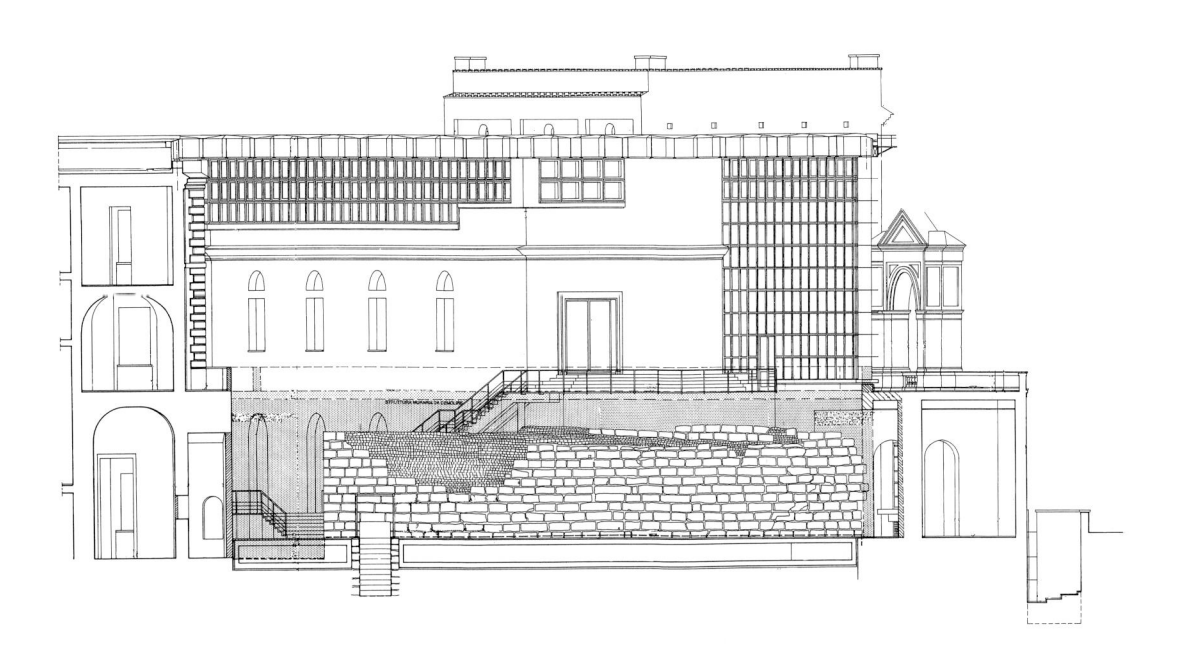

FROM ABOVE: Section A-A; section B-B; OPPOSITE, FROM ABOVE: Roof plan; upper level plan; ground level plan

BIOGRAPHY

Born in Rome in 1926, Carlo Aymonino graduated from the Faculty of Architecture (Rome) in 1950, where he has been Professor of Architectural Composition since 1967. He has continually worked as an architect, with studios in Rome and Venice, and has taught at the Venice University Institute of Architecture where he was Dean from 1974-79. He taught Architectural Composition at the Faculty of Architecture at the 'Sapienza' University in Rome from 1980-93, when he was called back to the IUAV. From 1981-85 he was Councillor for the interventions in the Historic Centre of Rome and is president of the Academy of San Luca. He was invited to take part in the XIII and XV Milan Triennale and the Venice Biennale in 1976 and 1985 respectively. From 1984-87 he edited the column 'L'Architettura' in the weekly *L'Europeo*.

COMPLETE WORKS

1950-52
- INA Casa Quarter, Tiburtino, Rome: C Chiarini, M Fiorentino, F Gorio, M Lanza, S Lenci, PM Lugli, C Melograni, GC Menichetti, G Rinaldi, M Valori; Group leaders: L Quaroni M Ridolfi.

1951-54
La Tartaruga, small residential unit: L Quaroni.

1952
- Co-ordinating plan, Basilicata region, preliminary study: L Quaroni, P Moroni.

1953
- Residential units, Stefer employees, Via Tuscolana, Rome, competition design: L Anversa, S Lenci, C Morelli, P Moroni.
- Residential units, Stefer employees, Ostia Lido, competition design: L Anversa, S Lenci, C Morelli, P Moroni.

1954
- Covered market, Pescara, competition design: G Belardelli, G Malatesta.
- Residential complex, Matera, competition design: C Chiarini, M Girelli, S Lenci, M Ottolenghi.

1956-58
- Tratturo dei Preti residential complex, Foggia: C Chiarini, B de Rossi, M Girelli, GRP, Brindisi, S Lenci, G Peretto.

1956-60
- Chamber of Commerce, Industry and Agriculture, Massa-Carrara: C Chiarini, B de Rossi, M Girelli.

1958
- Residential unit, Via Tommaso Salvini, Rome: S Lenci.
- Residential unit, Lungotevere degli Inventori, Rome: M Aymonino, A de Rossi, B de Rossi
- Paediatric hospital, Bari, competition design: C Chiarini, M Girelli.

1958-61
- Law Courts, Brindisi: S Lenci.
- INA Casa Quarter, Commenda Ovest district, Brindisi: C Chiarini, B de Rossi, M Girelli, L Poti.

1959
- Piazza della Guerra, Empoli.
- National Library, Rome, competition design: M Aymonino, B de Rossi, P Espagne.
- CEP Quarter, Barene di San Guiliano, Venice, competition design: M Aymonino, C Chiarini, B de Rossi, M Girelli.

1959-60
- Orione, Vega and Cassiopea residential co-operatives, Lecce: F Cicirillo, G Marasco.
- Residential unit, Via Citerni, Rome: M Aymonino, A de Rossi, B de Rossi.
- Venere, Domus, Nettuno and Nuove Brindisi residential co-operatives, Brindisi: F Cicirillo, G Marasco.
- Pegaso residential co-operative, Lecce: F Cicirillo, G Marasco, A de Rossi.

1959-61
- INA Casa Quarter, Via Ofanto, Foggia: C Chiarini, B de Rossi, M Girelli.

1960-61
- Residential unit, Via Arbia, Rome: M Aymonino, B de Rossi.
- F Vandone Pavilion, Spallanzani Hospital, Rome: M Aymonino, A de Rossi, B de Rossi, C Melograni.

1960-62
- Technical Industrial Institute, Brindisi: C Chiarini, B de Rossi, M Girelli.

1961
- Law Courts, Lecce: M Aymonino, F Cicirillo, B de Rossi, G Marasco.

1962
- Centre, Breuil, competition design: C Melograni.
- Commercial centre in Bologna, preliminary study: P Giordani.
- Business centre, Turin, competition design: M Aymonino, F Berlanda, F Battimelli, B de Rossi.

1962-63
- Residential unit, Via Anagni, Rome: M Aymonino, A de Rossi, C Chiarini, B Conti, M Vittorini.

1962-63
- Technical Industrial Institute, Lecce: G Marasco.

1963
- Restructuring, San Paolo Hospital, Savona, competition design: F Berlanda.

1963-64
- Tor Carbone residential co-operative, Rome: M Aymonino, A de Rossi, B de Rossi.
- Residential co-operative, Savona: M Aymonino, A de Rossi, B de Rossi.

1964
- Reconstruction, Paganini Theatre, Parma, competition design.
- Multi-purpose building, Viale C Colombo, Rome: M Aymonino, A de Rossi.
- Plan, Tor de Cenci Quarter, Rome: L Anversa, A de Rossi.
- School complex, Ferrara, competition design.

1966
- Offices, Chamber of Parliament, Rome, competition design: B de Rossi, N di Cagno, P Moroni, M Vittorini.
- Street and environmental arrangement for the area limited by Viale C Colombo, Valle Caffarella and Via C Baronio, Rome, competition design: F Battimelli, C Chiarini, B de Rossi, N di Cagno, P Moroni, M Vittorini.

1967
- Psychiatric hospital, Mirano, competition design: C Dardi.

1967-72
- Residential complex, Monte Amiata Gallaratese Quarter 2, Milan: M Aymonino, A de Rossi, I Messare.

1968
- Banca d'Italia, Grosseto, design.

1970
- Pompidou Centre, Paris, competition design: I Messare
- Unitarian design, college campus, Pesaro.

1970-73
- G Marconi Science College, Pesaro.
- Business centre in Reggio Emilia, competition design: C Dardi.
- Florence University, competition design: G Ciucci, C Dardi, V de Feo, U de Martino, M Manieri Elia, G Morabito, F Pierobon, A Zattera.
- Fontivegge Business Centre, Bellocchio, Perugia, competition design: C Dardi, G Morabito.

1971-74
- Plan, historic centre, Pesaro: C Dardi, G Fabbri, M Lena, R Panella, GU Polesello, L Semerani.

1972
- Cagliari University, competition design: G Ciucci, B Conti, V de Feo, M Manieri Elia, R Panella, ML Tugnoli.

1972-1974
- School, Abbiategrasso, Milan.

1973
- Calabria University, competition design: G Ciucci, B Conti, C Dardi, V de Feo, C di Pascasio, A Latini, GC Leoncilli, M Manieri Elia, G Morabito, R Panella, ML Tugnoli.
- Restructuring, Piazza XX Settembre, Fano, Pesaro, design.
- Cassa di Risparmio, Fano, Pesaro, design.
- Departmental building for biology, Piovego, Padua, competition design: P Roncali.

1976
- Plan, Semirurali, Bolzano: S Unterberger, R Venieri, O Zöggeler.

1976-79
- Civic Centre, Pesaro, design: C Montanari, ML Tugnoli.

1977
- Post Office, Genzano.
- Restructuring, Prager Platz, Berlin, design.
- Business centre, Florence, competition design: A Aymonino, A Rossi, G Braghieri, M Bosshard, A Cantafora, J Kirschenfeld, V Savi, C Sumi, GL Vimercati Sanseverino.
- Plan, Zone 7A, Vigne Nuove, Rome: C Chiarini, P Mazzacurati, D Prantera.

1977-84
- Court House, Ferrara: A Torti.

1978-79
- Restructuring, Saffa, Cannareggio Ovest, Venice, design: V Fraticelli, C Magnani.
- Istituto Bancario San Paolo di Torino, Lecce: ML Tugnoli.

1978-81
- Casa Parcheggio, Pesaro: ML Tugnoli.

1979
- Plan, Area 7, historic centre, Pesaro: G Fabbri, GU Polesello, L Semerani.

1979-1983
- Semirurali residential complex, Bolzano: ML Tugnoli.

1980
- Benelli Business centre, Pesaro: F Battimelli, E Giannini; plans: R Panella.

1981-86
- New hospital, Mestre-Venice, design: L Calcagni, GP Mar, G Tamaro.

1982
- IMA, design: A Veronese, ML Tugnoli.
- Plan, Abano Terme, historic centre, Padua: R Panella, C Magnani, S Rocchetto.
- Reclamation plan, Pomposas Abbey: G Barbini, A Torti, P Zambelli.
- Largo Firenze, Ravenna, competition design: A Aymonino, C Baldisseri, G Barbini, R Evangelisti, N Pirazzoli, L Sarti, M Scarano.

1982-84
- The Colossus, Rome: A Aymonino, S Giulianelli, ML Tugnoli.

1983
- Arrangement for the area adjacent to the San Cristoforo and Antonini squares, Via Gemona and Via Palladio, Udine, competition design: G Barbini.
- Restoration, Palazzo Scattolari, Pesaro: F Doglioni, ML Tugnoli.

1984
- Urban design, Campo di Marte, Giudecca Island, Venice, competition design: G Barbini.

1985
- Plan, Pontelagoscuro, Ferrara, design: C Cannata, ML Tugnoli, A Veronese.
- Intervention, St Mark's Basin, Venice.
- Third International Exhibition of Architecture, Venice Biennale, design: G Barbini, F Frison, P Mazzoleni, L Salce, A Sandi.
- Three piazzas, Terni, design: ML Tugnoli.
- Covered market and square, Massa barracks, Lecce: ML Tugnoli.

1986
- Market parking, Orte: A Balducci, ML Tugnoli.
- Second university, Tor Vergata, Rome, competition design: L Calcagni, GP Mar, G Tamaro, ML Tugnoli.
- La Villette urban park, Paris, competition design: GG Dardia, V Fraticelli, G Mainini, R Nicolini, A Zattera.
- Pirelli-Bicocca area, Milan, competition design: G Barbini, ML Tugnoli, S Amorosini, G Conte, C Gibone, P Leon, G Longhi.
- Restructuring, Riccione centre, design: G Barbini.
- Restoration and refurbishment, Mario Valentino, Venice: G Barbini.

1986-88
- Consultancy and reclamation plans, commune of L Aquila.

1987
- Largo Firenze, Ravenna, design: A Aymonino, C Baldisseri, G Barbini, R Evangelisti, N Pirazzoli, L Sarti, M Scarano.
- House, La Giudecca, Venice: G Barbini.
- Avellino Theatre: M Aurigemma, G Ferraro, A Aymonino, E Pitzalis, ML Tugnoli.
- Cassa di Risparmio, Jesi, competition design: ML Arlotti, A Aymonino, C Baldisseri, M Beccu, P Desideri, F Raimondo, M Saito, L Sarti, C Andriani.
- Offices, Veneziana Gas, San Francesco della Vigna, Venice, design: G Barbini.

1987-88
- Campi Bisenzio Elementary School, Florence, design: E Pitzalis, ML Tugnoli.
- School, Caposele, Avellino: E Pitzalis, ML Tugnoli.

1988
- Andrisani Mill, Matera: PG Corazza, R Panella.
- Sotto Napoli, Monte Echia, Naples: ML Tugnoli, A Zattera, MR Pinto, A Morone.
- Expansion and restructuring, Faculty of Architecture, Rome, competition design: P Angeletti, M Angelini, A Orlandi, R Panella, G Remiddi, A Terranova.
- Setiapolis Sports Centre, Sezze Romano, design: A Musacchio, F de Pisa, S Miura, F Ottone, E Pitzalis, M. L Tugnoli, D Bugli.

1989
- Il Trincerone transportation and parking system, Salerno, competition design: G Giannattasio, ML Tugnoli.
- Trade centre, San Giovanni Teadino, design: L Trotta, D Merlino.
- Offices, Via Ostiense, Rome: A Jazzetti, ML Tugnoli.
- Urban and architectural intervention, San Lorenzo, Greve, Scandicci, Florence, design: G Barbini, P Martini.
- Selvas Pavilion, Venice, scientific restoration: G Barbini.
- Marcian area, Venice, design: G Barbini.

1990
Urban and architectural intervention, former Papa plant, San Dona di Piave: G Barbini, G Zorzenoni.
- Urban and architectural arrangement, Fossovalle residential complex, Scanzano Jonico, design: ML Arlotti, A Aymonino, P Desideri.
- Restructuring, Palazzo Genovese, design: G Barbini.
- Palazzo del Cinema, Venice Biennale, competition design: G Barbini, G Paolini.
- Plan and general design, university, Forli: G Barbini.
- Model for a technological park, Trieste: G Barbini.
- Urban infrastructure design, Todini-Pavan, Pordenone: G Barbini.

1991
- Austrian National Bank, Vienna, competition design: G Barbini, K Helleweger, E Pitzalis, A Stradella, M Tassoni.
- Barialto residential complex design: ML Tugnoli, G Hanssen.
- GRP, Bacoli, Naples.
- Restoration, Italian Embassy, Berlin, competition design: G Barbini.
- Master plan and restoration, Catanzaro sea front: MD Alessandro.

1992
- Urban and architectural consultancy, Torretta dei Massimi, Rome: L Ascarelli.
- Italian Embassy, Washington DC, competition design: G Barbini, A Stradella, M Tassoni.
- Project, Seven Hills Tunnel, Rome: B Castelli, A Croce, G Gullini, G Ottolenghi, D Rossi.
- Multi-purpose building, Lecce, design: G Hanssen, ML Tugnoli.
- Restoration, Villa Tittoni-Traversi; Library design, Desio, Milan: G Barbini.
- Consultancy and technical support, Bocche di Porto, Consorzio Venezia Nuova, Venice.

– Palazzo dei Conservatori, Campidoglio, Rome: ML Tugnoli, G Hanssen.
– Spreebogen area and Bundestag, Berlin, competition design: M Angelini, A Orlandi, A Terranova.
1993
– School, Piedicastello, Trento, competition design: G Barbini.
– Italian Pavilion, 45th Biennale, Venice: G Barbini.
– GRP, Sassari: G Barbini, engineer: G Uneddu.
– Theatre, Barialto, Bari, design: G Hanssen, ML Tugnoli.
– Project for the completion of de S Carlo Sacromonte, Arona.
1994
– Restructuring, Apollo Theatre, Lecce, design: G Hanssen, ML Tugnoli.
1995
– Hertzian Library, Rome, competition design: G Hanssen, ML Tugnoli.
– Urban renewal, industrial complex, Via Salaria 207, Monterotondo Scalo, Rome, design: G Hanssen, V de Santis, ML Tugnoli.
– Prado Museum, Madrid, competition design: G Barbini, , A Stradella, M Tassoni.
1996
– Design consultancy, urban and architectural restoration, Autovox Industrial Park, Monterotondo Scalo: G Barbini.
– New GRP, Jesolo, competition design: G Barbini.
– New GRP, Marciana, Elba: G Barbini, S Cacciapaggia.
– Consultancy, Pietralata complex, Territorial Policies Council, SDO Special Office, Rome: ML Tugnoli.
– Territorial Policies Council, SDO Special office.

The above schemes are realised unless specified otherwise. Information from M Tafuri and F Dal Co, *Architettura Contemporanea*, Electa, Milan, 1976, pp400-403 (English translation: Abrams, New York, 1979, pp394-97).

SELECTED WRITINGS BY CARLO AYMONINO
1953
– 'The Heart of the City', *Contemporaneo*, no 24.
1954
– 'The Pillage of Rome', *Contemporaneo*, no 2.
– 'The Architecture of Walter Gropius', *Contemporaneo*, no 10.
– 'The City and the Countryside', *Contemporaneo*, no 29.
1955
– 'The History of Rome's Plan', *Contemporaneo*, no 5.
– C Aymonino, C Chiarini, M Girelli, S Lenci, C Melograni, F Vandone, 'Popular Housing Estates in Naples', *Casabella-continuità*, no 205, May/June, p31.
1956
– 'The Meeting of Cities', *Contemporaneo*, no 5.
– 'The Tendenza', *Contemporaneo*, no 14.
– 'Marcel Breuer', *Contemporaneo*, no 20.
– 'From Utopia to Science', *Contemporaneo*, no 27.
1957
– 'History and Chronicles of the Tiburtino Quarter', *Casabella-continuità*, no 215, April/May, pp19-22.
– Carlo Aymonino, S Lenci, 'Architectural Investigations on Italian Cities: Brindisi', *Casabella-continuità*, no 222, November/December, pp21-28.
1958
– 'City Planning in Copenhagen', *Contemporaneo*, no 4.
– 'Rome Disembowelled', *Paese Sera*, 29 March.
– C Aymonino, M Aymonino, C Chiarini, A and B de Rossi, M Girelli, 'Design for the Competition for the Residential Quarter of the Barene di San Giuliano, Venice-Mestre', *Casabella-continuità*, no 242, August, pp50-51.
1961
– C Aymonino, C Chiarini, B de Rossi, M Girelli, 'Residential Unit in Trattauro dei Preti, *Foggia*, 1957-58', *Casabella-continuità*, no 249, March, pp24-35.
1962
– 'The Co-operative Movement in Italy in the Sixties', *Argomenti Architettura*, no 4.
– 'The End of the City-Garden?', *L'Unita*, 22 December.
1964
– *La Città Territorio: Un Esperimento Didattico*, Editrice Leonardo da Vinci (Bari).
– 'Faculty of Tendenza?', *Casabella-continuità*, no 287, May, p11.
– 'An Open City', *Casabella-continuità*, no 288, June, pp53-55.
1965
– *Gli Alloggi della Municipalità di Vienna 1922-1932*, Dedalo (Bari).
– *Origini e Siluppo della Città Moderna*, Marsilio (Padua).
1969
– 'Bari's General Regulatory Plan', *Lotus*, no 6.
1970
– 'The Formation of the City', *Lotus*, no 7.
1975
– *Il Ruolo delle Città Capitali nel XIX Secolo: Parigi e Vienna*, Officina (Rome).
– *Il Significato delle Città*, Laterza (Bari).
1977
– 'Matter and Materials', *Lotus*, no 15.
– 'Reflections Beyond the Venice Experience', *Casabella*, no 423, March, pp37-38.
– C Aymonino, PL Cervellati, 'The Historic Centre Between Political Design and Architectural Design', *Casabella*, no 428, September, pp13-14.

– 'Institute for the Facilitation of Residential Building; Executional Plan for the Semi-Rural Areas, 1977; Project for Bolzano with S Untenberger, R Veneri, O Zöggeler and with the collaboration of C Unterberger, N Anders', *Casabella*, no 428, September, pp32-35.
1978
– Carlo Aymonino, A Rossi, G Braghieri, 'Design for the Directional Area in Florence', *Casabella*, no 434, March, pp26, 30, 40-43.
1979
– 'The Socialist City', *Casabella*, no 446, April, pp10-13.
1980
– 'The Difficulty of a Project', Cluva (Venice).
– 'Monument, Modern Architecture, Contemporary City', *Casabella*, no 459, January, pp10-11.
– 'Bolzano: Typological Complexities and the Order of Settlements', *Casabella*, no 459, June, pp46-51.
– 'Options for the Competition for the Set Up of the Halles Quarter', *Casabella*, no 460, July/August, pp43-45.
1981
– *The Historical City and the Political City in Rome: Continuity of the Ancient: The Imperial Forum within the Design of the City*, Electa (Milan).
1982
– *Rome's Historic Centre. Four essays by Carlo Aymonino and a Debate*, Officina Edizioni (Rome).
– 'Berlin for Example', *Casabella*, no 480, May, pp36-37.
– 'Archaeology and Urban Design', *Casabella*, no 482, July/August, pp36-37.
1983
– *Carlo Aymonino and Raffaele Panella: A Design for Rome's Historic Centre*, Officina (Rome).
– C Aymonino, Raffaele Panella, 'Rome, A City Aside: Utilizing the Historical Delay to Build a Different Capital', *Casabella*, no 487/488, January/February, pp90-97.
– 'The Competition for the Railway Junction in Bologna', *Casabella*, no 497, December.
1985
– 'Ten Opinions on Type: An Intervention by Carlo Aymonino', *Casabella*, no 509/510, January/February.
– 'Sergio Crotti, Enrica Invernizzi: Houses in Alzano Lombardo. Building in the Historic Centre', *Casabella*, no 526, July/August.
1988
– *Italian Squares*, ed F dal Co, Electa (Milan).
– 'Inside the Cave: Ideas in Competition for Naple's Underground', *Phalaris*, no 1.
1989
– *Planning Rome*, ed P Desideri, F Leoni, Laterza (Bari).
– *No More Models but Solutions*, Laterza (Bari).
– 'How Time Flies . . . Kenzo Tange in Rome?', *Phalaris*, no 2.
1990
– *Carlo Aymonino*, ed Giancarlo Priori, Zanichelli (Bologna).
1991
– *Architettura di Carlo Aymonino*, ed Giancarlo Priori, Nuova Alfa Editoriale (Modena).

SELECTED WRITINGS ON CARLO AYMONINO
Foreign publications
1964
– 'Roman School', *The Architectural Review*, (London, England) no 801.
1971
– G Laslo, 'The City of Padua', *Revue d'Historie de l'Architecture et de la Conservation des Monuments d'Art*, (Budapest, Hungary) vol XV; no 2.
– 'Le Centre de Direction de Bologne', *Espace et Societe*, (France) March.
1972
– 'Architekten: Carlo und Maurizio Aymonino, Alessandro de Rossi, Buro – und Wohngebaude in Savona, Italien', *Werk*, (Switzerland) no 10.
1974
– M Tafuri, 'L'Architecture dans le Boudoir: The Language of Criticism and the Criticism of the Language', *Oppositions*, no 3.
1975
– 'La Génération de l'Incertitude', *L'Architecture d'Aujourd'hui*, (France) no 181.
– A Kanne, 'Carlo Aymonino: Sozialer Wohnbau in Gallaratese', *Rationale Architektur*, (Austria) no 4.
1976
– F Gelabert, 'Progetto nel Quartiere Gallaratese a Milano', *Jano Architettura*, June.
1977
– PL Nicolin, 'Presentation of Carlo Aymonino's Projects', *Global Architecture*, Ada Edita, (Tokyo, Japan) no 45.
1978
– *Rational Architecture*, Editions des Archives d' Architecture Moderne, (Brussels, Belgium), p68.
– 'The Gallaratese Quarter, Milan', *A+U*, (Japan) no 88, February.
1980
– P Nicolin, 'Carlo Aymonino, Aldo Rossi: Housing Complex at the Gallaratese Quarter in Milan', *Global Architecture*, Ada Edita, (Tokyo, Japan).
– 'Scientific College and Technical Institute, Pesaro', *A+U*, (Japan) October.
1982
– *The Charlottesville Tapes*, Rizzoli International Publications (New York).
– 'Projektubersicht Stadterneuerung und Stadneubau-Stand', *Internazionale Bauausstellung, IBA*, (Berlin, Germany) no 84-87, October.
1983
– 'Il Quartiere Gallaratese', *The Bulletin of the association of Greek Architects*, Messaré, (Greece) no 17, May.
1984
– 'Ferrara: Rehabilitacion de la Iglesia y Convento del Gesu', *Periferia*, (Spain) no 1, June.
1986
– 'Carlo Aymonino: Architecture de la Ville et Projets Urbains', *Forces*, (Canada) no 74.
– 'Institute of Technics and Commerce, Pesaro', *A+U*, (Japan) May.
1987
– F dal Co, *Carlo Aymonino: Projects in Ancient Cities*, ed R Einaudi, Cornell University, College of Architecture.
– 'New Hospital in Mainland Venice', *GA Document*, GA International, (Japan) no 18.
– 'Project Report: Prager Platz', *Internazionale Bauausstellung IBA*, (Berlin, Germany).
1988
– 'Die Semirurali in Bozen', *Baumeister*, (Germany) no 9, September.
1989
– 'Design for the New Hospital in Mestre, Venice', *Zodiac*, (Florence, Italy) no 1.
1992
– 'Designing the University', *Zodiac*, (Florence, Italy) no 7.
– 'Carlo Aymonino', *Arquitectos Jornal*, Rivista dell'Ordine Degli Architetti Portoghesi, Associaçao dos Arquitectos Portugueses, no 112, June.
1994
– *La Ville, Art et Architecture en Europe, 1870-1993*, Editions du Centre Pompidou (Paris).

SELECTED WRITINGS ON CARLO AYMONINO
Italian publications
1956
– F Tedeschi, 'Competition for a Covered Market in Pescara', *L'Architettura – Cronache e Storia*, no 4.
1959
– F Tentori, 'Exceptional Probity in the Masses of Roman Palazzine', *L'Architettura – Cronache e Storia*, no 14.
1960
– I Insolera, 'Competition for the National Library in Rome', *Casabella-continuità*, no 239.
– 'Competition for the Residential Complex at the Barene in San Giuliano, Venice', *Casabella-continuità*, no 242.
– 'Theatre, Cinema and Housing in a New Quarter', *La Casa: Quaderni di Architettura e di Critica*, no 6.
– B Zevi, 'Standards against the Avant-garde', *L'Espresso*, no 31, December.
1961
– G Samoná, 'Chamber of Commerce, Industry and Agriculture in Massa-Carrara', *L'Architettura – Cronache e Storia*, no 17.
– M Girelli, 'Committed Architecture in the Roman Suburbs', *Casabella-continuità*, no 247.
– S Benedetti, P Portoghesi, 'Idea of the City', *Comunità*, no 94.
– B Zevi, 'Punished for Their Courage', *L'Espresso*, December.
1962
– M Tafuri, 'The Roman Architectural Vicissitudes 1945-1961', *Superfici'II*, no 5.
1963
– 'The Commitments of the New Generations', *Aspetti dell' Arte Contemporanea*, L'Aquila (Rome).
– S Benedetti, 'Problems of the Latest Roman Generations', *Aspetti dell' Arte Contemporanea*, L'Aquila (Rome).
– M Tafuri, 'Recent Activities of the Roman studio', *L'Architettura – Cronache e Storia*, no 93.
– P Portoghesi, 'Tendencies of the New Generations of Architects', *Comunità*, no 115.
– 'Competition for the Directional Centre in Turin', *L'Espresso*, 10 May.
1964
– F Tentori, 'Projects by Roman Architects: Design for the Courts of Law in Lecce 1961', *Casabella-continuità*, no 289.
– I Insolera, 'The City-Territory', *Comunità*, no 123.
1965
– S Anselmi, G di Toro, F Montuori, 'Didactics and Methodologies of Urbanistics', *La Citta Futura*, no 8.
– V Sermonti, 'On the Paganini Theatre – Aymonino', *Palatina*, no 31/32.
1966
– B Zevi, 'Competition for the New Paganini Theatre in Parma', *L'Architettura – Cronache e Storia*, no 129.
– GK Koenig, 'Montecitorio', *Casabella*, no 321.
– A Rossi, 'The Architecture of the City', *Marsilio* (Padua).
– 'Architecture in the USA: A Debate Between Aymonino, Benevolo and Tafuri', *Rassegna dell' Istituto di Architettura e Urbanistica*, vol III; no 7.
– B Zevi, 'Parma Sewn Back Together by an Architect', *L'Espresso*, 2 January.
– C Melograni, 'Two Cultures Even in Architecture', *Rinascita*, 6 January.
1967
– G Grassi, *The Logical Construction of Architecture*,

Marsilio (Padua).

1968
- M Tafuri, *Competition for the New Offices of the Chamber of Parliament*, Edizioni Universitarie Italiane (Bari).
- M Tafuri, *Theories and History of Architecture*, Laterza (Bari).
- L Benevolo, 'A More Defined Line in Architectural Research', *Rinascita*, no 26, April.
- C Dardi, 'Is the Problem Another One?', *Rinascita*, no 26, April.

1969
- E Saezano, *Town Planning and the Opulent Society*, Laterza (Bari).

1970
- P Sica, *The City Image from Sparta to Las Vegas*, Dedalo (Bari).
- A Rossi, *The Urban Analysis and the Architectural Project*, Clup (Milan).
- A Pica, 'The City of Padua', *Domus*, no 389.
- B Zevi, 'Everyone has Overcome Everything', *Cronache dell'Architettura*, Laterza, (Bari) vol III; no 304.
- A Villa, 'Architecture and the Formation of the Modern City', *Lotus*, no 7.

1971
 L Finolli, 'The City of Padua', *L'Architottura – Cronache e Storia*, no 180.
- M Tafuri, 'Social Democracy and Cities in the Weimar Republic', *Contropiano*, no 1.
- M Tafuri, 'Austro-Marxism and Cities', *Contropiano*, no 2.
- M Scolari, 'A Contribution for the Foundation of a New Urban Science', *Contropiano*, vol III; no 7/8.
- A Pica, 'Origins and Development of the Modern City', *Domus*, no 497.
- B Zevi, 'Neo-Rationalists Dethrone the Marble', *Cronache dell'Architettura*, Laterza, (Bari) vol IV; no 381.
- B Zevi, 'Second Prize to the Silent Protest', *Cronache dell'Architettura*, Laterza, (Bari) vol IV; no 399.
- A Terranova, 'Historiography and the Theory of Town Planning', *Storia dell' Arte*, no 7/8.
- F Berlanda, 'The Rational Housing', *Rinascita*, 21 May.
- B Zevi, 'Freedom does not Live in barracks', *L'Espresso*, 13 June.

1972
- M Cerasi, *City and Suburb*, Clup (Milan).
- 'International Competition for the Directional Centre in Fontivegge-Bellocchio', *Controspazio*, vol IV; no 1.
- M Folin, *The City of the Capital*, Laterza (Bari).
- B Zevi, 'A Body for the Continual Planning of Rome', *Cronache dell'Architettura*, Laterza, (Bari) vol V; no 565.
- L Bortolotti, 'Padua: Analysis of a City', *Rinascita*, 21 April.

1973
- R Bonicalzi, U Siola, 'Architecture and Reason', *Controspazio*, vol V; no 6.
- 'Cagliari's New University', *Controspazio*, vol V; no 3.
- B Zevi, 'Still Ahead of the Ville Radieuse', *Cronache dell'Architettura*, Laterza, (Bari) vol VIII; no 871.
- B Zevi, 'The Tattered Square Sewn Up', *Cronache dell'Architettura*, Laterza, (Bari) vol VI; no 610.
- B Zevi, 'Twelve Parliaments in One Republic', *Cronache dell'Architettura*, Laterza, (Bari) vol VI; no 686.
- B Zevi, 'Translate Sappho and Go Down to the Boutique', *L'Espresso*, 23 December.

1974
- C Dardi, 'Living in the Gallaratese Quarter in Milan', *L'Architettura – Cronache e Storia*, no 226.
- A Ferrari, 'Roofless Houses: Residential Complex at the Gallaratese 2, Milan', *Casabella*, no 391.
- 'The Gallaratese Quarter in Milan: Urban Development and Popular Participation', *Edilizia Popolare*, no 19.
- L Biscogli, 'Architecture and Urban Fabric', *L'Industria delle Costruzioni*, no 42.
- L Toccafondi, 'The Awakening of Forms', ed A Samonà, C Doglio, *Oggi l'Architettura* (Milan).
- PC Santini, 'Hard Life at Gallaratese 2', *Ottagono*, no 35.
- B Zevi, 'Luxury for Proletarians', *L'Espresso*, 5 May.

1975
- C Guenzi, 'An Open Debate: A Review of the Problems in the Relationship Between Avant-Garde and Popular Culture', *Artecontro*, no 2.
- B Zevi, 'Education in Terms of Territorial Asset', *Cronache dell'Architettura*, Laterza, (Bari) vol IX; no 1003.
- G Gresleri, 'Significance of the City', *Parametro*, no 42.

- F Papi, 'Form and Fruition: Considerations about the Gallaratese', *Rassegna dell'Istituto di Architettura e Urbanistica*, vol XI; no 31/32.
- 'The Phantom of Autonomy: The Myth of Aymonino in the Faculty of Architecture', *Valle Giulia* (supplement to *Il Manifesto*) no 1, 23 May.

1976
- C Dardi, *Simple, Linear, Complex*, Magma (Rome).
- G Rebecchini, 'The Discreet Charm of Capital Cities: Paris and Vienna in the 19th Century', *Controspazio*, vol VIII; no 3.
- C Forte, 'Carlo Aymonino: The Significance of Cities', *Economia e Territorio*, no 6.
- F Moschini, 'The Significance of Cities', *La Sapienza*, (Rome) no 13/14.
- PL Cervellati, 'The City: Advanced Ideas, Backward Laws', *Rinascita*, 23 January.
- P Portoghesi, 'The City Tells us of its Infancy', *Tempo*, 28 March.
- A Rossi, 'Capital Cities', *Rinascita*, 2 April.

1977
- R Cicala, 'The History of Padua Through its Land Registers', *AR*, no112.
 S Bassotti, A Biotti, O Zoeggeler, 'Bolzano: Urban History and Restructuring Projects; Plan for the Semi-Rural Area', *Casabella*, no 428.
- P Portoghesi, 'National Competition for the New Directional Centre in Florence: A Review of the Winning Designs', *Controspazio*, vol IX; no 6.
- F Moschini, 'Between Continuity and Disintegration: Two Interventions by Carlo Aymonino', *L'Industria delle Costruzioni*, no 73.
- PC Santini, 'Encounters with the Protagonists: Carlo Aymonino', *Ottagono*, no 44.
- 'A School from Scratch', *Parametro*, no 61.
- L Berni, 'Pesaro's Science College', *Panorama*, 12 July.

1978
- 'Designs for the Directional Area in Florence', *Casabella*, no 434.
- 'Fifty Years of *Casabella-continuità*', *Casabella*, no 440.
- 'Dreaming Florence: A Catalogue of Architecture', *Parametro*, no 63.
- G Contessi, 'The Nodes of Representation', *La Tradizione del Nuovo*, no 3.
- L Berni, 'National Competition for the Planimetric and Volumetric Design for a Directional Area in Florence', *Panorama*, 25 April.
- F dal Co, 'Florence: Projects Compared', *Rinascita*, 12 May.

1979
- *The Architectural Debate 1945-1975*, Bulzoni, (Rome).
- B Zevi, 'The Semantic Fission/Fixation of the Pyramid', Editoriali di Architettura (Einaudi, Turin).

1980
- C Conforti, *Carlo Aymonino: Architecture is Not a Myth*, Officina (Rome).
- F Moschini, *College Campus in Pesaro*, Kappa (Rome).

1981
- C Conforti, *The Gallaratese of Aymonino and Rossi 1966-1972*, Officina (Rome).
- G de Feo, E Valeriani, *Italian Architecture of the Seventies* (catalogue), De Luca (Rome).

1982
- G Polin, 'The Courts of Law in Ferrara', *Casabella*, no 444.

1983
- G Polin, 'The Benelli Directional Centre in Pesaro', *Casabella*, no 497.
- F Moschini, 'Over the Hedge', *Domus*, no 637.

1984
- P Melis, 'The Colossus' Enigma', *Domus*, no 651.
- F Moschini, 'Workshop in Ferrara', *Domus*, no 654.
- 'The New Law Court in Ferrara Ready to go Ahead', *Ferrara*, vol LXXXIV; no 8.
- 'Competition for the Dantean Area in Ravenna', *Casabella*, no 501, April.
- P Portoghesi, '*The new Courts of Law in Ferrara*', *Epoca*, 20 July.
- S Brandolini, 'The Technical College on the Campus in Pesaro', *Casabella*, no 507, October.
- V Gregoretti 'Pesaro, for Example', *Panorama*, 5 November.

1984
- PO Rossi, *Roma: Guida all'Architettura Moderna 1909-1984* (Bari).

1985
- M Tafuri, *History of Italian architecture 1944-1985*, Einaudi (Turin).
- C Magnani, 'Venice's IACP Competition Entry for the Campo di Marte at the Giudecca', *Casabella*, no 518.
- A Mendini, 'A Talk with Carlo Aymonino', *Domus*, no 658.
- G Vindigni, 'The Benelli Directional Centre in Pesaro', *L'Industria Italiana del Cemento*, no 591,

1987
- F Moschini, 'Carlo Aymonino: Fragments of Self Quotes', *L'Industria delle Costruzioni*, no 194.
- R di Caro, 'The Imaginary Naples', *L'Espresso*, 12 April.
- L Chierici, 'Naples: Fires at Sea', *Ambiente*, May.
- G Priori, 'Aymonino in Ancient cities', *L'Unita*, 13 December.

1988
- G Priori, *The Poetry of Listening*, Clear (Rome).
- F Moschini, 'Covered Market and Square of the Former Massa Barracks in Lecce', *Domus*, no 700.
- 'Project for the Area of Monte Echia' (catalogue), ed V Lampugnani, *Electa* (Milan).
- *Piazza d'Italia*, Electa (Milan).
- F dal Co, *The Projects of Carlo Aymonino*, Electa (Milan).
- 'Interview with Carlo Aymonino. The New Hospital in Mestre', *Galleria di Architettura*, Fondazione Masieri.
- C Conforti, 'Italian Squares: Designing the Open Spaces', *Piano Progetto Citta*, September.

1989
- 'Carlo Aymonino. Design for the Set Up of Largo Firenze in Ravenna', *Casabella*, no 557.
- M Pisani, 'There are Squares and there are Squares', *Rinascita*, 27 May.

1990
- 'Accounts on Ernest N Rogers Twenty Years after his Death', *Zodiac*, (Florence, Italy) no 3.
- M Gil, A Longo 'The Square', *Mondoperaio*, March.
- S del Pozzo, 'And the Lion Changes its Den', *Panorama*, 9 September.

1991
- R Panella, 'Aymonino, Panella, Corazza: Urban Complex in Matera', *Domus*, no 733.
- 'Competition for the New Palazzo del Cinema at the Lido in Venice' (catalogue), *Electa* (Milan).
- G Priori, 'Aymonino, the Colossus', *Phalaris*, no 15.
- 'Residential and Tertiary Complex at S Lorenzo in Greve', *Zodiac*, (Florence, Italy) no 5.

1992
- A Donti, *Architecture for the New City: A Comparison of Experiences*, Alinea (Florence).
- V Lampugnani, N di Battista, 'Interview with Carlo Aymonino: Theory, Architecture and Contradiction', *Domus*, no 739.
- 'Building complex in Piazza Kennedy by C Aymonino, R Panella, PG Corazza, 1988-1991', *Phalaris*, no 19.
- F Prodi, 'The New Hospital for 1080 Beds', *Progettare la Sanita*, no 10.
- 'Designing the University', *Zodiac*, no 17.

1993
- 'A Multi-Functional Building in S Paolo, Rome', *Edilizia Popolare*, no 227.
- 'Designs for the Completion of the Sacro Monte di S Carlo in Arona', *Zodiac*, (Florence, Italy) no 7.
- A Terranova, 'An Exhibition by Carlo Aymonino Opens in Rome', *Bollettino della Biblioteca del Dipartimento di Architettura e Analisi della Citta*, February.
- F Frison, 'The Re-employment of the Saint's Pavilion', *Recuperare*, Ediz Peg, (Milan) no 2, March.
- 'Competition Design for the Spreebogen in Berlin', *Casabella*, no 601, May.
- 'The New Chancellery of the Italian Embassy in Washington DC', *Casabella*, no 602, June.
- G Remiddi, 'The Story of a Lost Interview; Notes from a Conversation with Carlo Aymonino and Raffaele Panella', *Groma*, Apartimento Dipartimento di Architettura e Analisi della Citta, June.

1994
- M Fabbri, 'Urban Designs for a City Model: The Competition for Piazza Matteotti in Matera', *Controspazio*, no 3.
- A Belluzzi, C Conforti, *Guida all'Architettura Italiana 1944-1994*, Laterza (Bari).
- L Monica, Carlo Quintelli, *Criticism and Design: Seven Questions on Architecture*, Città Studi, May.